"This outstanding volume provides timely and thought-provoking insights into the constantly evolving nature of journalism, the fluid definitions and overlapping roles of occupational outsiders and insiders, and the existential questions practitioners face in navigating between tradition and change. Every chapter offers a fresh perspective on the 'received wisdom' of journalism studies about challenges and challengers. Some authors provide unusual takes on the usual suspects, from audiences to native advertisers; others investigate such unexpected 'barbarians' as ideological editors, foundations, even academics. Just what is journalism today, and who is a journalist? The answers suggested here are more nuanced, and more interesting, than you might think."

– Professor Jane Singer, *Professor of Journalism and Innovation, City, University of London*

"This collection of essays grapples with a curious but highly consequential fact: since the advent of professional journalism at the turn of the twentieth-century, there has never been more news produced than today, and never less of it by journalists. Over eleven wide-ranging chapters, the authors investigate what happens when journalists who once were able to patrol the boundaries of their field now find themselves cheek-to-jowl with political activists, advertisers, nonprofits, university newsrooms, the 'people formerly known as the audience,' and technologists, among others. The result is an incisive exploration of how and why the institution of journalism has blurred in the twenty-first century. A must-read for anyone interested in the future of news and the role journalism might play in that future."

– Professor David Ryfe, *Professor of Journalism and Mass Communication, University of Iowa*

THE INSTITUTIONS CHANGING JOURNALISM

Bringing together original contributions from a worldwide group of scholars, this book critically explores the changing role and influence of institutions in the production of news.

Drawing from a diverse set of disciplinary and theoretical backgrounds, research paradigms and perspectives, and methodologies, each chapter explores different institutions currently impacting journalism, including government bodies, businesses, technological platforms, and civic organisations. Together they outline how cracks in the autonomy of the journalism industry have allowed for other types of organizations to exert influence over the manner in which journalism is produced, funded, experienced and even conceptualized. Ultimately, this collective work argues for increased research on the impact of outside influences on journalism, while providing a roadmap for future research within journalism studies.

The Institutions Changing Journalism is an invaluable contribution to the field of journalism, media, and communication studies, and will be of interest to scholars and practitioners alike who want to stay up to date with fundamental institutional changes facing in the industry.

Patrick Ferrucci (PhD, University of Missouri) is an Associate Professor and the associate chair for graduate studies in the Department of Journalism in the College of Media, Communication and Information at University of Colorado-Boulder. His research primarily concerns itself with how shifting notions of "organization" in journalism lead to influence on journalism practice. Specifically, his work examines organization-level variables' impact on message construction. He is the author of *Making Nonprofit News* (Routledge).

Scott A. Eldridge II (PhD, University of Sheffield) is an Assistant Professor at the Centre for Media and Journalism Studies at the University of Groningen. He researches digital journalism and how non-traditional actors challenge the boundaries of the journalistic field. He is the author of *Online Journalism from the Periphery* (2018) and co-author with Miguel F. Santos Silva of *The Ethics of Photojournalism in the Digital Age* (2020), and is co-editor with Martin Conboy of *Global Tabloid: Culture and Technology* (2021) and with Bob Franklin, of the *Routledge Companion to Digital Journalism Studies* (2017) and *Routledge Handbook of Developments in Digital Journalism Studies* (2019). From 2018–2021 he was Associate Editor of *Digital Journalism*.

THE INSTITUTIONS CHANGING JOURNALISM

Barbarians Inside the Gate

Edited by Patrick Ferrucci and Scott A. Eldridge II

Routledge
Taylor & Francis Group

LONDON AND NEW YORK

Cover image: Getty image 1311443860

First published 2022
by Routledge
4 Park Square, Milton Park, Abingdon, Oxon OX14 4RN

and by Routledge
605 Third Avenue, New York, NY 10158

Routledge is an imprint of the Taylor & Francis Group, an informa business

© 2022 selection and editorial matter, Patrick Ferrucci and Scott A. Eldridge II; individual chapters, the contributors

The right of Patrick Ferrucci and Scott A. Eldridge II to be identified as the authors of the editorial material, and of the authors for their individual chapters, has been asserted in accordance with sections 77 and 78 of the Copyright, Designs and Patents Act 1988.

British Library Cataloguing-in-Publication Data
A catalogue record for this book is available from the British Library

Library of Congress Cataloging-in-Publication Data
A catalog record has been requested for this book

ISBN: 978-0-367-69085-4 (hbk)
ISBN: 978-0-367-69090-8 (pbk)
ISBN: 978-1-003-14039-9 (ebk)

DOI: 10.4324/9781003140399

Typeset in Bembo
by Taylor & Francis Books

From Patrick Ferrucci
To Erin, Owen and my parents, for everything
From Scott A. Eldridge II

To Martin, John, and Jairo, for encouraging me to think about these things

CONTENTS

ILLUSTRATIONS

Figures

Tables

CONTRIBUTORS

Stefan Baack is a research and data analyst at the Mozilla Foundation and an associate researcher at the Weizenbaum Institute in Berlin, Germany. His research is broadly about the implication of datafication for democratic practices. He studies the entanglements of civic tech and data journalism, transnational journalism networks and alternative data governance. His work has been published in journals including *Digital Journalism, Big Data & Society*, and *Journalism*.

Sandra Banjac is an assistant professor at the Centre for Media and Journalism Studies at the University of Groningen in the Netherlands. Her research explores the changing relationship between journalists and audiences, focusing in particular on journalistic roles and audience expectations. Her work has examined these in relation to the boundaries of journalism, lifestyle journalism, and intersectional approaches to exploring journalism's inequalities. She is also affiliated with the Journalism Studies Centre at the University of Vienna, Austria, as a research fellow on the project "Audience expectations of news in the digital age" funded by the Austrian Science Fund. Her work has been published in journals including *Digital Journalism, New Media & Society*, and *Journalism*.

Valérie Bélair-Gagnon is an associate professor and Cowles Fellow in Media Management at the Hubbard School of Journalism & Mass Communication and Affiliated Faculty in the Department of Sociology at the University of Minnesota. She is an Affiliated Fellow at the Yale Law School Information Society Project. Previously, she was Director of the Minnesota Journalism Center as well as Executive Director and Research Scholar and Postdoctoral Fellow at the Information Society Project at Yale Law School. She has been a fellow at Oslo Metropolitan University Digital Journalism Research Group and the Tow Center for Digital Journalism at Columbia University. Born in Montréal (Québec, Canada), she earned a BA in Sociology (honors) from McGill University, an MSc in Sociology from the Université de Montréal, and a PhD in Sociology from City, University of London.

David Cheruiyot is an assistant professor at the Centre for Media and Journalism Studies at the University of Groningen in the Netherlands. David has a specific interest in non-journalistic actors, for example mainstream media critics, and how they shape journalistic practice. His research has appeared in *Digital Journalism, Journalism Practice*, the *International Journal of Communication*, and *Media, Culture and Society*, and focuses on the following areas: digital media criticism, press accountability, media representation, among others.

Scott A. Eldridge II is an assistant professor at the Centre for Media and Journalism Studies at the University of Groningen. He researches digital journalism and how non-traditional actors challenge the boundaries of the journalistic field. He is the author of *Online Journalism from the Periphery* (2018) and co-author with Miguel Santos Silva of *The Ethics of Photojournalism in a Digital Age* (2020) and is co-editor with Martin Conboy of *Global Tabloid: Culture and Technology* (2021) and with Bob Franklin, of the *Routledge Companion to Digital Journalism Studies* (2017) and *Routledge Handbook of Developments in Digital Journalism Studies* (2019). From 2018–2021 he was Associate Editor of *Digital Journalism*.

Raul Ferrer-Conill is an associate professor of Journalism at the University of Stavanger, Norway and an assistant professor of Media and Communication Studies at Karlstad University, Sweden. His research investigates digital journalism, audience engagement, and the structural changes of the datafied society. His work has been widely published in journals such as *Digital Journalism, New Media & Society, Journalism Studies* and *Television & New Media*.

Patrick Ferrucci is an associate professor and the associate chair for graduate studies in the Department of Journalism in the College of Media, Communication and Information at University of Colorado-Boulder. His research primarily concerns itself with how shifting notions of "organization" in journalism lead to influence on journalism practice. Specifically, his work examines organization-level variables' impact on message construction. He is the author of *Making Nonprofit News* (2020, Routledge).

Tine Ustad Figenschou is professor of journalism at Oslo Metropolitan University. Figenschou's research interests include counter-hegemonic, alternative media; the news media and marginalized groups; mediatization of government and interest groups. Her work appears in international journals including *International Journal of Press/Politics, Journalism, Journalism Studies, Digital Journalism, European Journal of Communication, Media, Culture & Society* etc. Figenschou is co-leader of the Digital Journalism Research Group and part of the *Far Right Politics Online and Societal Resilience* (FREXO).

Andreas Hepp is professor of media and communications and head of ZeMKI, Centre for Media, Communication and Information Research, University of Bremen, Germany. He was Visiting Researcher and Visiting Professor at leading institutions such as the London School of Economics and Political Science, Goldsmiths University of London, Université Paris II Panthéon ASSAS, Stanford University, and others. He is the author of 12 monographs including "The Mediated Construction of Reality" (with Nick Couldry, 2017), "Transcultural Communication" (2015), and "Cultures of Mediatization" (2013). His latest book is *Deep Mediatization* (Routledge, 2020).

Alfred Hermida (PhD) is professor and former director (2015–2020) at the School of Journalism, Writing, and Media at the University of British Columbia, and co-founder of The Conversation Canada. With more than two decades of experience in digital journalism, his research addresses the transformation of news, media innovation, social media and data journalism. His books include *Data Journalism and the Regeneration of News* (Routledge, 2019), co-authored with Mary Lynn Young, and *Tell Everyone: Why We Share and Why It Matters* (DoubleDay, 2014). He was a BBC TV, radio, and online journalist for 16 years, including four in North Africa and the Middle East.

Karoline Andrea Ihlebæk is an associate professor of journalism at Oslo Metropolitan University. Her research interests include alternative media, boundaries, moderation, platforms and policy. Her work appears in international journals including *New Media & Society, Journalism, Journalism Studies, Journalism Practice, European Journal of Communication* and *Media, Culture & Society*. Ihlebæk is member of the Digital Journalism Research Group and co-leading the research project *Far Right Politics Online and Societal Resilience* (FREXO).

Magda Konieczna is an associate professor of journalism at Concordia University in Montreal. She is the author of *Journalism Without Profit: Making News When the Market Fails* (Oxford University Press, 2018), and was a reporter at the now defunct *Guelph Mercury* newspaper in Canada. Her research has been published in journals including *International Journal of Communication, Digital Journalism*, and *Journalism Studies*.

You Li is an associate professor of journalism at Eastern Michigan University. Her research traces the evolvement of journalism with a particular emphasis on the tension between the autonomous forces and heteronomous forces that shape and challenge journalism. Dr. Li draws theories from sociology, business, and journalism, and uses both qualitative and quantitative methods in her research. Her recent projects examine how native advertising may have affected journalistic autonomy and further blurred the boundaries between journalism and commercialism. Her current projects involve solutions journalism, computational content analysis, and interdisciplinary research on data science and data literacy in undergraduate education.

Wiebke Loosen is a senior journalism researcher at the Leibniz Institute for Media Research | Hans Bredow Institute (HBI) as well as a professor at the University of

Hamburg, Germany. Her major areas of expertise are the transformation of journalism within a changing media environment, theories of journalism, and methodology. Wiebke's current research focuses on the changing journalism-audience relationship, the datafication of journalism, forms of pioneer journalism and the emerging start-up culture in journalism, as well as algorithms' "journalism-like" constructions of public spheres and reality.

Jacob L. Nelson is an assistant professor at the University of Utah, and a fellow with the Tow Center for Digital Journalism at Columbia University. He is also the author of *Imagined Audiences: How Journalists Perceive and Pursue the Public* (Oxford University Press, 2021). He uses qualitative and quantitative methods to study the changing relationship between journalism and the public. Before completing his PhD at Northwestern University, he worked as an editor for Patch, a hyperlocal, online newspaper. He covered Highland Park, a small suburb north of Chicago.

Jonathan Peters is a media law professor at the University of Georgia, where he has faculty appointments in the College of Journalism and Mass Communication and the School of Law. He is the press freedom correspondent for the *Columbia Journalism Review*, and he has written for *Esquire, The Atlantic, Sports Illustrated*, Slate, *Wired*, and CNN. He has blogged about the First Amendment for the *Harvard Law Review* and the *Harvard Law and Policy Review*, and he is a frequent commentator on First Amendment issues for *The New York Times, The Washington Post, Vanity Fair*, CNN, NBC News, CBS News, NPR, and PBS. Peters is a co-author of the book *The Law of Public Communication* (Routledge, 2020), and his scholarship has appeared in journals published by the law schools at the University of California at Berkeley, Harvard, New York University, and the University of Virginia, among others. He is a volunteer First Amendment lawyer for the Student Press Law Center and the American Civil Liberties Union, and he has worked internationally on press freedom projects as a consultant to the United Nations Development Programme, the United States Agency for International Development, and the Organization for Security and Co-operation in Europe.

Frank M. Russell is an associate professor of journalism in the Department of Communications at California State University, Fullerton. His research, which has been published in *Digital Journalism* and *Journalism Studies*, concerns journalism's interactions with Twitter and other Silicon Valley platforms. He earned a PhD and was a Knight visiting editor and assistant professor at the University of Missouri School of Journalism. Previously, he was an editor and writer mainly specializing in technology and financial news at newspapers including the *San Jose Mercury News* and *The Seattle Times*.

Lisa Varano is an audience development editor at *The Conversation Canada* in Toronto. She previously worked as a news writer for CTV News Toronto and The Weather Network and as a reporter for the *Guelph Mercury* newspaper in southern Ontario. She has a Master of Arts in journalism from the University of Western Ontario and a Bachelor of Arts (honours) in political science from McGill University.

Tim P. Vos is professor and director of the Michigan State University School of Journalism. His research examines the roles of journalism, media sociology and gatekeeping, media history, and media policy. He has published over 60 journal articles and book chapters. He is co-author, co-editor, or editor of four books and the *International Encyclopedia of Journalism Studies*. He is the book series editor of Journalism in Perspective from the University of Missouri Press. He is past president of the Association for Education in Journalism and Mass Communication (AEJMC).

Andrea Wenzel is an assistant professor at Temple. She is the author of *Community-Centered Journalism: Engaging People, Exploring Solutions, and Building Trust* (University of Illinois Press, 2020). She co-founded the Germantown Info Hub and has been a fellow with Columbia University's Tow Center. Her research focuses on initiatives to create more connected and equitable communities and newsrooms through community-centered and antiracist journalism. Prior to completing her PhD at USC Annenberg, she spent 15 years as a radio producer at WBEZ and WAMU, and a trainer/project manager for organizations including BBC Media Action and Internews in Afghanistan, Sri Lanka, Iraq, and Ghana.

Mary Lynn Young (PhD) is professor, co-founder and board member of The Conversation Canada. She has held a number of academic administrative positions at the University of British Columbia, including Associate Dean, Faculty of Arts (2011–2016), and Director of the UBC School of Journalism (2008–2011). Her research interests include gender and the media, newsroom sociology, data and computational journalism, journalism startups and representations of crime. Her most recent co-authored book is with Candis Callison, PhD, entitled *Reckoning: Journalism's Limits and Possibilities* (Oxford, 2020).

ACKNOWLEDGEMENTS

Any book project is a testament to those who work on it and those whose work inspires it, and this book is no different. In that light, we are indebted to Bob Franklin, who in early discussions of some of the ideas now present in this book first encouraged Pat to reach out to Scott. In doing so, he brought together the two of us who, over video calls timed to take advantage of early evenings in the Netherlands and early mornings in Colorado, started crafting the outlines of the book in front of you. From that first foray, and over many months of defining our shared interests, while swapping stories of growing up in Massachusetts, we hashed out how each of us thought about the questions and challenges facing journalism and journalism studies, and how we could address these in new ways. One of the benefits of our field is the ways in which these conversations can give rise to new connections, and new ideas. In the best traditions of academic work, Bob's initial suggestion led to a fruitful and enjoyable collaboration which allowed us to make concrete those initial ideas.

It hopefully goes without saying that, in order to do realize the potential of those ideas, we would be nowhere without the contributors whose chapters give substance to the shape we outlined in developing this project. One of the benefits of working across the great distances between the two of us is each of us had a different group of scholars in our networks who we wanted to work with. It is one thing to have read the work of all those whose pages fill this book. It is quite a different thing, and a far more rewarding one, to work with those scholars to identify and then refine different ideas about journalism, its institutions, and change. We are particularly grateful for how this bringing together of voices has allowed this book to introduce a compelling set of dialogues between academics based in North America and in Europe, who speak to a global set of issues, and who do so with a wider set of perspectives than either of us could have offered on our own.

It is also worth acknowledging the contexts in which this book came together. For Scott, the last book project he worked on was meant to be his 'Covid book', and in wrapping up that project in late 2020, he and Martin Conboy thanked authors for weathering the challenges of writing, editing, and refining while managing life in a pandemic. We had thought this experience might shape up differently. It did not. Were it not for the resilience of all involved, who wrote chapters between vaccine doses and who responded to edits and feedback while balancing childcare alongside work, again, we would have a far less compelling set of discussions than what appears in front of you. To their contributions, and to their efforts and enthusiasm despite all the challenges faced, we are forever grateful.

Finally, to the team at Routledge from Margaret Farrelly, who first helped us bring this book into shape, to Priscille Biehlmann who helped us manage all the steps along the way, to the production and design teams. Any project is a testament to all those who work on it, and this one is no different.

INTRODUCTION

Journalism coming into being: The timbers and planks of a changing institution

Scott A. Eldridge II

When we say "journalism",[1] what are we referring to? Perhaps an awkward start to a book that is deeply concerned with journalism, but in light of slipping threads binding journalism's central tenets, it is a question that has gained renewed attention. In witnessing and studying what has changed over our decades of speaking about journalism, this question reflects ongoing struggles to outline the shape of journalism. Whether addressing the definitional boundaries defining its space or making sense of new entrants' place within it, it also reflects a lack of certainty over what journalism was historically and what it is now. On one level, this question conveys a challenge of description, as in larger and smaller ways the journalism we see around us is hardly recognizable when compared to its forebears. Media technologies have changed, as has the nature of news work. The roles journalists find themselves performing have changed, as have the ways in which these manifest, as have the ways people access news and content.

Dig a bit deeper and the question becomes more fundamental, as dependencies of journalism on its own and other institutions in society have become more complex, blurring distinctions that used to separate the institution of journalism from those surrounding it. Where two decades ago new actors and institutions from "j-bloggers" (Singer 2005) to audiences (Singer 2009) were seen as outsiders challenging the field, as "barbarians" storming its gates (Singer 1997) and threatening the independence of journalism itself (Singer 2007), in this book we posit that these interlopers are now firmly within the field.

However, the fact that such outsiders now appear to be more firmly seated within our conversations about journalism does not mean their place within the field is clear, nor does it resolve the uncertainty that always accompanies change, uncertainty in what we mean by "journalism" when we say it, when we study it, and as we account for change after incremental change, what we imagine "journalism"[2] to be becoming. In this book we will address these changes, and how

DOI: 10.4324/9781003140399-1

they shape our imaginations of journalism. From the material changes to how journalism reaches us, to the societal changes underpinning its place in our lives, we approach change in this volume by examining how different institutions have come to play a greater role in shaping the field of journalism. As Patrick Ferrucci outlines in his conclusion, this includes embracing a research agenda that seeks to make sense of the drivers of change themselves, looking not just at journalism but also at those institutions coming into its orbit. In this introductory chapter I establish key conceptual landmarks that can be used to navigate change after subsequent change. In doing so, I argue that adjoining our emphasis on what was to our attention on what is offers an opportunity to see journalism as something that is constantly becoming.

Journalism's changing planks

To begin, we can imagine journalism as a modern-day "Ship of Theseus" (Scaltsas 1980). In this classic thought experiment we are asked to imagine a hypothetical ship, floating in a harbor as a tribute to the triumphs of its captain, Theseus. Over time, each of its wooden planks slowly rots and is replaced, one by one, with a new, identical piece of wood, so as to maintain Theseus' legacy as it had originally been remembered. As each plank is renewed, however, questions surface about whether the original ship is being preserved, or if it is instead becoming something new. If so, at what point does Theseus' ship cease to be *Theseus'* ship? And, at what point does it become a new ship entirely? Perhaps not when the first plank has been replaced, as it is still mostly the original ship, but what about two? Ten? Fifty? Does it become a "new ship" when the majority of its planks and timbers are new, or only when the last original piece has been replaced?

The answers to these questions tend to differ, as people grapple with the nature of identity and existence. While at first glance a ship with one plank replaced seems largely the same, a ship with all its planks replaced seems quite different. And while a ship's legacy and original purpose can be reflected in new planks and timbers, they are, nevertheless, new, and at that level can signal something altogether different. Philosophers ask whether it matters whether change is gradual, rather than sudden, and whether the nature and identity of being Theseus' ship is tied not to its make-up, or to each of its original components, but to the historically imbued specific purpose and identity each plank represents. Is a ship's identity one that can survive incremental and, eventually, total change, so long as each new plank refers to its predecessor in some symbolic fashion? If each new piece is a testament to the ship's original purpose, is that purpose maintained, no matter the scale and scope of change?

These questions about incremental change and original purpose are analogous to our aims with this book, exploring whether referring to "journalism" continues to hold clear symbolic meaning and purpose as newer and newer planks contribute to its shape. From legal concerns (Peters, Chapter 3), to political actors (Figenschou and Ihlebæk, Chapter 1), civic organizations (Baack, Cheruiyot, and Ferrer-Connill, Chapter 7), modes of knowledge production (Hermida, Varano, and Young,

Chapter 4), and revenue streams (Konieczna, Chapter 6; Li, Chapter 2), the new considerations we need to account for in understanding journalism are many, and each adds new complexities. In other versions of this thought experiment, philosophers ask what if each rotted timber is replaced with one made of metal, acknowledging a different technology might stand the test of time a bit better (Biro 2017; Worley 2019). With historical markers of journalism now being replaced by newer technologies, where media platforms (Russell and Vos, Chapter 11), technologically-inclined actors (Hepp and Loosen, Chapter 8), modes of measuring traffic (Bélair-Gagnon, Chapter 10) and engagement (Nelson and Wenzel, Chapter 9), provide audiences new voice (Banjac, Chapter 5), can we say journalism is still the same thing we previously referred to? And as journalism continues to undergo change after change, what do we do when it has been entirely rebuilt?

Through this analogy, we can approach journalism as a ship defined on the one hand by the historically imbued value and purpose it has long benefited from, and by the continuous transformations that it has endured on the other. From print technologies to those of the web, and from mass media newspapers and broadcasters to a range of digital outlets, we can identify change quite readily. What can be harder to pin down is the enduring legacy that new institutions might *also* refer to when aligning themselves with journalism, and what doing so means for either understanding journalism as something that remains steadfast despite newer and newer components, or as something entirely new given the raft of changes it has experienced. Through this analogy, and thinking through legacy and change, we can also confront one of journalism's recurring paradoxes; that is, journalism has benefitted from a seemingly agreed-upon social status, its legacy, even though that status is cordoned by ever-contested, ever-changing, boundaries and myriad ways of defining it. This has led us, among many, to ask why journalism has continued to matter so much, even as the ways it has mattered are so difficult to make concrete. Stephen Reese highlights this in *The Crisis of the Institutional Press*, saying journalism and the institution of journalism have historically been "notoriously difficult to define" (2021: 59). Matt Carlson and Seth Lewis (2020: 123) offer that "the questions regarding the contours of journalism lack obvious or agreed-upon answers" (2020: 123), and separately Carlson argues that to the degree that we can understand "journalism" through the ways we refer to it, it is a particularly "unstable referent" (2015: 8). Wolfgang Donsbach (2010) describes this in terms of a gap between journalism's clear societal importance and our abilities to define its boundaries and competencies, a task Jane Singer notes, "has never been easy and gets harder by the day" (2019: 487).

With these challenges in mind, we set about to explore where and how we make sense of something like "journalism", a term that seemingly refers to an institution defined by its historical status, imbued with purpose and value, while simultaneously being subject to constant change and increasing uncertainty. In the spaces between agreed-upon importance and elusive boundaries, and between historic legacy and newer components, however, we can see journalism constantly coming into being through interaction and change, and through revisiting what it is that has given this particular ship its identity. In doing so, we gain firmer purchase when trying to grasp what, exactly, has changed, and can better interrogate both what it might be we pine for when we say "journalism", and what it is we are newly embracing.

The social institution of journalism: Value and stability

If we are to begin with the legacies that give journalism status, we should unpack one of the more edificial metaphors that has been leaned on to make sense of journalism, one that will recur throughout this volume: journalism as an institution. Seeing journalism as an institution hearkens to its reputational highpoint, its era of "high modernity" (Hallin 1992). Specifically in the United States and particularly in the latter twentieth century, this was, as Pamela Shoemaker and Stephen Reese describe,

> a period when newsworkers pledged obeisance to codes of professionalism and claimed their news coverage was independent of the financial interests of the large corporations, then beginning to consolidate their grasp on the media landscape and eventually to hold it in thrall.
>
> *(Shoemaker and Reese 2014: xi)*

In this setting and during this period, the institution seemed clear, and much of the work that has peered through the institutional lens towards journalism has built from this moment to address either US contexts,[3] or stretched a particular US-centric conception of the institution further afield. Reese (2021: ix) notes this partly reflects different traditions that took hold in the academy in the US, where a cultural studies tradition was prevalent in journalism scholarship, and the critical theoretical traditions that took hold in Europe. As the field of journalism studies has expanded, there are fewer ties between theoretical and geographic "containers" within which scholars located in the US, Europe, or anywhere else, operate (Reese 2008). Where we can still see traces of these geographic homes, it is when institutionalism is embraced in scholars' efforts to rescue journalism from its own hand within the highly-commercial media systems of the US (Alexander, Butler Breese, and Luengo 2016), or when examining journalistic institutions in the context of US-style commercialization (e.g. in Australia; see Harrington 2021). Henrik Örnebring captures this well, noting that while Reese's (2021) reflections on the crisis facing the journalistic institution list towards a US-centered understanding, they highlight the implications of "hav[ing] given a private institution a public role" (2021: 2). In other words, while this act of "having given" might not be an exclusively US dynamic, it often has a uniquely American flavor.

Metaphorically, describing journalism as an institution suggests status, and stasis. This is not incidental. Institutions depends on it. "Institutions are stable by definition," Reese writes, adding: "But stability alone is not sufficient to lay claim to public support and full institutionality" (2021: 62). For that, stability needs also to be met with public acknowledgement of the value an institution holds. In

Shoemaker and Reese's hierarchy of social influences, this manifests for journalism through,

> a relatively homogenous social practice, with similar concerns over legitimacy and commercial success, glossing over organizational differences in favor of making broader statements about the media in general, considering how journalistic practices are more alike than different.
>
> *(2014: 99)*

In this definition, we see stability in journalism's shared concerns and in journalists' adherence to certain practices, and value in terms of both legitimacy and commercial success.

Alongside allusions to value and stability, institutionalism also requires interaction. In particular, the institution of journalism depends on interaction between journalism and other external, "extra-media" institutions. As Shoemaker and Reese write:

> The *social institution* level describes the influences arising from the larger trans-organizational media field, how media organizations combine into larger institutions that become part of larger structured relationships as they depend on and compete with other powerful social institutions.
>
> *(2014: 8)*

This interactivity has been expanded upon within other strands of institutionalism as well. New institutionalism in particular offers ways of describing journalism as a political institution through its interactions with politics (c.f. Cook 1998; Sparrow 1999). Discursive institutionalism offers another path, showing where discursive interaction undergirds a sense of journalism coming into formation through the ways it is discussed and described collectively (Hanitzsch and Vos 2017; c.f. Schmidt 2010).

Across these approaches to seeing journalism through an institutional lens, there is an effort to build from individuals, to organizations, towards seeing something more substantive in what we refer to when we say "journalism," including by looking at how value and stability are shaped interactively. We might even be so bold as to think of the institutional label as a shorthand for the complex social interactions that drive shared practices among practitioners. Institutionalism, it seems, is perhaps at its contradictory best when downplaying the status of the institution itself, and focusing more on the practices that give it shape. Laura Ahva argues such attention to practice can help avoid an "overemphasis of the role of institutions or norms" (2017: 1525), especially when trying to account for journalistic actors outside more established organizational settings. By focusing instead on practices, scholarship can reinforce the *social* in institutions, offering a window into how individuals' routines can shape our perceptions of journalism as an institution, practices that can be shared by both more formal and more peripheral journalistic actors.

What this greater emphasis on interaction and influence encourages, and what Ryfe (2019) among others (Eldridge 2019) advocate for explicitly, is recognizing journalism is not now nor has it ever been, truly, a fixed space or place in our societies. Rather it is the product of an interweaving of journalism's recognized value and those actors who embrace it. It is also something that can change over-time, rendering stability a more open question. Inasmuch as journalism is an institution at all, in the end that perspective depends on all those who recognize journalism this way. Sparrow argues this recognition is built on the *appearance* of similarity; an "aggregate" of familiar approaches to doing newswork according to "shared norms and informal rules" (2006: 155). Hanitzsch and Vos reflect on this as the *articulation* of shared belonging, within "a struggle over discursive authority in conversations about the locus of journalism in society" (2017: 116). In each of these we are encouraged to consider how appearances of a consolidated idea of journalism are shaped, but also how they are not to be assumed as inherent or lasting. Within this emphasis, we can also see journalism's shape is not predicated on certain actors being involved, but rather on the role of interaction between all those involved. These dynamics are contextual, allowing us to see journalism shaped in each moment through interactions with other social forces and actors, and disrupted by the same. Journalism operates in a space alongside other institutions "who may do battle with one another", where each puts forward a dominant vision of society they wish to convey, and where each shapes the other as they do so (Bourdieu 2005: 31).

Institutions and fields, boundaries and borders

Critical reflections on institutional approaches have built upon this interactivity, showing that while the institutional lens allows us to talk about "journalism" as something coherent, that cohesion is not in and of itself explanatory, regardless tendencies towards that finding. As Ryfe comments:

> Study after study had shown that across organization, geography, size, and kind of news outlet, the news is extraordinarily homogeneous. Why such homogeneity in the news? Largely, this literature concluded, because journalism is defined by a shared set of organizational routines and practices.
>
> *(2006: 135).*

Such conclusions miss a trick, Ryfe argues further, one embedded in the impetus for new institutionalist approaches. That is, "the idea of homogeneity, and that it is caused by organizational and professional imperatives, ought to be a beginning, not an end, of discussion" (2006: 135). Finding homogeneous routines and practices should offer us a starting point for new inquiry *into* homogeneity within the institution, and in doing so avoiding the trap of work that "simply assumed it and gone on to examine homogeneity's various "effects," principally on policymaking and public opinion" (Ryfe 2016: 135). From this admonition we can approach the appearance of similarity in certain moments as offering focal points to explore where status has been confronted by change, and where coherence has been ruptured by new institutions and actors who claim allegiance to the legacy of journalism, doing so in altogether novel ways.

This line of inquiry has been central to theoretical approaches for accounting for the relative consistency we find when trying to define and describe journalism not through metaphors of place, i.e. the *institution of journalism*, but through metaphors of space, i.e. the *field of journalism* (c.f. Benson 2006; Bourdieu 2005). In their similarities, approaches to both institutions and fields place attention on how journalism comes into being in part through individuals and organizations rallying around a dominant vision of what it is to belong. Benson (2006) makes this dialogue explicit. Reese (2021) does so as well. Both locate commonalities between field theory's and institutionalism's "attention to intra- and inter-field dynamics", with clear differences between institutionalism's "static, stable view of the journalistic space" and field theory's "dynamic struggle, as one field tries to assert its autonomy by differentiating itself from others" (Reese 2021: 68). Each also emphasizes how, whether as a field or as an institution, journalism benefits from a consolidated outward-facing vision of journalism to the wider public. This vision provides journalists a point around which they can measure their belonging, and a central reference to call upon when projecting an idea of journalism to society, while paying heed to the distinct ways each theoretical metaphor draws our attention towards seeing this vision as more-or-less stable (Eldridge 2018: 107).

In their similarities, both institutionalist and field approaches guide our thinking about journalism as being shaped by societal interaction, including by focusing on inter-, intra-, and extra- media actors contesting the lines drawn around the field (Perreault and Ferrucci 2020). These lines become important, as Shoemaker and Reese argue, in the ways "fields and institutions bring up questions of where the boundaries lie among these institutions as they jockey for power", both of these approaches can be conducive to building our understanding of journalism, as: "Whether between fields or institutions, borders have become particularly relevant" (Shoemaker and Reese 2016: 402–403). Indeed, borders have been something of a concern not only in thinking through field and institutional metaphors for understanding journalism, but in considering how such boundaries are effectively exertions of power, resisting change and drawn by tradition (Wahl-Jorgensen 2014). It was a similar focus on power that inspired Reese's institutional curiosity about the journalistic institution (2021: xi), also embedded in theorizations of the journalistic field among several "fields of power" (Bourdieu 2005).

While attention on boundaries between institutions (or fields) has been a fruitful avenue for understanding journalism in the context of change, the lines themselves pose complications when it comes to thinking through journalism in a manner that remains cognizant of both legacy and change. Boundaries tend to place attention on the distinctions being drawn, rather than on the interactive forces and motivations behind them (Eldridge 2019: 9). Cook (2006: 16) reflects on this as a possible negative outcome of his own work, writing: "Thinking of the news media as a political institution, I fear, emphasizes the image of walls too much and downplays the portrait of interpenetrating journalistic and governmental realms too much". Later work, perhaps mindful of this lament, made these dynamics more central to discussions of journalism and boundaries, including in work conceptualizing such boundaries (Carlson and Lewis 2015, 2020), making sense of how these are challenged (Eldridge 2014), again and again (Nygaard, 2020), by actors seen as internal and external to journalism (Banjac and Hanusch 2020), and those found someplace in-between (Bélair-Gagnon and Holton 2018). This has, at least to a degree, moved our conversations away from focusing on journalism as either static, or bounded by stable lines, and has drawn our attention towards the "interpenetrating" forces that have given journalism at moments an appearance of institutional stability, and at others the impression of a field undergoing immense change. Nevertheless, there seems to be space for more being done along this trajectory.

Returning to our analogous ship, we are reminded that despite their contributions to our shared understandings of journalism, history and legacy are impermanent, and "that institutions, just because they have certain enduring attributes, do not automatically deserve to endure in the same form" (Reese 2021: vii). Or, put differently, while "institutions persist" (Sparrow 2006: 152) and so too might the institution of journalism, this does not say anything about how it will persist. Planks will be replaced, and newer ones might call into question whether or not we are referring to the same thing we once were. Institutional approaches to journalism, then, might best be seen as a jumping off place. They allow us to see that even though there are points of similarity across journalism's disparate actors and organizations, homogeneity is not alone an answer and the institution is itself more concept than concrete.

Nevertheless, as a way of reflecting on "journalism", the institutional lens allows us to indulge curiosity, and to examine legacy and change in finer detail. While change can call into question journalists' identities (Ferrucci and Vos 2017), and our bases for reckoning with the field at large (Eldridge 2019), focusing on how change reflects tradition can also help us make sense of journalism as a field in society that has frequently mapped its socio-informative functions and public contributions to new modes of delivery (Conboy 2021: 11; Conboy and Eldridge 2017: 171). The back-and-forth between historical value and new imaginations also allows us to mark transition from an era of "high modernity" (Hallin 1992), appreciating the foundation for journalism's esteem and professional repute, to the more uncertain times we now find ourselves in, with journalism "experiencing upheaval and uncertainty in many parts of the world" (Carlson, Robinson, and Lewis 2018: 7).

In the absence of certainty and clear boundaries, approaching journalism through looking at what has changed offers a way to recognize what we are building from and what feels familiar. This appreciates that despite its legacy in our modern societies, many of our understandings of journalism have rested not on strict criteria, but on a sense of familiarity between participants in the field. Whether that is familiarity in terms of their identities (Aldridge and Evetts 2003), routines (Konow-Lund 2019), organizations (Riedl 2021), or interpretations of news (Zelizer 1993), familiarity helps us see how many of our conversations about journalism are built on a tacit agreement journalists are doing something distinct, societies' agreement to shared reference points of what journalism is, and other institutions' agreement to abide the boundaries that have thus far maintained journalism's shape. Seeing familiarity not as a superficial recognition, but as the product of interactions between institutions and actors, adds substance to the way we study journalism, allowing us to see how a casual recognition of journalism-as-something-familiar underlies a more complex understanding of the dynamics that shape that familiarity.

There is a point, however, where a comfortable, familiar, sense of journalism begins to falter. This occurs when it runs headlong into new institutions surrounding the field or those that are becoming more firmly situated within its boundaries and which appeal to journalism's long legacy. While on the one hand we can find some solace in these clashes, recognizing that journalism's traditional timbers continue to provide inspiration to new actors who seek to also be seen as journalists (Eldridge 2014), on the other there remains something unsettling about the amount of change that overlays this shape; the new and newer planks shaping journalism's composition seem to differ so wholly from their predecessors in terms of form, function, and mode of operation (Tandoc 2019). In response, scholars tend towards a focus *either* on old timbers in ways which mourn their passing, or on newer planks which confront legacy with rebirth (c.f. Conboy and Eldridge 2014). The former privileges a historically imbued status of journalism, centered around a purpose-driven approach to informing the public and holding power to account. But it risks prioritizing tradition in guiding our evaluations of new actors and new institutions. The latter encourages us to recognize that any historical impression of journalism was itself shaped by influences internal and external to the actual work of journalists and journalism, and that any idea of a stable institution of journalism is built upon "fundamental complicities" that smooth over these dynamics (Bourdieu 2005: 36). But this can lead to a too-expansive imagination of journalism that renders its boundaries meaningless in order to wrap in all novel approaches.

Journalism, a ship coming into being

Perhaps this needn't be an either-or proposition, in favor of either tradition or that which is new. Looking between tradition and novelty, as we do in this volume, can lead us to recognize, and not for the first time (Zelizer 1993), that we can gain a deeper understanding of journalism from observations of change when these are weighed against tradition, with each playing a role in the complexity of interactions shaping our societies (Eldridge and Bødker 2019). This shifts our attention from the observation of what has emerged, or what has changed, towards interactions, conceptually and materially: between the familiar and the new, between tradition and alternatives, and between exogenous and endogenous forces within and without the journalistic field that have long shaped our understanding of "journalism". At any given moment, this helps us see how journalism is defined by pointing to its historical claims of independence (Karppinen and Moe 2016; Tuchman 2014: xi), while also acknowledging its "structured dependency relationships with other major systemic players: including the state, public relations, and advertising" (Reese and Shoemaker 2016: 402), and new technological platforms which have "become themselves institutional actors" (Reese 2021: 20).

If we are able to take up this shift to adjoin tradition and change, we can then permit ourselves to think of journalism as something neither fully tied to a historical tether, nor fully needing to accommodate each new change agent. Rather, we can see journalism as ontogenetic; a journalism in a constant "state of becoming" (Kitchin 2017: 18).[4] This gives us latitude to think of journalism as something that is "never fixed in nature, but [is] emergent and constantly unfolding", and allows us to recognize that journalism can be morphologically distinct from other aspects of our societies and trade on its long history, as long as we recognize it is also something that is defined "contextually, reactive to input, interaction and situation" (Kitchin 2017: 21).

Such an ontogenetic approach aligns with much of our scholarly reflection on "journalism", as working within this field we are constantly in a space where we need to assess context (De Maeyer and Le Cam 2014) and reactions to contexts (Godler 2020), input (Steensen 2019), and interactivity (Zamith 2019) in the many situations in which we define journalism as an object of study we are all concerned with (Eldridge et al. 2019). This shifts attention from the traditional walls which have been the focus of our own and colleagues' attention, towards the interpenetrating forces that have rendered the walls if not obsolete, permeable. This encouragement towards journalism as "constantly unfolding" also aligns with calls to de-center our thinking about "journalism" away from those with institutional largesse (Schapals, Maares, and Hanusch 2019), away from the geographical contexts where attention is most often paid (Mitchelstein and Boczkowski 2021), and even away from journalism itself (Broersma 2019). It allows us to make sense of this ship we have in front of us, and the mix of older timbers and newer planks that keep it afloat.

While seeing journalism as something that comes into being, constantly, can be an intellectual comfort as it draws from the best traditions of journalism scholarship that weigh its history alongside its development, it is also quite demanding to reorient from seeing change as disruption to seeing change as a process of "becoming". To some, this will seem to be an abandonment of legacy, and of the stability that gave journalism as an institution its status and regard. However, permitting ourselves to think about any particular object of journalism through both similarities with other markers of belonging (including tradition) and difference between actors and approaches (including technological novelty), we can then consider how each plays a role in defining journalism's place in society. Seeing journalism as constantly becoming recognizes that we can reorient our understanding of journalism in uncertain times by working *through* its fluctuations, defining journalism through the way small differences and dynamics of constant change have shaped both journalism's societal position and our perceptions of it. Journalism is neither a ship that has changed, nor one that is changing into something. It is one that is in a constant process of taking shape.

The chapters that follow explore institutions that each in their own way call into question what we mean when we talk about "journalism". Each asks us to refine our thinking as we reflect on changes journalism has experienced, and where we can benefit from re-examining what we are referring to when we say "journalism". In doing so, we consider boundaries, fields, and institutions more complexly, using the conceptual tools we have in front of us to measure both legacy and novelty, and to consider both tradition and change, each, as factors affecting how journalism takes shape. In doing so, we see a journalism confronted by new actors and how these confrontations set the stage for dynamics of boundary challenging, crossing, and revision that have allowed us to see journalism through new lenses, through the changes it has experienced. As Jane Singer writes in theorizing digital journalism, we are best advised to recognize that journalism is not now, if it ever had been, a "fixed object of study", for "the digital environment is in some ways like Heraclitus' river: It can never be stepped in twice, for it is constantly changing, and so are those it touches" (Singer 2021: 487). Journalism in a constant state of becoming. A ship whose planks are continuously being renewed, where with each new addition we are again asked to consider what it means when we say "journalism".

Notes

1   In putting "journalism" in scare quotes when I refer to the ways we refer to it, I am intentionally drawing on a tradition (Predelli 2003, 4) of using these to acknowledge a specific debate around the term, one that goes on between the many approaches that have been used to define it, and then to argue over its definitions.
2   My use of scare quotes continues here to make it clear that in this chapter I think this argument is far more interesting than quickly resolving it would be. This is also done with a nod to Carlson (2017: 204, f. 73) who muses briefly over marking "journalism" in quotation marks in his own work so as to indicate its unstable definitions, with a nod to Morozov (2013), who himself is nodding to Lawrence Lessig. After that, it's turtle nods all the way down.
3   See Ryfe (2006) and Reese (2021) for insights into this literature.
4   My gratitude to Rik Smit, who raised this perspective over coffee and, by doing so, helped break a logjam in the development of this chapter.

References

Ahva, Laura. 2017. "Practice Theory for Journalism Studies: Operationalizing the concept of practice for the study of participation." *Journalism Studies* 18 (12): 1523–1541.

Aldridge, Meryl and Julia Evetts. 2003. "Rethinking the concept of professionalism: the case of journalism." *British journal of Sociology* 54 (4): 547–564.

Alexander, Jeffrey C., Elizabeth Butler Breese, and María Luengo. 2016. *The crisis of journalism reconsidered: Democratic culture, professional codes, digital future.* New York, NY: Cambridge University Press.

Banjac, Sandra and Folker Hanusch. 2020. "A question of perspective: Exploring audiences' views of journalistic boundaries." *New Media & Society.* doi:10.1177/1461444820963795.

Bélair-Gagnon, Valérie and Avery Holton. 2018. "Boundary Work, Interloper Media, And Analytics in Newsrooms." *Digital Journalism* 6 (4): 492–508.

Benson, Rodney. 2006. "News Media as a 'Journalistic Field': What Bourdieu Adds to New Institutionalism, and Vice Versa." *Political Communication* 23 (2): 187–202.

Biro, John. 2017. "Saving the Ship." *European Journal of Analytical Philosophy* 13 (2): 43–54.

Bourdieu, Pierre. 2005. "The Political Field, The Social Science Field, and the Journalistic Field." In: *Bourdieu and the Journalistic Field.* Rodney Benson and Erik Neveu (eds) Cambridge: Polity, pp. 29–47.

Broersma, Marcel. 2019. "Epilogue: Situating Journalism in the Digital: A Plea For Studying News Flows, Users, and Materiality." In: *The Routledge Handbook of Developments in Digital Journalism Studies.* Scott Eldridge and Bob Franklin (eds). London: Routledge, pp. 515–526.

Carlson, Matt. 2017. *Journalistic Authority.* New York: Columbia University Press.

Carlson, Matt. 2015. "The many boundaries of journalism." In *The Boundaries of Journalism*. Matt Carlson and Seth Lewis (eds). London: Routledge, pp. 1–18.

Carlson, Matt, Sue Robinson, Seth C. Lewis, and Daniel A. Berkowitz. 2018. "Journalism Studies and its Core Commitments: The Making of a Communication Field." *Journal of Communication* 68 (1): 6–25.

Carlson, Matt and Seth Lewis. 2020. "Boundary work." In *Handbook of Journalism Studies*. Karin Wahl-Jorgensen and Thomas Hanitzsch (eds). London: Routledge, pp. 123–135.

Carlson, Matt and Seth Lewis. 2015. *Boundaries of Journalism*. London: Routledge.

Conboy, Martin. 2021. "Tabloid culture: Parameters and debates." In *Global Tabloid: Culture and Technology*. Martin Conboy and Scott Eldridge (eds). London: Routledge, pp. 1–15.

Conboy, Martin and Scott Eldridge. 2017. "Journalism and public discourse: Navigating complexity." In *The Routledge Handbook of Language and Media*. Colleen Cotter and Daniel Perrin (eds.) London: Routledge, pp. 164–177.

Conboy, Martin and Scott Eldridge. 2014. "Morbid Symptoms: Between a dying and a re-birth (apologies to Gramsci)." *Journalism Studies* 15 (5): 566–575.

Cook, Timothy. 2006. "The News Media as a Political Institution: Looking Backward and Looking Forward." *Political Communication* 23 (2): 159–171.

Cook, Timothy. 1998. *Governing with the news: The news media as a political institution*, Chicago: University of Chicago Press.

De Maeyer, Juliette and Florence Le Cam. 2014. "The Material Traces of Journalism: A socio-historical approach to online journalism." *Digital Journalism* 3 (1): 85–100.

Donsbach, Wolfgang. 2010. "Journalists and their Professional Identities." In *The Routledge Companion to News and Journalism*. Stuart Allan (ed). London: Routledge, pp. 38–59.

Eldridge, Scott. 2019. "Where do we draw the line? Interlopers, (Ant)agonists, and an Unbounded Journalistic Field." *Media and Communication* 7 (4): 8–18.

Eldridge, Scott. 2018. *Online Journalism from the Periphery: Interloper Media and the Journalistic Field*. London: Routledge.

Eldridge, Scott. 2014. "Boundary Maintenance and Interloper Media Reaction." *Journalism Studies* 15 (1): 1–16.

Eldridge, Scott and Henrik Bødker. 2019. "Confronting Uncertainty: The Contours of an Inferential Community." *Journalism & Communication Monographs* 21 (4): 280–349.

Eldridge, Scott, Kristy Hess, EdsonTandoc, and Oscar Westlund. 2019. "'Navigating the Scholarly Terrain: Introducing the Digital Journalism Studies Compass." *Digital Journalism* 7 (3): 386–403.

Ferrucci, Patrick and Tim Vos. 2017. "Who's in, who's out? Constructing the identity of digital journalists." *Digital Journalism* 5 (7): 868–883.

Godler, Yigal. 2020. "Post-Post-Truth: An Adaptationist Theory of Journalistic Verism." *Communication Theory* 30 (2): 169–187.

Hallin, Daniel. 1992. "The Passing of the "High Modernism" of American Journalism." *Journal of Communication* 42 (3): 14–25.

Hanitzsch, Thomas and Tim Vos. 2017. "Journalistic Roles and the Struggle Over Institutional Identity: The Discursive Constitution of Journalism." *Communication Theory* 27 (2): 115–135.

Harrington, Stephen. 2021. "Recent shifts in the Australian tabloid landscape: Fissures and new formations." In *Global Tabloid: Culture and Technology*. Martin Conboy and Scott Eldridge (eds). London: Routledge, pp. 125–136.

Karppinen, Kari and Hallvard Moe. 2016. "What We Talk About When Talk About "Media Independence." *Javnost – The Public* 23 (2): 105–119.

Kitchin, Rob. 2017. "Thinking critically about and researching algorithms." *Information, Communication & Society* 20 (1): 14–29.

Konow-Lund, Maria. 2019. "Negotiating Roles and Routines in Collaborative Investigative Journalism." *Media and Communication* 7 (4): 103–111.

Mitchelstein, Eugenia and Pablo Boczkowski. 2021. "What a Special Issue on Latin America Teaches Us about Some Key Limitations in the Field of Digital Journalism." *Digital Journalism* 9 (2): 130–135.

Morozov, Evgeny. 2013. *To Save Everything: Click here.* New York: PublicAffairs.

Nygaard, Silje. 2020. "Boundary Work: Intermedia Agenda-Setting Between Right-Wing Alternative Media and Professional Journalism." *Journalism Studies* 21 (6): 766–782.

Örnebring, Henrik. 2021. "Book Review: The Crisis of the Institutional Press." *Digital Journalism.* doi:10.1080/21670811.2021.1983727.

Perreault, Gregory and Patrick Ferrucci. 2020. "What Is Digital Journalism? Defining the Practice and Role of the Digital Journalist." *Digital Journalism* 8 (10): 1298–1316.

Predelli, Stefano. 2003. "Scare Quotes and Their Relation to Other Semantic Issues." *Linguistics and Philosophy* 26 (1): 1–28.

Reese, Stephen. 2021. *The Crisis of the Institutional Press.* Cambridge: Polity.

Reese, Stephen. 2008. "Theorizing a Global Journalism." In *Global Journalism Research.* Martin Löffelholz and David Weaver (eds). Oxford: Blackwell, pp. 240–252.

Reese, Stephen, and Pamela Shoemaker. 2016. "A Media Sociology for the Networked Public Sphere: The Hierarchy of Influences Model." *Mass Communication and Society* 19 (4): 389–410.

Riedl, Martin Johannes. 2021. "Journalism as a profession of conditional permeability: A case study of boundaries in a participatory online news setting." *Journalism.* doi:10.1177/14648849211043488.

Ryfe, David. 2019. "The Warp and Woof of the Field of Journalism." *Digital Journalism* 7 (7): 844–859.

Ryfe, David. 2016. *Journalism and the Public.* Cambridge: Polity.

Ryfe, David. 2006. "Guest Editor's Introduction: New Institutionalism and the News." *Political Communication* 23 (2): 135–144.

Scaltsas, Theodore. 1980. "The Ship of Theseus." *Analysis* 40 (3): 152–157.

Schapals, Aljosha Karim, Maares, Phoebe, and Hanusch, Folker. 2019. "Working on the Margins: Comparative Perspectives on the Roles and Motivations of Peripheral Actors in Journalism." *Media and Communication* 7 (4): 19–30.

Schmidt, Vivien. 2010. "Taking ideas and discourse seriously: explaining change through discursive institutionalism as the fourth 'new institutionalism'." *European Political Science Review* 2 (1): 1–25.

Shoemaker, Pamela and Stephen Reese. 2014. Mediating the Message in the 21st Century. London: Routledge.

Shoemaker, Pamela and Stephen Reese. 1991. *Mediating the Message: Theories of Influences on Mass Media Content.* London: Longman.

Singer, Jane. 2021. "Border patrol: The rise and role of fact-checkers and their challenge to journalists' normative boundaries." *Journalism* 22 (8): 1929–1946.

Singer, Jane. 2019. "Theorizing Digital Journalism." In *The Routledge Handbook of Developments in Digital Journalism Studies.* Scott Eldridge and Bob Franklin (eds). London: Routledge, pp. 487–500.

Singer, Jane. 2009. "Barbarians at the Gate or Liberators in Disguise? Journalists, Users and a Changing Media World." In *Actas do Seminário "JORNALISMO: Mudanças na Profissão, Mudanças na Formação".* Universidade do Minho (Braga): Centro de Estudos de Comunicação e Sociedade (CECS).

Singer, Jane. 2007. "Contested Autonomy: Professional and popular claims on journalistic norms." *Journalism Studies* 8 (1): 79–95.

Singer, Jane. 2005. "The political j-blogger: 'Normalizing' a new media form to fit old norms and practices." *Journalism* 6 (2): 173–198.

Singer, Jane. 2003. "Who are these Guys?: The Online Challenge to the Notion of Journalistic Professionalism." *Journalism* 4 (2): 139–163.

Singer, Jane. 1997. "Still Guarding the Gate? The Newspaper Journalist's Role in an Online World." *Convergence: The Journal of Research into New Media Technologies* 3 (1): 72–89.

Sparrow, Bartholomew. 2006. "A Research Agenda for an Institutional Media." *Political Communication* 23 (2): 145–157.

Sparrow, Bartholomew. 1999. *Uncertain Guardians: The news media as a political institution.* Baltimore: Johns Hopkins University Press.

Steensen, Steen. 2019. "Journalism's epistemic crisis and its solution: Disinformation, datafication and source criticism." *Journalism* 20 (1): 185–189.

Tandoc, Edson. 2019. "Journalism at the Periphery." *Media and Communication* 7 (4): 138–143.

Tuchman, Gaye. 2014. "Forward." In *Mediating the Message in the 21st Century.* Pamela Shoemaker and Stephen Reese. London: Routledge.

Wahl-Jorgensen, Karin. 2014. "Is Wikileaks Challenging the Paradigm of Journalism?" *International Journal of Communication* 8: 2581–2592.

Worley, Peter. 2019. *The If Machine.* London: Bloomsbury.

Zamith, Rodrigo. 2019. "Transparency, Interactivity, Diversity, and Information Provenance in Everyday Data Journalism." *Digital Journalism* 7 (4): 470–489.

Zelizer, Barbie. 1993. "Journalists as interpretive communities." *Critical Studies in Mass Communication* 10 (3): 219–237.

PART I

The historical influencers

1

KNOCK, KNOCK! RIGHT-WING ALTERNATIVE MEDIA IS AT THE DOOR

Institutional boundary work in a hybrid media environment

Karoline Andrea Ihlebæk and Tine Ustad Figenschou

What constitutes the core of the institutional press, and how are institutional boundaries challenged and protected in a hybrid media environment? Studies have warned that the news institution is under pressure due to dramatic technological disruptions, financial struggles, and the proliferation of content producers (Carlson 2017; Reese 2021). Alongside these challenges, the institution of journalism has been confronted by an increase in right-wing alternative media (Figenschou and Ihlebæk 2019; Holt 2020; Roberts and Wahl-Jorgensen 2021) and populist actors (Carlson, Robinson, and Lewis 2020), that engage in ideological and political critique to undermine the authority of the press while they compete for attention and impact with their own production of news and views. Overall, right-wing alternative media are unpredictable and antagonistic actors with whom professional journalism has struggled with understanding and responding to (Krämer and Langmann 2020; Nygaard 2021), both in terms of their ideological position and criticism, their semi-professional practices, and their relationship to the journalistic field.

This chapter investigates professional-alternative relations and boundary work processes from an institutional perspective in the context of the Norwegian media system. More specifically we look at inclusion and exclusion mechanisms as right-wing alternative media actors move closer to the professional field, and how the journalistic institutions react in a system characterized by strong press associations, consensus about professional ethical standards, and self-regulatory mechanisms guarding these principles (Hallin and Mancini 2004; Syvertsen et al. 2014). Based on in-depth interviews with both editors of right-wing alternative media and representatives from key press organizations in Norway, this chapter demonstrates how institutional regulative and constitutive rules are employed and understood by both insiders and outsiders of the journalistic institution.

The chapter takes a critical incident (Carlson 2020; Zelizer 1993) as a point of departure, specifically restrictions made in the statutes of the formalized self-regulatory

DOI: 10.4324/9781003140399-3

system for the press (Norwegian Press Council) which meant that only members of key press associations was included in the arrangement. First, these changes had implications for how the boundaries for the self-regulatory system and, ultimately, the journalistic institution were drawn. Second, the new requirements had consequences for key press associations, as controversial right-wing alternative media actors responded by applying for membership. In sum, this chapter demonstrates how institutional rules were reaffirmed by clarifying and tightening the boundaries between professional and alternative journalism.

Journalistic rules, codified ethics and critical incidents

Although the day-to-day institutional rules of journalism are primarily guided by implicit, common-sense news values and practices, codified and formalized professional codes of ethics also play a crucial part (Hafez 2002). Ethical codes consolidate *the regulative* and *the constitutive* rules of journalism (Ryfe 2006), emphasizing both legitimate modes of journalistic practice and attitudes and assumptions concerning what journalism ought to be. Codes of ethics serve as points of reference in debates about professional practice, institutional autonomy, and legitimacy, and while they might differ somewhat across national and journalistic cultures, Ward (2019: 6) underlines the general commitment that professional journalism adheres to "factual truth-telling in an objective manner." This shared understanding is deeply rooted in the ideology that journalism works for the public good, seeking to portray facts in a neutral way (Deuze 2005). Professional associations have since the 19th century played a key role in developing and securing codes of ethics, stating common principles of journalistic practice that are formative of the institution (Ward 2019). The codes are guided by press councils, meaning "nongovernmental bodies for professional self-regulation" (Brurås 2016), which monitor misconduct. Even though press councils take on many different shapes and forms across the world, with different levels of legitimacy and support, it represents a key feature of autonomous and independent media systems. We argue that professional codes of ethics and the associations that protect them, represent powerful points of reference in institutional boundary making processes, specifically following critical incidents when the rules of the institution are challenged and disputed (Ryfe 2006, 2016).

Traditionally, institutional approaches emphasize social institutions' durability over time by studying how patterns of behavior become internalized and routinized and how resources (material and symbolic) and rules (informal and formal) guide behavior and provide individuals with identities and professional roles (Ryfe 2016). While stability is at the core of how we perceive institutions, they are not static entities; disruptions or critical incidents can "shock" the system, potentially leading to significant change or reconfirming shared understandings (March and Olsen 2011). These incidents are characterized by uncertainty, pushing important and powerful actors within institutions to make decisions. Stressing empirical variations, Ryfe (2016) underlines the need to study critical incidents in different national contexts, as both threats to journalism and institutional responses are unevenly distributed across the globe. Our point of departure is that when journalistic values, routines and practices are disrupted by controversies or "critical incidents," such incidents cause people to question, challenge, and negotiate the boundaries of appropriate practice and attitudes (Carlson 2020; Zelizer 1993). In other words, when journalists are pushed to think about their roles and rules and to give them meaning, institutional identity is defended discursively (Hanitzsch and Vos 2017). For researchers, then, critical incidents are well-suited empirical cases to reveal how boundaries of the journalistic institution are challenged and defended, and to identify both continuity and change as potential outcomes.

It has been extensively documented that digitalization has disrupted journalism in several ways, having an impact on both structures and practices, even though continuity is also an important part of the picture (Ryfe 2019). In the context of this chapter, we emphasize two important developments that have been identified as a challenge to the journalistic institution. The first is related to the changing boundaries of journalism due to digitalization (Carlson 2015). Numerous studies have pointed to the dramatic proliferation of actors producing content on the borderline of journalism, including content marketing, alternative media, bloggers, fake news sites, that compete for attention and impact (Eldridge 2018; Holt, Figenschou, and Frischlich 2019). Consequently, the competition for audiences and revenues have become fiercer and it has become more difficult to define what journalism is, as new actors that enters the media sphere might or might not share or follow the constitutive or regulative rules of the institution (Carlson 2015; Culver 2017; Ward 2015, 2016, 2019). The second (and related) dimension is that journalism is under attack, and its authority and legitimacy is being questioned (Carlson 2017; Reese 2021). Particularly relevant here is far-right actors' harsh criticism of journalists and specific news organizations (Figenschou and Ihlebæk 2019) as well as the institution of journalism more broadly (Holt 2020; Reese 2021). Anti-institutionalism or counter-institutionalism fundamentally challenge the structures of journalism, questioning perceptions of facts, truth, objectivity, and neutrality (Carlson, Robinson, and Lewis 2020; Reese 2021). The worry is how such attacks influence trust in journalism. Falling levels of trust in journalism have prompted widespread concern that the institution of journalism is in crisis (see Newman et al. 2019; Strömbäck et al. 2020), with audiences positioned to the right of the political center having comparatively higher distrust in established news media (Tsfati and Ariely 2014).

In the context of this chapter, these two developments extend to the scholarly discussion of right-wing alternative media and how they should be understood in the wider media environment. At one level, it has been pointed out how right-wing alternative media is on the rise and that they manage to set the agenda on social media platforms with content that is often partisan and pushing the ethical standards of the mainstream press (Benkler, Faris, and Roberts 2018; Sandberg and Ihlebæk 2019; Wischnewski, Bruns, and Keller 2021; see also Russell and Vos, this volume). As such they compete with professional news organizations for agenda-setting power. At another level, these kinds of news producers have a dubious relationship with the journalistic institution. It has been pointed out that alternative media demarcate their position by emphasizing their role as a "self-perceived corrective" to the mainstream (Holt et al. 2019; Mayerhöffer 2021). This counterposition is specifically visible in how alternative media engage in media criticism or cynicism as part of their publication strategy, claiming that the established media is biased and not trustworthy (Cushion, McDowell-Naylor, and Thomas 2021; Figenschou and Ihlebæk 2019; Mayerhöffer 2021). At the same time, the antagonism is paradoxical, as alternative media sites often refer to or recontextualize content from established media sources and copy their style in terms of lay-out and practices (Haanshuus and Ihlebæk 2021). It is also necessary to distinguish between those actors that are deviant and those that are closer to the professional field. Extreme actors are more likely anti-institutional, but it is far more common to support the constitutive rules but criticize the practice of professional journalists (Figenschou and Ihlebæk 2019).

Previous research has indicated that the professional field has struggled with how to understand and respond to such competitors (Krämer and Langmann 2020; Nygaard 2021), and it becomes specifically complex when this kind of actors that want to be an alternative approach the professional field and engage in mainstreaming processes. Von Nordheim and Kleinen-von Königslöw (2021) refer to the metaphor of "the parasite" to explain how a subsystem relates to the host which it is simultaneously dependent and critical of. Moving from an outsider to an insider position, the danger is that the parasite might threaten the integrity or the legitimacy of the system. That being said, it is important to acknowledge how an insider or outsider distinction in a journalistic context has not only a symbolic value in terms of who is perceived as a professional or non-professional actor, but also that it has an impact at the material level, for instance on who gets access to professional associations, press subsidies, press conferences, or sources, a point we will return to in the analysis.

Case: Institutional boundary work

To better understand the relevance of our case as a critical incident and what it can tell us about institutional boundary work, it is first necessary to describe the core features of the Norwegian journalistic institution. Nordic societies, including Norway, Sweden, Denmark, Finland, and Iceland, have been described as having a *democratic corporatist model* characterized by (1) a strong press with high newspaper circulation and early development of mass-circulation press; (2) an active state that supports journalism through strong subsidies and public-service broadcasting and has equally strong protections for press freedom; (3) political parallelism, meaning a history of intimate structural ties between the newspaper industry and political sphere; and (4) strong professionalization of the media sector through institutionalization and self-regulation systems (Hallin and Mancini 2004: 67; Brüggemann et al. 2014). Similarly, Ahva et al. (2017) argue that journalists in Nordic countries work under "similar systemic conditions," and share strikingly similar visions of what it means to be a journalist.

The Norwegian media system and the development of journalism as an institution within it are inherently linked to the role of professional associations, reflecting the traditionally strong corporatist structures of Norwegian society (Rommetveit 2017). Professional associations in the Nordic media system have a comparatively stronger position than in other media systems (Hallin and Mancini 2004: 170–178), and they were key drivers of the establishment of a strong, formalized self-regulatory system for the press (Brurås 2016). Contrary to developments elsewhere, press associations continue to play a powerful role in defending key journalistic principles, functioning as the primary representatives of the journalistic institution in public debates and policy processes. Wide support for the Norwegian Press Council (PFU) and the Code of Ethics for the Norwegian Press (hereafter referred to as the Code of Ethics) is another key characteristic of the system (Hallin and Mancini 2004). The Press Council's main purpose is "to supervise and promote the ethical and professional standards of the Norwegian press" (*presse. no,* n.d.), and it manages complaints against misconduct by the news media. If a media organization is found to have breached the Code of Ethics, it must publish a public apology on its news site. In this way, the system holds the institution of journalism accountable for its practices. The formalization of the Code of Ethics illustrates the consolidation and expansion of the Norwegian journalistic institution, including how its boundaries are marked, legitimacy is claimed, and self-reflexive debates are encouraged (Sørum et al. 2012). The Press Council is solely financed by members of the Norwegian Press Association, an umbrella organization comprised of all the unions and associations for media professionals in Norway.[1] The Norwegian Press Association and the Press Council represent powerful non-governmental bodies that secure the autonomy of the journalistic field and independence from state intervention (Brurås 2016, Hallin and Mancini 2004; Sørum et al. 2012).

The Press Council: tightening the boundaries

It used to be that the Norwegian Press Council managed any complaint made against any content producer for failing to adhere to the Code of Ethics. However, as the number of media actors with an unclear relationship to press ethics increased, there was a drastic growth in the number of complaints, ultimately exhausting the system. In response, the Norwegian Press Association initiated a discussion about whether they needed to limit their oversight. The original text of the statutes reads as follows, with the two final sentences serving as the subject of debate:

§ 1 The Norwegian Press Council is established by the Norwegian Press Association to supervise and secure the ethical and professional standard of the Norwegian media. As part of this work, the Press Council evaluates complaints made against the Norwegian media and makes public statements. The same applies to independent publishers that are not members of The Norwegian Press Association, but that follow the *Code of Ethics*. Other media can be evaluated if they agree.[2]

Whether or not restrictions were needed was discussed for several months in different fora before being accepted by a unanimous board in 2018, and the two last sentences were deleted and changed to the following sentence: "All editorial-driven media that is affiliated to the Norwegian Press Association can be reported to the Press Council." Consequently, inclusion in the self-regulatory system was limited to those who were affiliated with the Norwegian Press Association through membership in the Association of Editors or the Association of the Media Industries. It was also stressed that it was not enough for specific journalists to be part of the Norwegian Union for Journalists.

Two main reasons were given for the change in the statutes. The first was based on resources, as the secretary-general of the Norwegian Press Association explained:

> First, we need to use the resources on those that actually contribute to the self-regulatory system, and it is not just about those that call themselves alternative media, but many other publications too, like bloggers, podcasts, etc., that do not follow the Code of Ethics or the Code for Editors. There were a lot of people complaining against these forms of media, and we are a self-regulatory system, we are financed by the established media, so it was a pragmatic decision.
>
> *(Personal communication, informant 5)*

The second argument was related to questions of professional legitimacy. The secretary-general of the Norwegian Press Association argued that the association did not want unprofessional actors, who were often accused of ethical misconduct, to "borrow" the legitimacy of professional journalists by claiming they followed the Code of Ethics. In other words, it was necessary to make a clearer distinction between those who *said* that they followed ethical principles and those who *did* so: "we need to protect the media that want to follow the press ethics, because journalism is ethics, and that is our view in this debate" (Personal communication, informant 5). At the same time, it was acknowledged that restricting their statutory oversight would have some risky consequences. For example, the public would be left with limited opportunities to complain about misconduct, which could lead to calls for a parallel complaint system or state intervention (e.g., establishment of a press ombudsman). Were this to occur, it would weaken the autonomy of the self-regulatory, non-governmental system.

As the symbolic boundaries determining who is understood to be part of the professional field were tightened, the secretary-general of the Norwegian Press Association explained, the two most important associations, the Association of Editors and the Association of the Media Industries, would probably receive applications from actors that were defined as "outsiders." This is exactly what happened. In the following, we will explore why editors of right-wing alternative media sought membership in professional organizations, the process that followed, and the outcomes.

Right-wing alternative media seeking insider status

In 2018, the editors of controversial right-wing alternative news sites *Document.no* and *Resett.no* applied for membership in the Association of Editors and, later on, *Resett.no*, applied for membership in the Association of the Media Industries. *Document.no* was established as a right-wing blog in 2003 by the editor, Hans Rustad, who had previously worked in the professional press. It has expanded over the years, and now has several writers regularly publishing news and opinions. It describes itself as a "conservative, independent and national media house for news, political analysis and comments," and emphasizes that they prioritize "the current big and defining issues, like mass immigration to Norway and the integration problems this leads to" as well as the US, the climate change debate, the Middle East, and religion, particularly Islamism, which they argue represents "the most dangerous totalitarian movement" (*Document.no*, n.d.). *Resett.no* was established in 2017 as a tabloid, alternative news site by Helge Lurås, a former strategic analyst with no previous experience in journalism. The site describes itself as a political independent media channel that represents "the voice of those that are not heard" and aims to be "an alternative to the established media" (*Resett.no,* n.d.). Both editors point out that they have been inspired by the populist right-wing movement in Europe and that they are especially concerned about the negative consequences of immigration and Islam on Norwegian culture (personal communication, informant 1 and 4). Both news sites have received public attention and criticism for their provocative reporting, especially on these topics (Nygaard 2020).

Before we look more closely at their processes, it is necessary to explore why these two editors, who clearly positioned themselves as stern media critics and as an alternative to the mainstream media, want to become members in professional associations, and consequently, be included in the self-regulatory complaint system. Why would they risk their "contract" with their dedicated audiences, who value their outsider position, to become part of the mainstream? Our analysis showed that both symbolic and material resources are at stake. First, both editors stressed that even though they are critical of the news media and have made media criticism part of their editorial strategy, they support the self-regulatory system and the Press Council, which gives the public the opportunity to complain and publications the potential to learn from their mistakes. As the news editor of *Resett.no* explains:

> We receive a lot of criticism and many people react to what we write for both good and bad reasons. It would have been an advantage for them and those people that we write about, and particular those that are most hostile towards us, that their complaints had been tested by the Press Council.
>
> *(Personal communication, informant 2).*

In other words, the editors are not anti-institutionalist; they do not oppose the constitutive or regulative rules of the press institutions. They are, however, critical of how these rules are adapted and practiced by those on the inside. Specifically, they critique what they see as a biased and elitist form of journalism. An important motivation for their applications was to be taken seriously and to gain influence and legitimacy. This form of mainstreaming was, they acknowledged, not without risk since their audiences value their outsider position. Nevertheless, they believed they could balance their alternativeness with their insider position. Importantly, membership in the associations also provides formalized access to, for example, specific court cases, the parliament, and press conferences. In other words, membership does not just represent the crossing of symbolic boundaries, but material ones. A final point that is less-often articulated, but important, is the value of creating attention; these actors publicly announced that they had applied and followed up by reporting on the application process and, when it was made, the decision.

Decisions: Yes, then no, no, and no again

Their membership applications received mixed responses by professional actors. While some argued that it was wise to include the editors to hold them accountable to the Code of Ethics, others feared that these actors were not serious, that they would challenge the system from within, and that they would not respect institutional rules. The applications also represented something new for the associations. Normally, membership applications are administered by the secretary of the associations, but if they are complicated or controversial, they are sent to the board for further investigations. From interviews with those involved, it was clear that the application from the editor of *Resett.no* was viewed as particularly difficult. The deputy chairman of the Association of Editors explained, "*Resett.no* represents something new. It is different. It's not like anything else that we see, and it is not about politics, it is about practice" (personal communication, informant 9). This was also emphasized by the Association of the Media Industries: "We have never had that type of application before (…). Previously it has only been necessary to make a more general assessment of the members who have joined" (personal communication, informant 11).

The Association of Editors first accepted the application for membership from the editor of *Document.no* in 2018, but rejected the editor of *Resett.no* later the same year. The editor of *Resett.no* applied again in 2019, but the application was unanimously rejected by the board in 2020. *Resett.no* then applied for membership in the Association of the Media Industries but was again turned down. One of the reasons why the editor of *Document.no* was accepted in the Association of Editors and the editor of *Resett.no* was not, according to an interview with the Chairman of the Board (personal communication, informant 8), was the latter's lack of professional training and experience from the professional field. She also added that the association would soon launch a course for editors of new publications with no professional background. In other words, coming from a professional background function as a safeguard in terms of understanding the rules of the institution and what it entails. Informants from the Association of Editors pointed out that nevertheless a systematic analysis of the sites was carried out for both sites to evaluate the editorial practices, and they had invited the editors to meetings to discuss issues they were concerned about. According to the Deputy Chairman, the core question was: "Is this journalism or not? Is it outside or inside the criteria that form our basis?" (personal communication, informant 9). The Chairman of the Board further outlined,

> At a time when journalism is under pressure from so many fronts, there must be some who insist that everything that is available online is not journalism. And what defines journalism in relation to all other types of information, that is, among other things, the Code of Ethics, which is tested by the Press Council. And maintaining the quality of journalism is more important than ever at a time when we also see that fake news is flourishing and is a serious threat to democracy and our society
>
> *(Personal communication, informant 8).*

The rejections were based on two arguments. The first relates to the regulative rules of the press institution, and more specifically, instances of what was perceived as serious journalistic misconduct. Examples included a lack of moderation in the comment sections of the website, an attempt to pay a source a considerable amount of money to talk about a sex scandal, the use of anonymous writers, personal attacks on particular people, as well as inappropriate commercial promotion of a book written by the editor. The other argument is more closely related to the constitutive rules of journalism and was perceived as particularly grave: the editor of *Resett.no* had made a call for boycotts of other news media. In an interview with the former Chair of the Board and the Secretary-General of the Association of Editors, who was involved in evaluating the first application, they emphasized that the call for boycotts of other news media was a serious breach to the association's overall aim to secure the conditions for free speech (Statutes, §2).[3]

> Of course, you can criticize editorial-driven media, you can also warn against concrete forms of journalistic practices. But you cross a line when you call for a general boycott.
>
> *(Personal communication, informant 7)*

> It is contrary to the purpose (of the association), because we do not boycott, we do not encourage boycotts. We want a wide number of editorial-driven media.
>
> *(Personal communication, informant 6)*

Even though both board decisions were unanimous, it became clear from the interviews that it had not been easy, and there had been disagreement and discussion between board members. One difficult issue was whether it would be better to allow the editor of *Resett.no* into the association and let the Press Council take care of future misconduct on the same terms as other members post-publication.

The rejection from the Association of the Media Industries was also based on an inquiry to determine whether *Resett.no* adhered to "ordinary publishing principles" (personal communication, informant 10). In order to do so, as stated by the Head of Business Policy, they had to more clearly operationalize what this meant:

> What does it mean to be a publicist actor, as we consider it? Based on our statutes, right? When we say that we must strengthen and protect freedom of expression, freedom of the press and freedom of information as fundamental values in a democratic and open society. According to our statutes, what does this mean in terms of being a publicist?
>
> *(Personal communication, informant 11)*

To perform the evaluation, they made a list of core journalistic principles, including the importance of "safeguarding anonymity, protection of sources, promoting free dissemination of information, and open, honest and truth-seeking journalism" (personal communication, informant 11). Furthermore, they emphasized that journalists had to clearly distinguish between facts and opinion, clearly stating what is editorial content and what is commercial material, and work according to the ethical guidelines for Norwegian media (i.e., the Code of Ethics).

The informants from *Resett.no* argued that the rejections were expected. They acknowledged that some of their reporting crosses boundaries, but stated that they had followed the advice given during the application processes. In their coverage of the process, they accused the associations of making their decisions on an ideological basis and a desire to keep them on the outside because of their political views, a point that was vehemently denied by the informants from the associations. Also, the informants from *Resett.no* explained that their outsider position hinders access to press conferences and court cases. However, this line of reasoning should not be the primary aim for becoming a member, the informants from the Association of Editors argued; the overall ideals of journalism and its function (i.e., constitutive rules) are valued over material concerns.

Conclusion: You may (not) come in

In this case study, we have examined institutional boundary work in the context of media systems with strong press associations and strong support for shared ethical codes (Hallin and Mancini 2004; Syvertsen et al. 2014). We have argued that even though the rules of journalism are formed by day-to-day practices and routines, the role of codified ethics and the system that guards it constitutes a powerful reference point when it comes to institutional work and negotiation of boundaries. In the chapter, we show boundary work from two sides, both the insider and the outsider position. On the one hand, our study explores how the institution responds when "outsiders" prey on the legitimacy of the institution. Tightening the criteria for inclusion in the self-regulatory system through the status of the Press Council means that actors need to demonstrate their loyalty, both material and symbolically, by becoming members in a professional association. The examined case also illustrates that the position of professional associations as powerful gatekeepers guarding the boundaries of the journalistic institution is reaffirmed and strengthened. Faced with applications from antagonistic actors that have an unclear relationship with the regulative and the constitutive rules of journalism, the criteria for membership and how they are interpreted was re-evaluated. Pre-evaluations of how applicants adhere to the Code of Conduct, which are normally conducted by the Press Council post-publication, are unprecedented and signal a more active role of key stakeholders in protecting the legitimacy and the boundaries of the institution.

On the other hand, our study documents how right-wing alternative media actors, characterized by their antagonistic position, frame their motivation for seeking insider status and their experiences of institutional boundary work. This shows that it is important to distinguish between right-wing actors that are *anti-institutional* and those that are not. It is the latter category that most probably will move closer to the professional field. The informants explain that the motivations for mainstreaming and seeking insider status are of a material and symbolic nature. Being part of the self-regulatory system through membership in professional association, signifies legitimacy and potential impact, but also access and privileges. While they acknowledge that the paradoxical position might be questioned by their followers, they do not see this as a significant threat. Being kept on the outside is interpreted as a political move and the associations are accused of having dubious motivations.

In sum, the chapter shows how institutional work is played out when antagonistic actors knock on the door. If there are doubts about why you have come and how you are going to behave based on your previous actions, you might not be let in. Closing the door could be the safe move, but it is not without its risks. Being left on the outside, you can certainly make some noise that makes it uncomfortable for those on the inside. At least until you decide to knock again.

List of informants

Resett.no

1.   Chief Editor, Helge Lurås (5.8.2019 and 18.11.2020)
2.   News Editor, Lars Akerhaug (16.05.2019 and 24.11.2020)
3.   Editor, Shurika Hansen (19.06.2019)

Document.no

4.   Chief Editor, Hans Rustad (20.06.2019)

Norwegian Press Association

5.   Secretary-General, Elin Floberghagen (21.05.2019)

Association of Editors

6. Secretary-General, Arne Jensen (21.5.2019, 16.11.2020)
7. Former Chairman of the Board, Harald Stanghelle (20.05.2019)
8. Current Chairman of the Board, Hanna Relling Berg (16.11.2020)
9. Deputy chairman of the Board, Eirik Hoff Lysholm (25.11.2020)

Association of the Media Industries

10. Chairman of the Board, Pål Nedregotten (19.11.2020)
11. Head of Business Policy, Bjørn Wisted (24.11.2020)

NTB – The Norwegian News Agency

12. Chief Editor, Mads Yngve Storvik (24.11.2020)

Notes

1 The Norwegian Press Association is an umbrella organization supported by all the key unions and associations in Norway, including the Norwegian Union for Journalists, the Association of Editors, the Association of Media Industries, the Association of the Trade Press, the Association of Local Newspapers, the Association of Local Radio, the public service broadcasters NRK and TV2, Magasin, Discovery Norway, and the Nent Group.
2 https://presse.no/pfu/slik-klager-du-til-pfu/vedtekter/.
3 https://www.nored.no/Om-NR/Vedtekter.

References

Ahva, Laura, Arjen van Dalen, Jan Fredrik Hovden, Guðbjörg Hildur Kolbeins, Monica Löfgren Nilsson, MortenSkovsgaard, and Jari Väliverronen. 2017. "A Welfare State of Mind?" *Journalism Studies* 18 (5): 595–613. doi:10.1080/1461670X.2016.1249005..

Benkler, Yochai, Robert Faris, and Hal Roberts. 2018. *Network Propaganda Manipulation, Disinformation, and Radicalization in American Politics.* Oxford: Oxford University Press.

Brüggemann, Michael, Sven Engesser, Florin Büchel, Edda Humprecht, and Laia Castro. 2014. "Hallin and Mancini Revisited: Four Empirical Types of Western Media Systems." *Journal of Communication* 64 (6): 1037–1065. doi:10.1111/jcom.12127..

Brurås, Svein. 2016. "Normative Features of a Successful Press Council." *Journal of Media Ethics* 31 (3): 162–173.

Carlson, Matt. 2015. "Introduction: The Many Boundaries of Journalism." In *Boundaries of Journalism: Professionalism, Practices and Participation*, edited by Matt Carlson and Seth C. Lewis, pp. 1–19. London and New York: Routledge.

Carlson, Matt. 2017. *Journalistic Authority: Legitimating News in the Digital Era.* New York: Columbia University Press.

Carlson, Matt. 2020. "Journalistic Critical Incidents as Boundary Making and the Making of Boundaries Around Critical Incidents." In *Critical Incidents in Journalism*, edited by Edison C Tandoc, Joy Jenkins, Ryan J. Thomas, and Oscar Westlund, pp. 28–42. New York: Routledge.

Carlson, Matt, Sue Robinson, and Seth C. Lewis. 2020. "Digital Press Criticism: The Symbolic Dimensions of Donald Trump's Assault on U.S. Journalists as the 'Enemy of the

People'." *Digital Journalism*, 5 November 2020. Online before print. doi:10.1080/21670811.2020.1836981.

Culver, Kathleen Bartzen. 2017. "Disengaged Ethics." *Journalism Practice* 11 (4): 477–492. doi:10.1080/17512786.2015.1121788..

Cushion, Stephen, Declan McDowell-Naylor, and Richard Thomas. 2021. "Why National Media Systems Matter: A Longitudinal Analysis of How UK Left-Wing and Right-Wing Alternative Media Critique Mainstream Media (2015–2018)." *Journalism Studies* 1–20. doi:10.1080/1461670X.2021.1893795..

Deuze, Mark. 2005. "What is Journalism?: Professional Identity and Ideology of Journalists Reconsidered." *Journalism* 6 (4): 442–464. doi:10.1177/1464884905056815..

Eldridge, Scott. 2018. *Online journalism from the Periphery: Interloper Media and the Journalistic Field*. Oxon and New York: Routledge.

Figenschou, Tine Ustad, and Karoline Andrea Ihlebæk. 2019. "Challenging Journalistic Authority." *Journalism Studies* 20 (9): 1221–1237. doi:10.1080/1461670x.2018.1500868..

Haanshuus, Birgitte P., and Karoline Andrea Ihlebæk. 2021. "Recontextualising the news: How antisemitic discourses are constructed in extreme far-right alternative media." *Nordicom Review* 42 (1):37–50. doi:10.2478/nor-2021-0005.

Hafez, Kai. 2002. "Journalism Ethics Revisited: A Comparison of Ethics Codes in Europe, North Africa, the Middle East, and Muslim Asia." *Political Communication* 19 (2): 225–250. doi:10.1080/10584600252907461..

Hallin, Daniel C., and Paolo Mancini. 2004. *Comparing Media Systems: Three Models of Media and Politics*. Cambridge: Cambridge University Press.

Hanitzsch, Thomas, and Tim P. Vos. 2017. "Journalistic Roles and the Struggle Over Institutional Identity: The Discursive Constitution of Journalism." *Communication Theory* 27 (2): 115–135. doi:10.1111/comt.12112..

Holt, Kristoffer. 2020. *Right-Wing Alternative Media*. London: Routledge.

Holt, Kristoffer, Tine Ustad Figenschou, and Lena Frischlich. 2019. "Key Dimensions of Alternative News Media." *Digital Journalism* 7 (7): 860–869. doi:10.1080/21670811.2019.1625715..

Krämer, Benjamin, and Klara Langmann. 2020. "Professionalism as a Response to Right-Wing Populism? An Analysis of a Metajournalistic Discourse." *International Journal of communication* 14: 1932–8036.

March, James G., and Johan P. Olsen. 2011. "Elaborating the 'New Institutionalism'." In *The Oxford Handbook of Political Institutions*, edited by Robert E. Goodin, pp. 1–19, Oxford: Oxford University Press. doi:10.1093/oxfordhb/9780199604456.013.0008.

Mayerhöffer, Eva. 2021. "How do Danish Right-wing Alternative Media Position Themselves Against the Mainstream? Advancing the Study of Alternative Media Structure and Content." *Journalism Studies* 22 (2):119–136. doi:10.1080/1461670X.2020.1814846..

Newman, Nic, Richard Fletcher, Antonis Kalogeropoulos, and Rasmus Kleis Nielsen. 2019. *Reuters Institute Digital News Report 2019*. Oxford: Reuters Institute for the Study of Journalism.

Nygaard, Silje. 2021. "On the Mainstream/Alternative Continuum: Mainstream Media Reactions to Right-Wing Alternative News Media." *Digital Journalism*:1–17. doi:10.1080/21670811.2021.1894962..

Nygaard, Silje. 2020. "Boundary Work: Intermedia Agenda-Setting Between Right-Wing Alternative Media and Professional Journalism." *Journalism Studies* 21 (6): 766–782. doi:10.1080/1461670X.2020.1722731..

Reese, Stephen D. 2021. *The Crisis of the Institutional Press*. Cambridge: Polity Press.

Roberts, Jason, and Karin Wahl-Jorgensen. 2021. "Breitbart's Attacks on Mainstream Media: Victories, Victimhood, and Vilification." In *Affective Politics of Digital Media: Propaganda by*

Other Means, edited by Megan Boler and Elizabeth Davis, pp. 170–185. New York: Routledge.

Rommetveit, Hilmar. 2017. "Scandinavian Corporatism in Decline." In *The Nordic Models in Political Science: Challenged, but Still Viable?*, edited by Oddbjørn Knudsen. Bergen: Fagbokforlaget.

Ryfe, David M. 2006. "The Nature of News Rules." *Political Communication* 23 (2): 203–214.

Ryfe, David M. 2016. "News Institutions." In *Sage Handbook of Digital Journalism*, edited by edited by Tamara Witschge, Chris W. Anderson, David Domingo, and Alfred. Hermida, pp. 370–382. London: Sage.

Ryfe, David M. 2019. "The Warp and Woof of the Field of Journalism." *Digital Journalism* 7 (7): 844–859.

Sandberg, Linn, and Karoline Andrea Ihlebæk. 2019. "Exploring the Link Between Right-wing Alternative Media and Social Media During the Swedish 2018 Election." *Statsvetenskaplig Tidsskrift* 12 (3): 421–440.

Strömbäck, Jesper, Yariv Tsfati, Hajo Boomgaarden, Alyt Damstra, Elina Lindgren, Rens Vliegenthart, and Torun Lindholm. 2020. "News media trust and its impact on media use: toward a framework for future research." *Annals of the International Communication Association*:1–18. doi:10.1080/23808985.2020.1755338..

Syvertsen, Trine, Gunn Enli, Ole J. Mjøs, and Hallvard Moe. 2014. *The Media Welfare State: Nordic Media in the Digital Age.* Ann Arbor: The University of Michigan Press.

Sørum, Kathrine Y., Terje Rasmussen, Kathrine Amarloui, and Åste H. Alnæs. 2012. "Presseetikk og autonomi: Pressenormers bidrag til journalistikkens selvstendiggjøring" [Press Ethics and Autonomy]. *Norsk Medietidsskrift* 19 (2): 130–150.

Tsfati, Yariv, and Gal Ariely. 2014. "Individual and Contextual Correlates of Trust in Media Across 44 Countries." *Communication Research* 41 (6): 760–782. doi:10.1177/0093650213485972..

von Nordheim, Gerret, and Katharina Kleinen-von Königslöw. 2021. "Uninvited Dinner Guests: A Theoretical Perspective on the Antagonists of Journalism Based on Serres' Parasite." *Media and Communication* 9 (1): 88–98. doi:10.17645/mac.v9i1.3419.

Ward, Stephen J. A. 2015. *The Invention of Journalism Ethics: The Path to Objectivity and Beyond.* Montreal, Kingston, London, and Chicago: McGill-Queen's University Press.

Ward, Stephen J. A. 2016. "Digital Journalism Ethics." In *Sage Handbook of Digital Journalism*, edited by Tamara Witschge, Chris W. Anderson, David Domingo, and Alfred. Hermida, pp. 35–43. London: Sage.

Ward, Stephen J. A. 2019. *Disrupting Journalism Ethics: Radical Change on the Frontier of Digital Media.* London: Routledge.

Wischnewski, Magdalena, Axel Bruns, and Tobias Keller. 2021. "Shareworthiness and Motivated Reasoning in Hyper-Partisan News Sharing Behavior on Twitter." *Digital Journalism*: 1–23. doi:10.1080/21670811.2021.1903960..

Zelizer, Barbie. 1993. "Journalists as Interpretive Communities." *Critical Studies in Mass Communication* 10 (3): 219–237.

2

THE INTEGRATION OF NATIVE ADVERTISING IN JOURNALISM AND ITS IMPACT ON THE NEWS-ADVERTISING BOUNDARY

You Li

Journalism in the 21st century has been transformed not only by technological disruptions, but also by outside institutions. One such institution is advertising, which has shared the physical space with news and fueled news production since the early days of print newspapers but has now evolved into more seamless forms. Journalism has been in a contested relationship with advertising ever since the latter became a major source of revenue for the press (Baldasty 1992). With a figurative boundary established between news and advertising at the turn of the twentieth century to ensure editorial autonomy and operational efficiency (Mari 2014), a so-called wall between the editorial team and the advertising staff was built (McManus 1992). However, despite clear labeling of editorial sections and advertising sections in print, advertisers never ceased in attempting to influence editorial decisions and content (Soley and Craig 1992; Hays and Reisner 1990). In recent decades, this editorial-advertising boundary has diminished into an ethical myth and rhetorical symbol at a time when the survival of journalism is in question (Coddington 2015). The norm of separation has gradually evolved into a culture of collaboration between the editorial side and the business side to improve the adaptability, financial sustainability, and efficiency of a journalistic entity (Artemas, Vos, and Duffy 2016; Cornia, Sehl, and Nielsen 2018).

The rise of native advertising exemplifies the newest breach on the news-advertising boundary with unprecedented challenges and opportunities. Native advertising on news websites resembles the news content to lure readers while disclosing the commercial nature to warn them (Ferrer-Conill and Karlsson 2018). While journalists have insisted on clear differentiation between news and advertising to preserve journalistic autonomy and credibility (Schauster, Ferrucci, and Neill 2016; Li 2019), pro-business managers and publishers have assembled editorial content and staffing with advertising to maximize revenue potential (Glasser, Varma, and Zou 2019). The tension between the transparency and deception of

DOI: 10.4324/9781003140399-4

the news-advertising boundary illustrates the power asymmetries between the editorial side and the business side. The preservation of the editorial-business boundary depends on the execution of native advertising, whether the production, integration, and presentation of native advertising adhere to an ethical and clear disclosure.

This chapter begins by explaining the uniqueness of native advertising and revisiting the roots and practices of integrating native advertising into media as an attempt to blur the news-advertising boundary. The focus is on native advertising on news media platforms and its challenge to the boundary of journalism. Then, the chapter will show conceptually the disclosure practices that defend the boundary of journalism. This chapter concludes with the impact of native advertising on journalism practices. The objective is to observe the renegotiation of the boundary between journalism and commercialism in the face of native advertising, discuss the implications of the blurred lines, and offer scholarly and managerial recommendations.

What is native advertising?

Native advertising is at the intersection of marketing and journalism; it is hybrid commercial content blended into editorial content and congruent with the appearance and behavior of the hosting media platform. Native advertising is not the same as content marketing, as the former places commercial content on a media platform, whereas the latter can occur at all possible platforms, including owned, earned, and paid (Pulizzi 2013). For advertisers, one advantage of native advertising is to leverage the audience base and credibility of the hosting media. But to media critics, that mere advantage misleads audiences and impedes upon editorial integrity (see Banjac, this volume).

Online native advertising is not the first attempt of advertising to challenge the news-advertising boundary. In the 19th century, advertising agencies often requested a specific placement of advertising with other content (e.g., next to regular newspaper articles and not next to other ads) (Baldasty 1992). Many publishers, enticed by the revenue, welcomed the ads disguised as news in reading notices and produced them in the same typeface as their news articles (Baldasty 1992). The "advertorial," a special combination of advertising with simulated editorial material, appeared in newspapers as early as 1915 and gained popularity in broadcasting and magazines in the 1980s (Stout, Wilcox, and Greer 1989). In a survey conducted in the late 1990s, 97% of 148 daily newspapers produced advertorials as a part of the papers' regular business, and nearly half of them had internal departments producing the special section (Shaver and Louise 1997). When newspapers transitioned online in the early 2000s, advertising on news websites evolved to e-sponsorship where promotional messages and sponsored links featuring brands were inserted in an online news story (Rodgers, Cameron, and Brill 2005; Rodgers 2003). Debuting around 2010, native advertising inherited a similar trait of discreet placement and advanced on delivering a cohesive experience from design to content.

Native advertising may take various forms in execution, depending on the characteristics of the hosting media environment. The Interactive Advertising Bureau condensed the six forms of native advertising initially defined in 2013 into four core formats in its recent report outlined in Table 2.1 (Interactive Advertising Bureau 2019).

Regardless of format, native advertising has one essential characteristic. The word "native" differentiates it from traditional display ads in both content and presentation: The content is organic, relevant, engaging to audiences, and yet the presentation is nonpromotional and nonintrusive so that audiences tend to feel that the ads belong to the hosting environment. Compared to deceptive patent medicine ads, native advertising should provide truthful information. In other words, native advertising should meet the same basic editorial quality for journalism: authenticity and accuracy (Taiminen, Luoma-aho, and Tolvanen 2015). Compared to an advertiser-centric approach in traditional display ads and advertorials that feature products and services, native advertising adopts an audience-centric approach that focuses on providing information relevant to audiences (Matteo and Dal Zotto 2015). Native ads may not glorify or promote a brand or product but instead, increase audiences' awareness of certain issues and provide tips to ease their everyday life (Wang and Li 2017). Mirroring the content features of their hosting media, native advertising resembles infotainment, service, or civic engagement roles to simulate the functions of their hosting media to serve target audiences (Li 2019). Moreover, compared to short, sponsored content (e.g., tweets, posts, e-sponsorship), native advertising in the form of branded/native content posts simulates editorial length and design and incorporates journalistic story-telling techniques (Wang and Li 2017).

Technically, native advertising only refers to content on digital platforms, primarily on websites and mobile sites. Like other digital editorial content, it is interactive,

TABLE 2.1 The Formats of Native Advertising

Formats	Placement	Destination	Producer
In-feed native ad link	Appear among editorial headline links and article feeds on home page	External URL ad page or internal publisher page	Advertiser
In-content native ad link	Appear among the paragraphs of an article, usually resembling editorial designs	External URL ad page or internal publisher page	Advertiser
Content recommendation ad link	Appear on homepage or an article page in an isolated spot separate from the other editorial content and with distinctive visual designs	External URL ad page or internal publisher page	Advertiser
Branded/native content post	Appear on an article page resembling editorial designs	Internal publisher page	Content agency; content solution team; editorial team

social, fluid, shareable, and spreadable. Unlike traditional advertising often being produced by external agencies, native advertising may come from both external and internal agencies where dedicated writers and even editorial staff produce native advertising copies (Matteo and Dal Zotto 2015). In essence, the "native" character requires that native advertising not only follows the natural design, location, and content behaviors of the environment in which it appears (Interactive Advertising Bureau 2019), but also imitates editorial content characteristics and functions at a deeper level than sponsored content, which may require the collaboration of the editorial side to share space, resources, and staff with the business side.

The integration of native advertising into news media

Amid declining ad revenue in the 21st century, native advertising has provided publishers with the hope of a new revenue stream. The global spending of native advertising is estimated to jump from $85.83 billion in 2020 to $402 billion by 2025, with the US taking a third of the global share (Clementi 2019). In 2018, 53% of 148 news executives from 53 countries reported that they already adopted native advertising service and another 14% said they were most likely to adopt it in the near future (Laursen 2018). The degree of integration, however, was not uniform across all media, ranging from structural integration of space, procedural integration of resources, to cultural integration of the editorial and business sides.

The pro-business and more market-oriented news publications were the early adopters of native advertising in the United States. One such pioneer is Forbes. Launched in 2010, AdVoice, later renamed BrandVoice, produced and ran paid content pieces for advertisers. BrandVoice 360 mixed and matched the print, video, and digital editorial elements of Forbes with related BrandVoice content (DVorkin 2016). Although BrandVoice did not share resources or recruit personnel from *Forbes*' newsrooms, it used its editorial logic, focusing on a topic instead of a brand and correlating with readers' concerns and the news cycle (Feng and Ots 2018). Online-only media, such as The Huffington Post and BuzzFeed, soon joined the gold rush in 2010 and 2012 respectively (Matteo and Dal Zotto 2015; Almohammad 2017), followed by legacy news media outlets since 2013. American legacy newspapers gradually expanded native advertising from online homepages and section pages to mobile and print platforms to foster a cross-channel campaign.

FIGURE 2.1 The Timeline of Adopting Native Advertising in Major US Media Outlets

The integration of native advertising also changed the relationship between publishers and advertisers. The incentive of native advertising revenue compelled some publishers to migrate from working with advertising agencies to taking on ad production internally, through either their own design studios or editorial teams. According to The Native Advertising Institute (Laursen 2018), 18% of the 148 news executives worked with ad agencies in native advertising production in 2018, down from 26% in 2016. Meanwhile, 42% of executives handled native advertising through their own content studios in 2018, up from 33% in 2016. Publishers have shared editorial resources with advertisers via three popular models (see Table 2.2).

In the *platform model*, publishers outsource native advertising production to companies, ad agencies, and freelancers, lending them access to editorial tools and platforms. For instance, Forbes introduced a program called "Special Features," which allowed advertisers to create their own custom-designed, interactive feature pages, and gave advertising clients access to all the editorial production tools (Sass 2015a).

In the *agency model*, publishers assemble their own content teams and produce native ads internally using editorial tools and journalistic storytelling techniques on behalf of advertisers who would contribute ideas and approve content. Although those publishers do not have editorial crews working on native advertising directly, they do not shy away from recruiting people with editorial backgrounds to work in their content solution teams. For instance, the Tribune Company's Content Solutions team included editors, writers, marketers, strategists, and tech specialists (Sass 2015b). By recruiting personnel with editorial experience, the agency model adds the storytelling value to the creation of native content while shielding editorial staff from direct involvement in native advertising, which to some extent maintains the departmental division of news and advertising.

TABLE 2.2 The Models of Integrating Native Advertising

Models	Separation	Integration	Impact on journalistic autonomy
The platform model	Advertisers produce native ad content	Advertisers share the same editorial tools and platforms with editorial teams	Journalism shares content creation and distribution authorities with advertisers.
The agency model	The publisher has a separate team to produce native ads on advertisers' behalf	The advertising team uses editorial tools and techniques. Advertisers contribute ideas and approve content.	Journalism maintains an editorial-business departmental boundary but allows advertisers' intervention over the content
The aggregated model	The only distinction left is clear labeling of sponsored content.	Editorial staff work on native ads and report to advertising and sales.	Journalism loses financial and editorial autonomy to business interests.

In the *aggregated model*, editorial staff directly work on native advertising. The editorial involvement in advertising production forces the business-oriented logic and conduct into editorial routines, despite the will of the editorial staff (Li 2019). For instance, both UK-based newspapers in Atal's study (2018) let reporters and editors from related beats work on branded content to earn extra income. Globally, 29% of executives (n=43) in 53 countries said their editorial teams produced native content in 2018, down from 47% (n=100) executives in 2017 and 42% (n=65) in 2016 (Laursen and Stone 2016; Laursen et al. 2017; Laursen 2018).

Beneath the surface of the anecdotal phenomena was a power struggle between journalistic autonomy and economic imperative with the latter conquering the former and becoming the dominant power in the journalistic field. The pro-business mindset has pushed forward the editorial-business integration as an efficient resource-sharing configuration that leverages an organization's editorial expertise and excellence (Li 2019). The shift from division to collaboration between the editorial side and the business side depicts a decades-long trend of media response to digitalization, market turmoil, and declining advertising revenue that has further escalated since the 2008–2009 recession, as evidenced by publishers' aggressive move to native advertising. For most news organizations in the post-recession era, the question becomes less about whether they prioritize serving the public or the market, and more about how they could save their bottom line without compromising their public service mission. The financial insecurity gave rise to a series of pro-business discourses that attempted to delegitimize the boundary between editorial and business as "obsolete, irrelevant and obstructive" to the survival of the media business in the digital age (Li 2019: 12; Ferrer-Conill 2016).

The melting of the editorial-business boundary as seen in the integrated production process, seamless placement, and the congruent look and function of native advertising have led to serious concerns on the impact of journalistic autonomy and credibility. Research has shown that most audiences reported lower trust toward the hosting media when they learned about the presence of native advertising on the same platform (Lazauskas 2014; Jiang et al. 2019); the perceived media credibility went even lower when publishers did not clearly or correctly label native advertising as advertising and hence deceived the audiences to mistake it for news (Wojdynski and Evans 2015; Amazeen and Muddiman 2017). Even when the native ad is properly labeled, clicking on native ads and repeated exposure to native ads could lead audiences to perceive the news website as less trustworthy (Aribarg and Schwartz 2020). Although one study found that audiences who recognized native advertising reported more favorable evaluations of journalism (Amazeen and Wojdynski 2018), another study found that recognition results in less trust of subsequent political news (Iversen and Knudsen 2017). Audiences who use news for information purposes reported more negative attitudes toward native advertising and the hosting media (Amazeen and Wojdynski 2019), and they have more negative perceptions toward the hard-news oriented native advertising than soft-news oriented native advertising (Amazeen 2019). In essence, native advertising leverages the reputation of hosting media, misleading audiences to believe the promoted messages are endorsed by the publishers and scrutinized by the same editorial standard. The "native" and unobtrusive blending of native advertising with news from placement to production may risk trading the long-term reputation of the media for short-term financial gains. Clear disclosure of native advertising seems to be a consensus among scholars, but how to effectively execute disclosure in practice without hindering economic interest remains a myth.

Clarifying the boundary: Distinguishing native advertising from news

The American Federal Trade Commission issued a native advertising guideline in December 2015 to address when and how an advertiser should disclose its involvement (Federal Trade Commission 2015). The guideline requires any advertising not readily identifiable as advertising be expressly identified as advertising. However, its "definition" of advertising seems to only include content that promotes a product or service and exclude promotional materials that do not feature a product or service or product placement with no mention of the features or benefits of the product. In that sense, an article titled "How to Sleep Better" produced by Sleep Number[1] on the *Huffington Post* website would not be required to disclose its commercial nature per the FTC guideline. This could create an unregulated vacuum since nearly half of the native ads in a content analysis study (Wang and Li 2017) connected article topics to goods or services provided by the sponsors in an indirect way, such as by promoting the whole industry/service category, providing how-to solutions, and explaining issues that are critical to a sponsor's mission. That the FTC guideline may not restrict the nonproduct-centric type of native advertising has left advertisers with the freedom and flexibility of labeling and disclosing native advertising in various ways. Only 57% of the 151 native ads published in three American newspapers' websites disclosed sponsors in a 2014 study (Wang and Li 2017). Similarly, only 63% of the 12,000 ad campaigns disclosed the sponsorship behind a paid article in a 2016 study (Krizelman 2017). Even when the websites did disclose sponsors, the language varied in expression and clarity. A study of sponsorship disclosures from 83 US media outlets found that only 12 media outlets used explicit wording containing "AD" or "pay" to disclose the commercial nature of native advertising (An, Kang, and Koo 2018). Most of the websites used the word "sponsor" in the greatest variations (An et al. 2018). A study of 373 native ads from 21 media outlets in five countries found that only a third of the ads explained the meaning of the disclosure label and nearly half did not disclose the sponsors explicitly (Ferrer-Conill, Knudsen, Lauerer, and Barnoy 2020). Clear labeling of native advertising is the first step toward clarifying the boundary of journalism. Publishers should disclose any paid commercial message with an advertiser's involvement as advertising, regardless of the content being product/service-centric or not.

The FTC guideline also requires the disclosure of native advertising to be clear and prominent in the language (i.e., in clear and unambiguous language), location (as close as possible to the native ads to which they relate), and visual designs (in a font and color that's easy to read; in a shade that stands out against the background). However, very few media outlets used prominent visual elements to differentiate native advertising from news. In An et al.'s study (2018), only two native ads used background shading to differentiate native ads from editorial content. Only about one-third of the media outlets added prominent visual cues, such as borders, to increase sponsorship disclosures (An et al. 2018). A content analysis of 60 popular US news websites found that 53% of native ads had similar fonts with news content in all dimensions (style, color, size, weight/thickness) and 27% of the cases were similar in three out of four dimensions (Keib and Tatge 2016). A recent study of 145 native ad links and 66 branded posts from 57 US websites found that the visual clarity of native advertising was still lacking (Li and Wang 2019, see Figure 2.2 and Figure 2.3). Likewise, Ferrer-Conill et al.

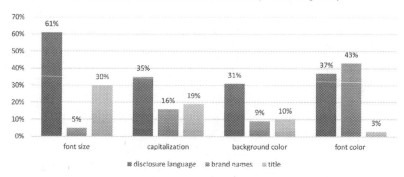

FIGURE 2.2 The Percentage of Native Ad Links Visually Differentiated from Editorial Links
Source: Adapted from Li and Wang (2019)

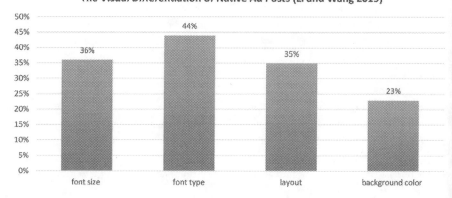

FIGURE 2.3 The Percentage of Native Ad Posts Differentiated from News Articles
Source: Adapted from Li and Wang (2019)

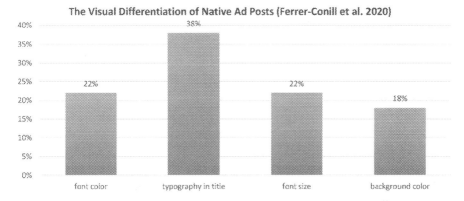

FIGURE 2.4 The Percentage of Native Ad Posts Differentiated from News Articles

(2020) found that many of the sampled ads lacked visual differentiation from editorial content on the same news websites (see Figure 2.4). Up-market media outlets were more likely to use different visual cues to differentiate native ads from the news. Native ads on the homepage of legacy newspapers were also more likely to stand out than the native ads on the homepage of online-only media outlets (Ferrer-Conill et al. 2020). In essence, the visual prominence of disclosing native advertising lacked consistency and clarity and differed vastly between the established elite-approach media outlets and the younger mass-oriented media outlets.

Audiences' recognition of native advertising

In practice, the effectiveness of disclosure should be measured by its performance – audiences' recognition of native advertising, primed by the degree of disclosure clarity and visual prominence. Research has shown that brand presence, clarity of sponsor, disclosure, and lack of deception can influence audiences' perceptions of sponsorship transparency; these factors are conceptually distinct, although correlated (Wojdynski, Evans, and Hoy 2018). Disclosure explicitness – how a native advertisement identified a sponsor – had the most substantial influence on advertising recognition (Amazeen and Wojdynski 2019). Sponsorship transparency, indicated by disclosure language and brand names, reduced the degree of unfavorable attitudes toward the messages and publishers (Amazeen and Wojdynski 2020; Li and Wang 2019; Brussee et al. 2019). The presence of a brand in prominent locations of an article, such as in the headline and the first paragraph, may increase audiences' advertising recognition without hindering the perceived credibility of the message or media. However, an increased presence of a brand in the content may decrease audiences' attitudes toward the brand, advertisement, and news website (Krouwer, Poels, and Paulussen 2017).

Besides disclosure clarity, the visual prominence of the disclosure also enhances audiences' ad recognition. Experiments have shown that audiences are more likely to recognize native advertising as an ad when the font size of disclosure text is bigger

(Wojdynski et al. 2017; Amazeen and Wojdynski 2020), or the background of the disclosure language and/or article is in greater contrast from the editorial content in color and shade (Amazeen and Wojdynski 2020; Aribarg and Schwartz 2020). Despite the non-universal application of the disclosure practices, research has shown that disclosure language alone explained less than 10% of the variance of audiences' advertising recognition in most experiments (Amazeen and Wojdynski 2018, 2020; Wojdynski and Evans 2015). Fewer than 1 in 10 audience members recognized an article as advertising in two experiments of 738 and 800 participants respectively (Amazeen and Wojdynski 2018, 2020). Participants either paid little attention to disclosure statements or barely remembered seeing disclosures (Boerman, van Reijmersdal, and Neijens 2012; Boerman, Willemsen, and Van Der Aa 2017; Wojdynski and Evans 2015; De Jans et al. 2018). These findings suggest that audiences need to learn to discern native advertising not only by disclosures implemented by publishers, but also to enhance their media literacy and experience, knowing the differences between news and advertising. For instance, the basic writing and reporting principle of journalism requires a news story to have a minimum of three independent sources, while native advertisements often cite the sponsor as a source or use fewer than three sources and/or rely on anonymous sources (Wang and Li 2017). The headlines of native advertising are also likely to use forward reference and click-bait headlines more often than editorial content. The narrative of native ads is less likely to involve primary sources, real people who are affected by or directly involved in concrete and time-sensitive events than news stories. Knowing those differences of article components and the purposes that they serve would activate audiences' recognition of native advertising even when disclosure practice is lacking or less effective.

Implications and conclusions

Journalism as a field is characterized by a low degree of autonomy and is receptive to a high degree of heteronomous influences from political and economic forces (Bourdieu 2005). The transformation to digital publishing has intensified the challenges for publishers to monetize content through digital subscription and ad revenue and opened doors for more interaction with and intervention of other actors who may reshape the boundary of journalism. As the power dynamics among actors in the field are always changing, depending on their positions and dispositions, the boundaries of journalism have been shifting, renegotiated, and transforming. To understand what native advertising means to journalism, one must understand the effects that the forces inside the field exert on one another, namely, the autonomous force that discerns the news-advertising boundary and the heteronomous forces of commercialism that blur the news-advertising boundary. In contrast to publishers' skeptical attitude toward external influences exerted by politics and traditional advertising, publishers' reaction to native advertising is collaborative and positive. Publishers allow native advertising to share editorial space, resources, and personnel with the editorial side and even assemble in-house teams consisting of people with editorial experiences and expertise to produce native advertising. The boundary that indicates where news ends and where advertising starts fades not only in the physical departmental division on the web but also in organizational culture, under which the editorial side and the business side collaborate to optimize economic return. Compared to the other covert content marketing techniques, what's unique about native advertising is that the editorial side of journalism gradually accepts, internalizes, and even embraces native advertising at some media organizations, which symbolizes an eventual submission of the autonomous force to the heteronomous forces inside the journalistic field. As native advertising resembles the form, content, feel, and roles of editorial content, audiences' perception of the news and advertising boundary also blurs. While some optimistic views claim that journalism extends its storytelling technique to native advertising, more critical views worry that the lack of clarity of the boundary will result in audiences' distrust of media credibility, the reputational damage of media brands, and cannibalization of audiences' attention to the news articles on the same platform.

Seeing the potential confusion and complications, regulators and media scholars have tried for years to improve the disclosure clarity of native advertising. Although dozens of media effect studies have identified effective disclosure practices that would help enhance audiences' recognition of native advertising and forecasted the negative consequences of ad recognition on media credibility, advertisers, and advertising messages, publishers' incorporation of the disclosure language and visual prominence in practice was far from clear, complete, or consistent. Publishers' lack of compliance, not lack of knowledge or strategies for disclosure, continues to blur the news–advertising boundary on the web and cast a shadow on the separation of editorial and business operations. Driven by the apparent economic imperative, publishers choose to prioritize survival over legitimacy even at the cost of compromising journalistic autonomy and integrity. Unless journalism builds up cultural capital, in the forms of professional recognition, editorial staffing size, and editorial content volume and quality, the boundary of journalism will be inevitably challenged, breached, and even dissolved. With media organizations enduring a financially challenging time during a global pandemic, the trend of retrenching editorial size and coverage seems irreversible, at least in the near future.

In addition to relying on publishers' consciousness, the public should gear up in their knowledge of native advertising to avoid deception and call out the confusing placement that may mislead audiences. The recognition of native advertising ultimately depends on audiences. Studies have shown that recognition was most likely among younger, more educated audiences who engaged with news media for informational purposes (Amazeen and Wojdynski 2018). It is also reasonable to expect that audiences who have more digital literacy may know how to navigate online information more effectively. Audiences with more media literacy acquired either from formal education or prior experiences may identify native advertising more easily from the news since the two differ in their ultimate purposes, communication strategies, and usages of sources. When audiences rely on not only structural features like disclosure conditions but also content characteristics to discern native advertising, the boundary of news and advertising would at least be more distinctive in the mindset of the message recipients, if not on the side of the message senders. Future research on native advertising may investigate ways of priming audiences with more media literacy and assess the consequent effects on rebuilding the boundary between news and advertising in the perception of audiences.

Note

1 "Produced by" was the exact "disclosure" term used by the *Huffington Post* when it presented the sponsored content, which exemplifies a vague and problematic disclosure language.

References

Almohammad, Rawan. 2017. "BuzzFeed Is Moving Away from Native Advertising." Medium.Com. https://medium.com/@rawan.almohammad/buzzfeed-is-moving-away-from-native-advertising-b4690bedbf0d.

Amazeen, Michelle A. 2019. "News in an Era of Content Confusion: Effects of News Use Motivations and Context on Native Advertising and Digital News Perceptions." *Journalism and Mass Communication Quarterly* 97 (1): 161–187. https://doi.org/10.1177/1077699019886589.

Amazeen, Michelle A., and Bartosz W. Wojdynski. 2018. "Reducing Native Advertising Deception: Revisiting the Antecedents and Consequences of Persuasion Knowledge in Digital News Contexts." *Mass Communication and Society* 22 (2): 222–247. https://doi.org/10.1080/15205436.2018.1530792.

Amazeen, Michelle A., and Bartosz W. Wojdynski. 2020. "The Effects of Disclosure Format on Native Advertising Recognition and Audience Perceptions of Legacy and Online News Publishers." *Journalism* 21 (12): 1965–1984. https://doi.org/10.1177/1464884918754829.

Amazeen, Michelle A., and Ashley R. Muddiman. 2017. "Saving Media or Trading on Trust? The Effects of Native Advertising on Audience Perception of Legacy and Online News Publishers." *Digital Journalism* 6 (2): 176–195.

An, Soontae, Hannah Kang, and S. R. A. Koo. 2018. "Sponsorship Disclosures of Native Advertising: Clarity and Prominence." *The Journal of Consumer Affairs* 53 (3): 998–1024. https://doi.org/10.1111/joca.12212.

Aribarg, Anocha, and Eric M. Schwartz. 2020. "Native Advertising in Online News: Trade-Offs Among Clicks, Brand Recognition, and Website Trustworthiness." *Journal of Marketing Research* 57 (1): 20–34. https://doi.org/10.1177/0022243719879711.

Artemas, Katie, Tim P. Vos, and Margaret Duffy. 2016. "Journalism Hits a Wall." *Journalism Studies* 19 (7): 1004–1020. https://doi.org/10.1080/1461670X.2016.1249006.

Atal, Maha Rafi. 2018. "The Cultural and Economic Power of Advertisers in the Business Press." *Journalism* 19 (8): 1078–1095. https://doi.org/10.1177/1464884917725162.

Baldasty, Gerald J. 1992. *The Commercialization of News in the Nineteenth Century*. Madison: University of Wisconsin Press.

Boerman, Sophie C., Eva A. van Reijmersdal, and Peter C. Neijens. 2012. "Sponsorship Disclosure: Effects of Duration on Persuasion Knowledge and Brand Responses." *Journal of Communication* 62 (6): 1047–1064. https://doi.org/10.1111/j.1460-2466.2012.01677.x.

Boerman, Sophie C., Lotte M. Willemsen, and Eva P. Van Der Aa. 2017. "'This Post Is Sponsored': Effects of Sponsorship Disclosure on Persuasion Knowledge and Electronic Word of Mouth in the Context of Facebook." *Journal of Interactive Marketing* 38: 82–92. https://doi.org/10.1016/j.intmar.2016.12.002.

Bourdieu, Pierre. 2005. "The Political Field, the Social Science Field, and the Journalistic Field." In *Bourdieu and the Journalistic Field*, edited by Rodney Benson and Erik Neveu, pp. 29–47. Malden, MA: Polity Press.

Brussee, E, Eva A. van Reijmersdal, Nathaniel J. Evans, and Bartosz W. Wojdynski. 2019. "Effects of Disclosing Online Native Advertising: A Test of Two Competing Underlying Mechanisms." In 69th International Communication Association Annual Convention. Washington DC.

Clementi, Alyssa. 2019. "The Native Advertising Market Will Be Worth over $400bn by 2025-Report." 5 March, Mobile Marketing. https://mobilemarketingmagazine.com/the-native-advertising-market-will-be-worth-over-400bn-by-2025-report.

Coddington, Mark. 2015. "The Wall Becomes a Curtain: Revisiting Journalism's News-Business Boundary." In *Boundaries of Journalism: Professionalism, Practices and Participation*, edited by Matt Carlson and Seth C. Lewis, pp. 67–82. London; New York: Routledge.

Cornia, Alessio, Annika Sehl, and Rasmus Kleis Nielsen. 2018. "'We No Longer Live in a Time of Separation': A Comparative Analysis of How Editorial and Commercial Integration Became a Norm." *Journalism* 21(2): 172–190. https://doi.org/10.1177/1464884918779919.

DVorkin, Lewis. 2016. "Inside Forbes: How Native Ads in Our Magazine Are Inspiring Digital and Video Ideas." Forbes. https://www.forbes.com/sites/lewisdvorkin/2016/08/30/inside-forbes-how-native-ads-in-our-magazine-are-inspiring-digital-and-video-ideas/#2012750f31ef.

Federal Trade Commission. 2015. "Native Advertising: A Guide for Businesses." https://www.ftc.gov/tips-advice/business-center/guidance/native-advertising-guide-businesses.

Feng, Songming, and Mart Ots. 2018. "Seeing Native Advertising Production via the Business Model Lens: The Case of Forbes's BrandVoice Unit." *Journal of Interactive Advertising* 18 (2): 148–161. https://doi.org/10.1080/15252019.2018.1491349.

Ferrer-Conill, Raul. 2016. "Camouflaging Church as State." *Journalism Studies* 17 (7): 904–914. https://doi.org/10.1080/1461670X.2016.1165138.

Ferrer-Conill, Raul, and Michael Karlsson. 2018. "Native Advertising and the Appropriation of Journalistic Clout." In *The Routledge Handbook of Developments in Digital Journalism Studies*, edited by Scott A Eldridge II and Bob Franklin, pp. 463–474. New York, NY: Routledge.

Ferrer-Conill, Raul., Erik Knudsen, Corinna Lauerer, and Aviv Barnoy. 2020. "The Visual Boundaries of Journalism: Native Advertising and the Convergence of Editorial and Commercial Content." *Digital Journalism*, DOI: 10.1080/21670811.2020.1836980

Glasser, Theodore L., Anita Varma, and Sheng Zou. 2019. "Native Advertising and the Cultivation of Counterfeit News." *Journalism* 20 (1): 150–153. https://doi.org/10.1177/1464884918807345.

Hays, Robert G., and Ann E. Reisner. 1990. "Ad vs. Edit: The Pressure Mounts. Folio: Magazines for Magazine Management." *Journalism and Mass Communication Quarterly* 67 (winter): 936–942.

Interactive Advertising Bureau. 2019. "The Native Advertising Playbook 2.0." https://www.iab.com/wp-content/uploads/2019/05/IAB-Native-Advertising-Playbook-2_0_Final.pdf.

Iversen, Magnus Hoem, and Erik Knudsen. 2017. "When Politicians Go Native: The Consequences of Political Native Advertising for Citizens ' Trust in News." *Journalism* 20 (7): 961–978. https://doi.org/10.1177/1464884916688289.

Jans, Steffi De, Ini Vanwesenbeeck, Veroline Cauberghe, Liselot Hudders, Esther Rozendaal, and Eva A. van Reijmersdal. 2018. "The Development and Testing of a Child-Inspired Advertising Disclosure to Alert Children to Digital and Embedded Advertising." *Journal of Advertising* 47 (3): 255–269. https://doi.org/10.1080/00913367.2018.1463580.

Jiang, Mengtian, Brigitte A. McKay, Jef I. Richards, and Wally Snyder. 2019. "Now You See Me, But You Don't Know: Consumer Processing of Native Advertisements in Online News Sites." *Journal of Interactive Advertising* 17(2): 92–108. https://doi.org/10.1080/15252019.2017.1399839.

Keib, Kate, and Mark Tatge. 2016. "Is That News Story an Ad? News Homepage Design May Mislead Consumers into Sponsored Content." In 99th Annual Conference of Association for Education in Journalism and Mass Communication.

Krizelman, Todd. 2017. "Native Advertising Continues to Grow, but Compliance Issues Remain." Media Radar. https://resources.mediaradar.com/newsroom/native-advertising-continues-to-grow-but-compliance-issues-remain.

Krouwer, Simone, Karolien Poels, and Steve Paulussen. 2017. "To Disguise or to Disclose? The Influence of Disclosure Recognition and Brand Presence on Readers' Responses Toward Native Advertisements in Online News Media." *Journal of Interactive Advertising* 17 (2): 124–137. https://doi.org/10.1080/15252019.2017.1381579.

Laursen, Jesper. 2018. "Native Advertising Trends in News Media." Native Advertising Institute. https://markedsforing.dk/artikler/pr-kommunikation/native-advertising-trends-2018.

Laursen, Jesper, Alexander Højfeldt, Dawn Mcmullan, and L. Carol Christopher. 2017. "Native Advertising Trends in News Media." https://nativeadvertisinginstitute.com/wp-content/uploads/2017/12/inma_2017NativeAdvertising.pdf.

Laursen, Jesper, and Martha L. Stone. 2016. "Native Advertising Trends 2016: The News Media Industry." https://nativeadvertisinginstitute.com/wp-content/uploads/2016/10/TrendReportNewsMedia16.pdf.

Lazauskas, Joe. 2014. "What You Need to Know about the WSJ's New Native Advertising Hybrid." Contently. https://contently.com/2014/03/25/what-you-need-to-know-about-the-wsjs-new-native-advertising-hybrid/.

Li, You. 2019. "Contest over Authority: Navigating Native Advertising's Impacts on Journalism Autonomy." *Journalism Studies* 20 (4): 532–541.

Li, You, and Ye Wang. 2019. "Understanding the Typology of Native Advertising on News Websites." In 102nd Annual Convention of the Association for Education in Journalism and Mass Communication. Toronto, Canada.

Mari, Will. 2014. "'Bright and Inviolate': Editorial–Business Divides in Early Twentieth-Century Journalism Textbooks." *American Journalism* 31 (3): 378–399. https://doi.org/10.1080/08821127.2014.936732.

Matteo, Stephane, and Cinzia Dal Zotto. 2015. "Native Advertising, or How to Stretch Editorial to Sponsored Content Within a Transmedia Branding Era." In *Handbook of Media Branding*, edited by Gabriele Siegert, Kati Förster, Sylvia M. Chan-Olmsted, and Mart Ots, pp. 169–185. Zurich: Springer International Publishing. https://doi.org/10.1007/978-3-319-18236-0.

McManus, John H. 1992. "What Kind of Commodity Is News?" *Communication Research* 19 (6): 787–805.

Pulizzi, Joe. 2013. *Epic Content Marketing: How to Tell a Different Story, Break through the Clutter, and Win More Customers by Marketing Less*. New York, NY: McGraw-Hill Education Publication.

Rodgers, Shelly. 2003. "The Effects of Sponsor Relevance on Consumer Reactions to Internet Sponsorships." *Journal of Advertising* 32 (4): 67–76. https://doi.org/10.1080/00913367.2003.10639141.

Rodgers, Shelly, Glen T. Cameron, and Ann M. Brill. 2005. "Ad Placement in E-Newspapers Affects Memory, Attitude." *Newspaper Research Journal* 26 (1): 16–27. https://doi.org/10.1177/073953290502600103.

Sass, Erik. 2015a. "'NYT' Public Editor Nails Native Ad Issues." MediaPost. https://www.mediapost.com/publications/article/262595/nyt-public-editor-nails-native-ad-issues.html?edition=87857.

Sass, Erik. 2015b. "Tribune Publishing Launches In-House Branded Content Agency." MediaPost. http://www.mediapost.com/publications/article/261576/tribune-publishing-launches-in-house-branded-conte.html.

Schauster, Erin E., Patrick Ferrucci, and Marlene S. Neill. 2016. "Native Advertising Is the New Journalism: How Deception Affects Social Responsibility." *American Behavioral Scientist* 60 (12): 1408–1424. https://doi.org/10.1177/0002764216660135.

Shaver, Mary Alice, and Lewis Regina Louise. 1997. "Role of Special Sections and Subsidiary Publications in Competitive Environment." *Newspaper Research Journal* 18 (3–4):16–30.

Soley, Lawrence C., and Robert L. Craig. 1992. "Advertising Pressures on Newspapers: A Survey." *Journal of Advertising* 21: 1–10. https://doi.org/10.1080/00913367.1992.10673381.

Stout, Patricia A., Bary B. Wilcox, and Lorrie S. Greer. 1989. "Trends in Magazine Advertorial Use." *Journalism & Mass Communication Quarterly* 66 (4): 960–964.

Taiminen, Kimmo, Vilma Luoma-aho, and Kristiina Tolvanen. 2015. "The Transparent Communicative Organization and New Hybrid Forms of Content." *Public Relations Review* 41 (5): 734–743.

Wang, Ye, and You Li. 2017. "Understanding Native Advertising from the Perspective of Communication Strategies." *Journal of Promotion Management* 23 (6): 913–929.

Wojdynski, Bartosz W., Hyejin Bang, Kate Keib, Brittany N. Jefferson, Dongwon Choi, and Jennifer L. Malson. 2017. "Building a Better Native Advertising Disclosure." *Journal of Interactive Advertising* 17 (2): 150–161. https://doi.org/10.1080/15252019.2017.1370401.

Wojdynski, Bartosz W., and Nathaniel J. Evans. 2015. "Going Native: Effects of Disclosure Position and Language on the Recognition and Evaluation of Online Native Advertising." *Journal of Advertising* 3367 (February): 1–12. https://doi.org/10.1080/00913367.2015.1115380.

Wojdynski, Bartosz W, Nathaniel J. Evans, and Mariea Grubbs Hoy. 2018. "Measuring Sponsorship Transparency in the Age of Native Advertising." *The Journal of Consumer Affairs* 52 (1): 115–137. https://doi.org/10.1111/joca.12144.

3

STAYING ABREAST OF THE LAW

Legal issues affecting journalism practice

Jonathan Peters

In 2021, voting technology companies Dominion and Smartmatic brought libel actions against Fox News, along with Donald Trump's allies and attorneys, for spreading harmful lies and conspiracy theories about fraud in the 2020 election (Grynbaum 2021). Claiming billions in damages, the companies alleged that Fox and several of its high-profile hosts effectively engaged in a disinformation campaign by originating or amplifying baseless assertions that the companies were corrupt or had rigged the election (Wemple 2021). Fox denied the allegations, saying it was "proud of [its] 2020 election coverage" (Collier 2021), and the network filed motions to dismiss the complaints arguing that the First Amendment and New York law protected Fox's reporting and commentary because they involved newsworthy issues of public concern (Grynbaum 2021).

These cases, which are pending as of this writing, arrived at a time of growing concern about the role of disinformation in US politics, and they could be consequential legally and practically. As one commentator put it: "If ... the defendants are able to resolve these suits with a relatively modest settlement payment and no admission of guilt, then the message might be to other speakers and broadcasters, '*Don't worry too much about defamation law*'" (Neal 2021: n.p.). But that would not be true if the cases went the other way, and no matter the outcome, their mere filing may be a reminder to news outlets that "there are some legal lines that cannot be crossed" (Neal 2021: n.p.).

The Dominion and Smartmatic suits also arrived amid a great many efforts to weaponize libel law in order "to generate publicity, to score political points, and to exact revenge on critics" (Peters 2021: n.p.). Consider a few examples. Rep. Devin Nunes, R-Calif., recently sued a number of news outlets, including CNN for $435 million and *Esquire* for $75 million, in response to stories and observations critical of him (Russell 2021; Laird 2020). Joe Arpaio, the notorious ex-sheriff in Arizona, sued *The New York Times* for nearly $150 million over an opinion piece calling him

DOI: 10.4324/9781003140399-5

"a sadist masquerading as a public servant" (Coble and Anglen 2018: n.p.). Shopping-mall enthusiast Roy Moore, of Alabama infamy, sued Showtime and Sacha Baron Cohen for $95 million after Moore was subjected to a fictitious pedophile-detection wand in an episode of Cohen's satirical show "Who Is America?" (Russell 2020). The list goes on.

Some of these actions have been dismissed, and the rest are highly unlikely to succeed on their merits as they go forward. They have the hallmarks of politically motivated and performative litigation, and they involve speech that plainly receives constitutional and other protections. The Dominion and Smartmatic claims, in contrast, are more serious and meritorious. Taken together, all of these colorful cases reveal not only libel law's complexity, but also the promise and limits of the First Amendment, which is rooted in the values that ideas should compete, and that "public discussion is a political duty" and "a fundamental principle of the American government."[1] The cases also expose some of the powerful socio-legal forces that can affect how journalists behave and how news outlets operate, especially to moderate the press's real and perceived excesses and mistakes. More broadly and directly, the cases illustrate how the law applies to the daily work of journalists and news outlets, an application that has never been more important to consider.

New communication technologies have been reshaping the gathering, production, and distribution of news (Downie and Schudson 2009), with the effect of challenging various long-held legal principles and government policies (Fargo 2021; Lewis, Sanders, and Carmody 2019; Stewart and Littau 2016). The contemporary political-cultural moment has presented its own law and policy challenges, too. Elected officials have denounced the press in stark and dangerous terms (Peters 2017a, 2017b). Reporters have been detained or arrested while covering protests (Jerreat 2020). They have been sued by the wealthy (Sorkin 2016; Peters 2014) and ensnared in leak investigations (Herb and Schneider 2021; Johnson 2013; Savage 2013). They have been denied access to open records (Fausset 2019), and their press credentials have been revoked in violation of due-process rights (Grynbaum and Baumgaertner 2018).

Against that background, this chapter explores how recent cultural, political, and technological changes have renewed and complicated efforts to regulate the modern practice of journalism, with a focus on the discrete issues that most often affect the press and influence news content, including prior restraints, privacy, defamation, access to information, and the protection of news sources and materials. These issues are explored from the perspective of US law because of its uniquely expansive constitutional protections for expression.

Prior restraints

The US Supreme Court has placed speech into categories and declared that some categories are unprotected by the First Amendment, while others receive varying degrees of protection. The categories of unprotected speech include obscenity, fighting words, incitement, and true threats, among others.[2] The question, then, is how to regulate harmful speech: before it is communicated or after? There is a clear preference in US law for the latter, because a prior restraint, a government action to prohibit speech in advance, is presumptively unconstitutional. This legal bias, in fact, predates the First Amendment's adoption. William Blackstone, the English jurist, wrote in the mid-1700s that freedom of the press "consists in laying no previous restraints upon publications" and that "[e]very freeman has an undoubted right to lay what sentiments he pleases before the public[,] ... but if he publishes what is improper, mischievous, or illegal, he must take the consequences" (Gifford 1820: 151–152).

The framers of the US Constitution and Bill of Rights adopted the First Amendment, in part, as a bulwark against prior restraints (Levy 1985), and later the Supreme Court observed that they "are the most serious and the least tolerable infringement on First Amendment rights."[3] The basic reason is that prior restraints are believed to be more inhibiting than post-speech penalties, which at least allow the offending speech to circulate and be considered by the public. Moreover, the threat of a post-speech penalty can seem more remote than that of a prior restraint, especially in a legal system in which prior restraints are widely used.

Historically, the presumption against prior restraints can be traced to the land-mark 1931 case *Near v. Minnesota*, in which the Supreme Court struck down a state statute authorizing injunctions to stop "malicious, scandalous and defamatory" publications.[4] Chief Justice Charles Evans Hughes, citing Blackstone, wrote in the majority opinion that journalistic irresponsibility "does not make any the less necessary the immunity of the press from previous restraint" and that "even a more serious public evil would be caused by authority to prevent publication."[5] Hughes did note that prior restraints might be permissible in limited circumstances (in wartime, for example, to halt speech that obstructs military recruiting), but other-wise he stressed that the proper redress was for a defamed official to sue after publication for libel. Legal journalist Anthony Lewis called *Near* the "first great press case" (Lewis 1991: 90), and 40 years later it featured prominently in the Court's decision in *New York Times Co. v. United States*, in which the justices held that the Nixon administration could not enjoin the *Times* and *The Washington Post* from publishing excerpts of a classified study, called the "Pentagon Papers," about US political and military involvement in Vietnam.[6]

Because of *Near* and its progeny, courts today strictly scrutinize all prior restraints that come before them. But they remain a significant issue, and they continue to affect the press and to influence news content. Modern prior restraints take many forms, of which the most common and compelling are injunctions and pre-publication agreements. First, courts will issue injunctions to prohibit the public communication of obscenity, false advertising, fraud, and other speech that lacks constitutional protection (Tribe 1988: 1048). Courts are less likely to issue a prior restraint on speech that relates to a matter of public concern, particularly in the area of politics. That said, from 2020 to 2021, CNN and the *New York Times* fought aggressive efforts by the Department of Justice to obtain email logs of their journalists as part of leak investigations (Savage 2021). Critically, the related court orders included an injunction preventing the lawyers and top editors at the news organizations from disclosing or reporting on the efforts to obtain the logs (Savage 2021). This surely will not be the last time the government makes such aggressive efforts, even though Attorney General Merrick Garland later issued a memo to limit when federal prosecutors may use subpoenas to obtain information about journalists (the memo could simply be rescinded by the next attorney general).

Second, prior restraints can take the form of a government contract or a pre-publication agreement that prohibits current and former employees from disclosing certain information to the public or to people not authorized to possess it. For example, federal employees in the executive branch routinely sign nondisclosure forms related to classified and even classifiable information, and CIA employees sign a contract subjecting them to a lifetime duty not to publish any material about the agency's intelligence activities without first submitting it to the CIA for review. Those who violate these obligations can lose their security clearances or jobs. They can also be sued for breach of contract (and be prosecuted, too, if the law makes it a crime to release the information at issue). Matt Bissonnette, a member of SEAL Team Six, learned this the hard way in 2016 after he published his account of the raid that killed Osama Bin Laden (Drew 2016). He was forced to forfeit nearly $7 million in book royalties and speaking fees because he failed to seek and receive the Pentagon's approval. Similarly, in 2020, a court found that the US government was entitled to more than $5 million in proceeds from Edward Snowden's memoir and paid speeches because he failed to submit his manuscripts, which discussed classified intelligence activities, for review (Slotkin 2020). These nondisclosure obligations, however necessary in some circumstances, have the effect of limiting the stock of information available to the press and public about newsworthy matters.

Privacy

In 1890, two Boston attorneys, Samuel Warren and Louis Brandeis, published an article in the *Harvard Law Review* arguing that technological advancements and changing journalistic norms had necessitated legal protections for privacy. As they put it: "Instantaneous photographs and newspaper enterprise have invaded the sacred precincts of private and domestic life," and "[n]umerous mechanical devices threaten to make good the prediction that 'what is whispered in the closet shall be proclaimed from the house-tops'" (Warren and Brandeis 1890: 195). Brandeis would go on to serve on the Supreme Court, and Warren was part of a powerful family, and they believed that a person had the "right to be let alone," to be free from publication of intimate or otherwise private information by the press (Warren and Brandeis 1890: 193). This idea reflected a respect for individual dignity that existed already in the law of trespass and copyright, both of which protected, in different ways, individual integrity and personality. The seeds Warren and Brandeis planted were slow to take root in US courts, but today all 50 states recognize a right of privacy in various forms (Lee, Stewart and Peters 2020: 187).

This right is found in laws that protect a person's spatial or physical privacy from peeping and snooping and from surreptitious surveillance; in laws that protect a person's right to forbid the unauthorized use of her name or likeness for commercial purposes; in laws that regulate the use and storage of personal data; in laws that protect a person's right to be portrayed publicly in an accurate manner; in laws that protect a person's right to be free from physical or technological intrusions while in a place of seclusion; and in laws that regulate the publication of intimate or embarrassing private facts about a person. But all of these laws are cast opposite a line of cases in which the US Supreme Court made clear that the government may punish a news organization for publishing lawfully obtained and truthful information about a matter of public concern only if the government can prove that the punishment is narrowly tailored "to further a state interest of the highest order."[7]

Privacy cases generally have colorful fact patterns. In 2016, for example, Terry Bollea, better known as the professional wrestler Hulk Hogan, won a lawsuit that ultimately shuttered Gawker and bankrupted its parent company after the gossipy news site published a video of Bollea having sex with his best friend's wife, prompting a jury to award Bollea $140 million in damages for invasion of privacy (Madigan 2016). The jury concluded that the post was highly offensive and rejected Gawker's claims that the video contained constitutionally protected news content and that Bollea waived his privacy interest in the video because he had bragged before in public comments about his sexual prowess (Eckholm 2016). Bollea and Gawker later settled for $31 million (Ember 2016), and it was even revealed that Peter Thiel, the conservative-libertarian tech investor and billionaire, had been "exorcising a deep grudge against Gawker by bankrolling [Bollea's] lawsuit to destroy" Gawker (Thompson 2018: n.p.).

In another case, in 2006, a judge let stand certain tort claims against US broadcaster NBC for the suicide of a Texas prosecutor who shot himself in the head as a Dateline crew waited outside his house with police to record his arrest for the program "To Catch a Predator" (Stelter 2008). The man's sister brought the claims, and the judge noted in his ruling that a reasonable jury "could find that NBC crossed the line from responsible journalism to irresponsible and reckless intrusion into law enforcement" (Stelter 2008: n.p.). In rejecting NBC's motion to dismiss, the judge observed that the "To Catch a Predator" journalists had likely violated several provisions of the Code of Ethics of the Society of Professional Journalists, including one that admonishes journalists to intrude into private lives only if there is an "overriding public need" for it.[8] Ultimately, the parties reached a confidential settlement before the trial could begin (Stelter 2008).

The colorful nature of many privacy cases is a cause for concern. Historically, US courts have deferred to journalists and editors in cases that have required them to consider what news to publish and how to present it (Calvert and Hayes 2012). But there is growing evidence that might be changing, thanks to "push-the-envelope media" that very often ignore traditional journalistic ethics (Gajda 2015: 157). Ours is an era of "pushback against media … excesses" and one in which "the public and many courts seem far less receptive to their First Amendment freedoms than ever before" (Gajda 2015: 219). Put differently, the alternative press is increasingly willing to push the boundaries of news values, and Hallin's (1986) spheres of information (consensus, legitimate controversy, and deviance) are shifting in the sense that what used to be considered deviant (that is, not publishable) is now very much publishable by certain organizations (Hopp and Ferrucci 2020). The core problem is that press freedom relies, in part, on a bargain between the media and the judiciary: that courts could defer to journalists and editors because they "could be trusted to regulate themselves through professional norms and standards" (Gajda 2015: 2). The "push-the-envelope media" are jeopardizing that bargain. At the same time, the US Supreme Court, the institution entrusted to safeguard press rights, is now less likely than in the past to talk about the press in its opinions, and when the Court does it is more often in a negative light, framing the press through its harmful impacts on, for example, personal privacy (Jones and West 2021).

Defamation

American law recognizes that reputation is a valuable personal possession and that its protection is an indication of the importance of the "dignity and worth of every human being."[9] The Supreme Court has said, in fact, that this principle is "at the root of any decent system of ordered liberty."[10] And in practice it allows any person, business, nonprofit, or association to bring an action against another for reputational harm – for printed or spoken words that incite "adverse, derogatory or unpleasant feelings or opinions" about them, or "diminish the esteem, respect, good will or confidence" that others have in them (Keeton, Dobbs, Keeton and Owen 1984: 773).

Nearly all defamation claims are civil actions for money damages under state law, subject to First Amendment limits. This means states can generally define for themselves the defamation law they want, on the condition that it does not violate the First Amendment (Peters 2015). What has emerged from this approach is a highly complex area of law in which it is not only difficult for a plaintiff to prevail but also expensive and time-consuming to bring a claim or to defend one (Lee, Stewart and Peters 2020:106). In the majority of states, a libel plaintiff must prove that the language at issue in a case is defamatory; that the defamation is about the plaintiff; that the defamation was published; that the defamation was published with fault; that the language is false, if related to a matter of public concern; and that the defamation caused injury to the plaintiff (Lee, Stewart and Peters 2020: 111). However, even if a plaintiff meets her burden of proof, she still might not prevail because the defendant can invoke privileges and defenses to overcome the plaintiff's case.

Defamation law is a source of significant financial risk to news organizations. Between 2010 and 2014 in the US, the average damage award for a defamation claim against a media defendant was $2.6 million, and the median was $1 million (Lee, Stewart and Peters 2020: 105). The largest award ever against a newspaper was nearly $223 million, in Texas in 1997, although it was eventually dismissed without payment of damages (Barrett 1999). It is common for media defendants to lose in a jury trial but to win on appeal, either by securing a reversal or a damages reduction. Most claims are withdrawn, dismissed, or settled. But merely litigating a defamation case, setting aside the specter of large damage awards, can cost hundreds of thousands of dollars, and sometimes millions of dollars, in attorney fees and other costs, depending on when and how a case is disposed (Lee, Stewart and Peters 2020: 105).

Consider the defamation case against the *Alton (Illinois) Telegraph*, a small paper that spent $600,000, a third of which was paid by insurance, defending itself unsuccessfully in a jury trial that produced a $9.2 million award for the plaintiff (Curley 1983). The *Telegraph* decided to settle while on appeal, for $1.4 million, to avoid the risk of bankruptcy. The knock-on effect of this case was that it sapped the paper's investigative spirit, and at least once its editor later refused to pursue a lead about official misconduct, offering this explanation: "Wouldn't you be gun-shy if you nearly lost your livelihood and your home?" (Curley 1983). Similarly, a Pennsylvania publisher who operated four weeklies stopped publishing investigative journalism pieces after being sued 11 times in seven years. As he later said: "I decided to abandon my obligation to the First Amendment and run my newspapers as a business" (Zucchino 1985).

The fear of costly defamation suits is a threat to robust accountability journalism, and it has become one of the most visible challenges facing journalists in the US, as politicians and other wealthy or powerful individuals (recall the discussion above of Devin Nunes, Joe Arpaio, and Roy Moore) have used the courts to try to intimidate and silence critics (Lee, Stewart and Peters 2020: 106). Moreover, although defamation law itself is relatively stable and protective of speech, particularly on matters of public concern, there are many reasons for journalists and their lawyers to keep vigilant. Justice Clarence Thomas wrote in 2019 that it was time for the Supreme Court to reconsider the landmark case *New York Times v. Sullivan* (Liptak 2019), which brought state defamation laws into the First Amendment's orbit and established a high fault standard for a public official plaintiff to meet.[11] Judge Laurence Silberman, of the US Court of Appeals for the DC Circuit, urged the Supreme Court in 2021 to overrule *Sullivan* (Luttig 2021). And the bar of lawyers who specialize in bringing claims against news organizations is also critical of *Sullivan*. Its members generally believe the lower courts have taken its central holding too far or believe that it encourages bad journalism (Peters 2019, 2021).

Access to information; protection of sources and materials

The First Amendment is a reliable source of rights to communicate information, but it is *not* a reliable source of rights of access to the information in the first place. For example, there is no constitutional right to attend a city council meeting or to obtain a state auditor's report about *quid pro quo* corruption in a prosecutor's office. There is, instead, a patchwork of access rights that covers everything from public records and meetings to judicial proceedings and records, to press briefings and facilities, and beyond. The sources of those rights are varied and include freedom-of-information laws, state constitutional provisions, common law principles, statutory privileges, administrative regulations, and the First Amendment. They are broadly grounded in American political theory and the idea that an informed and engaged electorate is essential to a healthy democracy (Lee, Stewart and Peters 2020: 557). But the patchwork of sources has come to be so uneven that access, as a practical matter, can be frustrating or unnavigable for citizens and journalists alike: those who simply want to learn "what their government is up to," which, as the Supreme Court once said, is "a structural necessity in a real democracy."[12]

Under any legal source, too, it is generally difficult to obtain access to information. To invoke access laws is "to deal with denials," not least because government secrecy "has been on the rise" for 40 years as agencies "have become savvy in managing the message and gaming the system" (Cuillier and Davis 2019: 104–107). Indeed, "[a] growing body of evidence indicates that all levels of government in the United States are becoming more secretive and controlling of information" (Cuillier and Davis 2019: 5). Consider the challenges of obtaining a public record under the federal Freedom of Information Act (FOIA). Backlogs, delays, and use of exemptions have increased since 1975 (Wagner 2016), and as recently as 2018 nearly four out of every five requests produced either fully redacted records or nothing at all (Bridis 2018). Noncompliance penalties are seldom or sporadically enforced (Stewart 2010), and a 2016 congressional report found that "FOIA is broken," chronicling a governmental culture with an "unlawful presumption in favor of secrecy" (Staff of House Committee 2016).

State and federal access laws can and do enable invaluable reporting, especially on public affairs, allowing journalists to document, for example, how local police chose not to pursue fugitives and how the Department of Justice responded to claims that its lawyers had misled a secret surveillance court (Editors 2018). But the many impediments to access are significant and make the job of reporting more difficult. This underscores the importance of the routine journalistic practice of developing sources that can provide information, often informally and sometimes confidentially. Which raises yet another legal issue: the protection from compelled disclosure of news sources and materials, such as notes or unpublished photographs and recordings (Peters 2016).

Normally, any person ordered to testify at a legal proceeding, or to produce documents relevant to one, is required to comply. But there are exceptions called privileges, and journalists in most jurisdictions can claim one (under the First Amendment, the common law, a procedural rule, or a state statute or constitution) that will exempt them from such testimony or production (Peters 2016). These privileges are a recognition of the public interest in encouraging disclosure of newsworthy information. Moreover, the press' credibility depends on its actual and perceived independence, and if journalists are regularly haled into legal proceedings, they might be seen as arms of governmental or private interests, causing the public to lose faith in their reporting and their sources to be loath to trust them (Peters 2016).

Notably, there is no statutory federal privilege, despite many attempts to get one passed, and innovations in technology have complicated the issue of defining journalists and journalism under all privilege sources. This is relevant because many privileges require the claimant to be a journalist or to be practicing journalism, but there is a range of definitions (Peters and Tandoc 2013). "Some ... are narrow and apply only to full-time employees of professional news outlets, while others are broad and extend to bloggers, filmmakers, freelancers, book authors, and student journalists" (Peters 2016: n.p.). WikiLeaks, for instance, has journalistic and non-journalistic features, so it is highly contested whether it would be able claim a reporter's privilege in any effort by the US government to compel its staff members to disclose the organization's confidential sources or unpublished materials (Peters 2011).

Beyond these issues, it is critical to understand today that protecting news sources and materials is as much about electronic security and technology as it is about any legal protections (Peters 2016). A 2015 survey found that 64% of US journalists believed the government had collected data about their phone calls, emails, or online communications; 80% believed that being a journalist increased the likelihood that their data would be collected; and 71% had "not much" or "no confidence at all" that Internet companies could protect their data from third parties (Holcomb and Mitchell 2015). The problem is that nearly everything a journalist does to communicate digitally leaves a trace, and in storing materials in the cloud a journalist is giving them to a third party to maintain. The risks come in the form of leaks and hacks and in the form of efforts to obtain the data through a subpoena served on the journalist or on the Internet service provider (recall the Department of Justice's 2020–2021 efforts, discussed above, to obtain email logs of journalists at CNN and the *New York Times*).

Conclusion

The law is an influential force in the making of news. It protects the rights of journalists to publish and broadcast, and it sets limits on the same. New technologies, along with political and cultural changes, have been reshaping journalism and, in turn, challenging long-held legal principles. And nowhere is that clearer than in the areas of prior restraints, privacy, defamation, access to information, and the protection of news sources and materials. Prior restraints may be presumptively unconstitutional, but they continue to impact news content through injunctions and prepublication agreements. The colorful nature of many privacy cases is jeopardizing the bargain between the media and the judiciary: that courts should defer to journalists and editors because their news judgment can be trusted. The fear of costly defamation suits is a threat to investigative reporting. It is difficult to obtain information through the patchwork of access rights that journalists have to navigate, and it is increasingly hard to protect news sources and materials from compelled disclosure and from digital hacks and leaks.

All of which is to say: "After a complex ... evolution over the past two hundred years, America has taken the ... concept of 'freedom of the press' ... and transformed it into a set of institutional protections" that gives journalists extraordinary freedom (Epps 2008: 17). But those protections are not absolute, and so the law ultimately influences the selection and shaping of news messages as they approach the gates and pass through or do not. In other words, the law is a significant part of a social system that affects the gatekeeping process, as editors and journalists navigate the risks and rewards of responding in various ways to laws that protect and restrict the making of news. That is the reality of the regulation of the modern practice of journalism, and it will remain so for the foreseeable future thanks to cultural, political, and technological change.

Notes

1 Whitney v. California, 274 U.S. 357, 375 (1927).
2 Brown v. Entertainment Merchants Association, 131 S.Ct. 2729, 2731 (2011).
3 Nebraska Press Association v. Stuart, 427 U.S. 539, 559 (1976).
4 Near v. Minnesota, 283 U.S. 697, 701 (1931).
5 *Id.* at 720–22.
6 New York Times Co. v. United States, 403 U.S. 713 (1971).
7 See, e.g., Smith v. Daily Mail Publishing Co., 443 U.S. 97, 103 (1979).
8 Conradt v. NBC Universal, 2008 U.S. Dist. LEXIS 14112, at *42 (S.D.N.Y. Feb. 26, 2008).
9 Rosenblatt v. Baer, 383 U.S. 75, 92 (1966).
10 *Id.*
11 New York Times Co. v. Sullivan, 376 U.S. 254 (1964).
12 U.S. Dep't of Just. v. Reporters Comm. for Freedom of the Press, 489 U.S. 749, 773 (1989); Nat'l Archives & Records Admin. v. Favish, 541 U.S. 157, 172 (2004).

Bibliography

Barrett, Paul M. 1999. "Libel Case Against Dow Jones Ends, As Plaintiff Asks for Suit's Dismissal." *The Wall Street Journal*, December 22. https://www.wsj.com/articles/SB945822461920337432.

Bridis, Ted. 2018. "U.S. Sets New Record for Censoring, Withholding Government Files." *Associated Press*, March 12. https://apnews.com/714791d91d7944e49a284a51fab65b85/US-sets-new-record-for-censoring,-withholding-gov't-files.

Brown v. Entertainment Merchants Association 131 S.Ct. 2729 (2011).

Calvert, Clay, and Justin B. Hayes. 2012. "To Defer or Not to Defer? Deference and Its Differential Impact on First Amendment Rights in the Roberts Court." *Case Western Reserve Law Review* 63 (1): 13–55.

Coble, Dani, and Robert Anglen. 2018. "Arpaio Sues *New York Times*, Claims Column Damages 2020 Senate Chances." *The Republic*, October 17. https://www.azcentral.com/story/news/politics/arizona/2018/10/17/arpaio-sues-new-york-times-claims-column-hurts-2020-senate-chance/1667392002/.

Collier, Kevin. 2021. "Fox News Sued by Dominion Voting Systems Over Election Fraud Claims." NBC News, March 26. https://www.nbcnews.com/tech/security/fox-news-hit-16-billion-lawsuit-election-fraud-claims-rcna520.

Cuillier, David, and Charles N. Davis. 2019. *The Art of Access: Strategies for Acquiring Public Records*, 2nd ed. Washington: CQ Press.

Curley, John. 1983. "How Libel Suit Sapped the Crusading Spirit of a Small Newspaper." *The Wall Street Journal*, September 29, 1.

Downie, Jr., Leonard, and Michael Schudson. 2009. "The Reconstruction of American Journalism." *Columbia Journalism Review*, November/December. https://archives.cjr.org/reconstruction/the_reconstruction_of_american.php.

Drew, Christopher. 2016. "Ex-SEAL Member Who Wrote Book on Bin Laden Raid Forfeits $6.8 Million." *New York Times*, August 19. https://www.nytimes.com/2016/08/20/us/bin-laden-book-seal-team-6.html.

Eckholm, Erik. 2016. "Legal Experts See Little Effect on News Media From Hulk Hogan Verdict." *New York Times*, March 19. https://www.nytimes.com/2016/03/20/business/media/legal-experts-see-little-effect-on-news-media-from-hulk-hogan-verdict.html.

Editors. 2018. "From Sex Abuse to Secret Surveillance, Freedom of Information Requests That Have Helped Uncover the Truth." *USA Today*, March 16. https://www.usatoday.

com/story/opinion/2018/03/16/sex-abuse-secret-surveillance-freedom-information-requests-have-helped-uncover-truth/431469002/.

Ember, Sydney. 2016. "Gawker and Hulk Hogan Reach $31 Million Settlement." *New York Times*, November 2. https://www.nytimes.com/2016/11/03/business/media/ga wker-hulk-hogan-settlement.html.

Epps, Garrett. 2008. *Freedom of the Press: The First Amendment: Its Constitutional History and the Contemporary Debate*. Amherst, NY: Prometheus Books.

Fargo, Anthony L. 2021. "The End of the Affair: Can the Relationship Between Journalists and Sources Survive Mass Surveillance and Aggressive Leak Prosecutions?" *Communication Law and Policy* 26 (2): 187–221. doi:10.1080/10811680.2021.1893100.

Fausset, Richard. 2019. "Former Atlanta Press Secretary Is Found Guilty of Violating Open Records Act." *New York Times*, December 19. https://www.nytimes.com/2019/12/19/us/jenna-garland-open-records-atlanta.html.

Gajda, Amy. 2015. *The First Amendment Bubble: How Privacy and Paparazzi Threaten a Free Press*. Cambridge: Harvard University Press.

Gifford, John. 1820. *Blackstone's Commentaries on the Laws and Constitution of England*. London: Sir Richard Phillips and Co.

Grynbaum, Michael M. 2021. "Fox News Files a Motion to Dismiss Dominion's Defamation Suit Over 2020 Election Coverage." *New York Times*, May 18. https://www.nytim es.com/2021/05/18/business/fox-news-dominion-election.html.

Grynbaum, Michael M., and Emily Baumgaertner. 2018. "CNN's Jim Acosta Returns to the White House After Judge's Ruling." *New York Times*, November 16. https://www. nytimes.com/2018/11/16/business/media/cnn-acosta-trump.html.

Hallin, Daniel. 1986. *The Uncensored War: The Media and Vietnam*. New York: Oxford University Press.

Herb, Jeremy, and Jessica Schneider. 2021. "Trump administration secretly obtained CNN reporter's phone and email records." CNN, May 20. https://www.cnn.com/2021/05/20/politics/trump-secretly-obtained-cnn-reporter-records/index.html.

Holcomb, Jesse, and Amy Mitchell. 2015. "Investigative Journalists and Digital Security Perceptions of Vulnerability and Changes in Behavior." Pew Research Center. February 5. https://www.journalism.org/2015/02/05/investigative-journalists-and-digital-security/.

Hopp, Toby, and Patrick Ferrucci. 2020. "A Spherical Rendering of Deviant Information Resilience." *Journalism & Mass Communication Quarterly*, 97 (2): 492–508. doi:10.1177/1077699020916428..

Jerreat, Jessica. 2020. "At Least 117 Journalists Detained, Arrested Covering US Protests This Year." *Voice of America*, December 14. https://www.voanews.com/press-freedom/lea st-117-journalists-detained-arrested-covering-us-protests-year.

Johnson, Kevin. 2013. "Appeals Court Orders 'New York Times' Reporter to Testify." USA *Today*, July 19. http://www.usatoday.com/story/news/politics/2013/07/19/risencia-iran-justice-department/2570125/.

Jones, RonNell Andersen, and Sonja, R. West. 2022. "The U.S. Supreme Court's Characterizations of the Press: An Empirical Study." *North Carolina Law Review 100* (2): 375–429.

Keeton, W. Page, Dan B. Dobbs, Robert E. Keeton and David G. Owen. 1984. *Prosser and Keeton on the Law of Torts*, 5th ed. St. Paul: West Group.

Laird, Rox. 2020. "Federal Judge Dismisses Nunes Defamation Case Over Iowa Farm." *Courthouse News Service*, August 6. https://www.courthousenews.com/federal-judge-dism isses-nunes-defamation-case-over-iowa-farm/.

Lee, William E., Daxton R. Stewart and Jonathan Peters. 2020. *The Law of Public Communication*, 11th ed. New York: Routledge.

Levy, Leonard. 1985. *Emergence of a Free Press*. New York: Oxford University Press.

Lewis, Anthony. 1991. *Make No Law: The Sullivan Case and the First Amendment*. New York: Random House.

Lewis, Seth C., Amy Kristin Sanders, and Casey Carmody. 2019. "Libel by Algorithm? Automated Journalism and the Threat of Legal Liability." *Journalism & Mass Communication Quarterly* 96 (1): 60–81. doi:10.1177/1077699018755983..

Liptak, Adam. 2019. "Justice Clarence Thomas Calls for Reconsideration of Landmark Libel Ruling." *New York Times*, February 19. https://www.nytimes.com/2019/02/19/us/politics/clarence-thomas-first-amendment-libel.html.

Luttig, J. Michael. 2021. "A Judge's Astonishing Attack on a First Amendment Precedent May End Up Strengthening It Instead." *The Washington Post*, March 25. https://www.washingtonpost.com/opinions/2021/03/25/federal-judges-dangerous-assault-free-press/.

Madigan, Nick. 2016. "Jury Tacks On $25 Million to Gawker's Bill in Hulk Hogan Case." *New York Times*, March 21. https://www.nytimes.com/2016/03/22/business/media/hulk-hogan-damages-25-million-gawker-case.html.

Neal, Jeff. 2021. "Disinformation on Trial: HLS Professor John Goldberg Explains 2020 Election Defamation Lawsuits Against Fox News, Rudy Giuliani, and Sidney Powell." *Harvard Law Today*, February 17. https://today.law.harvard.edu/disinformation-on-trial/.

Near v. Minnesota, 283 U.S. 697 (1931).

Nebraska Press Association v. Stuart, 427 U.S. 539 (1976).

New York Times Co. v. United States, 403 U.S. 713 (1971).

Peters, Jonathan. 2021. "Dominion's MyPillow and Smartmatic's Fox News Election Suits Put 'Disinformation' on Trial." NBC News, February 24. https://www.nbcnews.com/think/opinion/dominion-s-mypillow-smartmatic-s-fox-news-election-suits-put-ncna1258682.

Peters, Jonathan. 2020. "What the Lawyers Who Sue the Press Think of the Press, and Media Law." *Columbia Journalism Review*, July 30. https://www.cjr.org/analysis/lawyers-who-sue-the-press.php.

Peters, Jonathan. 2019. "I Also Consider Myself a First Amendment Lawyer." *Virginia Sports and Entertainment Law Journal* 18 (2): 109–126.

Peters, Jonathan. 2017a. "Trump Twitter Spreadsheet Tracks a Perpetual Campaign Against the Press." *Columbia Journalism Review*, December 21. https://www.cjr.org/united_states_project/trump-twitter-spreadsheet-pressattacks.php.

Peters, Jonathan. 2017b. "Trump and Trickle-Down Press Persecution." *Columbia Journalism Review*. Spring. https://www.cjr.org/local_news/trump-andtrickle-down-press-persecution.php.

Peters, Jonathan. 2016. "Shield Laws and Journalist's Privilege: The Basics Every Reporter Should Know." *Columbia Journalism Review*, August 22. https://www.cjr.org/united_states_project/journalists_privilege_shield_law_primer.php.

Peters, Jonathan. 2015. "Can I Say that? A Legal Primer for Journalists." *Columbia Journalism Review*, November 9. https://www.cjr.org/united_states_project/can_i_say_that_a_legal_primer_for_journalists.php.

Peters, Jonathan. 2014. "A Coal Magnate's Latest Lawsuit Was Tossed—But Ohio Can Do More to Defend Free Expression." *Columbia Journalism Review*, May 28. https://archives.cjr.org/united_states_project/murray_energy_defamation_lawsuits_huffington_post.php.

Peters, Jonathan, and Edson Tandoc Jr. 2013. "People Who Aren't Really Reporters At All, Who Have No Professional Qualifications: Defining a Journalist and Deciding Who May Claim the Privileges." *N.Y.U. Journal of Legislation & Public Policy* 2013: 34–63.

Peters, Jonathan. 2011. "WikiLeaks Would Not Qualify to Claim Federal Reporter's Privilege In Any Form," *Federal Communications Law Journal* 63 (3): 667–696.

Russell, Josh. 2021. "Devin Nunes Strikes Out With CNN Defamation Suit." *Courthouse News Service*, February 19. https://www.courthousenews.com/devin-nunes-strikes-out-with-cnn-defamation-suit/.

Russell, Josh. 2020. "Sacha Baron Cohen Ordered to Sit for Limited Interview in Suit by Judge He Pranked." *Courthouse News Service*, December 18. https://www.courthouse news.com/sacha-baron-cohen-ordered-to-sit-for-limited-interview-in-suit-by-judge-he-pranked/.

Savage, Charlie. 2021. "CNN Lawyers Gagged in Fight With Justice Dept. Over Reporter's Email Data." *New York Times*, June 9. https://www.nytimes.com/2021/06/09/us/poli tics/cnn-reporter-emails-justice-department.html.

Savage, Charlie. 2013. "Court Tells Reporter to Testify in Case of Leaked C.I.A. Data." *New York Times*, July 19. http://www.nytimes.com/2013/07/20/us/in-major-rulingcourt-order s-times-reporter-to-testify.html.

Slotkin, Jason. 2020. "Court Rules Edward Snowden Must Pay More Than $5 Million From Memoir and Speeches." NPR, October 1. https://www.npr.org/2020/10/01/ 919261319/court-rules-edward-snowden-must-pay-more-than-5-million-from-memoir-and-speeches.

Smith v. Daily Mail Publishing Co., 443 U.S. 97 (1979).

Sorkin, Andrew Ross. 2016. "Peter Thiel, Tech Billionaire, Reveals Secret War With Gawker." *New York Times*, May 25. https://www.nytimes.com/2016/05/26/business/dea lbook/peter-thiel-techbillionaire-reveals-secret-war-with-gawker.html.

Staff of House Committee on Oversight & Government Reform, 114th Congress. 2016. "FOIA is Broken: A Report." https://republicans-oversight.house.gov/WP-CONTENT/ UPLOADS/2016/01/FINAL-FOIA-REPORT-JANUARY-2016.PDF.

Stelter, Brian. 2008. "NBC Settles With Family That Blamed a TV Investigation for a Man's Suicide." *New York Times*, June 26. https://www.nytimes.com/2008/06/26/business/ media/26nbc.html.

Stewart, Daxton R., and Jeremy Littau. 2016. "Up, Periscope: Mobile Streaming Video Technologies, Privacy in Public, and the Right to Record." *Journalism & Mass Communication Quarterly* 93 (2): 312–331. doi:10.1177/1077699016637106..

Stewart, Daxton R. 2010. "Let the Sunshine in, or Else: An Examination of the 'Teeth' of State and Federal Open Meetings and Open Records Laws." *Communication Law & Policy* 15 (3): 265–310. doi:10.1080/10811680.2010.489858..

Thompson, Derek. 2018. "The Most Expensive Comment in Internet History?" *The Atlantic*, February 23. https://www.theatlantic.com/business/archive/2018/02/hogan-thiel-gawker-trial/554132/.

Tribe, Laurence. 1988. *American Constitutional Law*, 2nd ed. New York: Foundation Press.

Wagner, A. Jay Wallace. 2016. "A Most Essential Principle: Use and Implementation of the Freedom of Information Act, 1975–2014." November 2016. Ph.D. Dissertation, Indiana University (ProQuest).

Warren, Samuel D., and Louis D. Brandeis. 1890. "The Right to Privacy." *Harvard Law Review* 4 (5): 193–220.

Wemple, Erik. 2021. "Opinion: Dominion lawsuit outs Fox News' disinformation campaign." *The Washington Post*, March 30. https://www.washingtonpost.com/opinions/2021/03/30/ dominion-lawsuit-outs-fox-news-disinformation-campaign/.

Whitney v. California, 274 U.S. 357 (1927) 2016.

Zucchino, David. 1985. "Publish and Perish." *Washington Journalism Review*, July, 28.

4

THE UNIVERSITY AS A "GIANT NEWSROOM"

Not-for-profit explanatory journalism during COVID-19

Alfred Hermida, Lisa Varano and Mary Lynn Young[1]

The role and influence of academia in journalism has evolved against a backdrop of more than two decades of technological, cultural and economic transformation of media, presenting opportunities to circumvent the process of mediatization by traditional newsrooms. *The Conversation Canada* serves as an example of the increasing influence of the academic sector on the media, shifting from the edges of journalism to take on a more prominent role. It represents a peripheral news actor defined as "those who have not belonged to traditional journalism practice but have imported their qualities and work into it," (Holton and Bélair-Gagnon 2018: 70).

The not-for-profit independent digital journalism organization was launched as a digital-only media outlet in June 2017, with a mix of university, foundation, and research funding. It is part of a global network of *Conversation* sites that includes seven national partners, namely Australia, Indonesia, France, Spain, the UK, the US, and South Africa. In the *Conversation* model of journalism, articles are written by academics and edited by professional journalists. The content is then free to republish under a Creative Commons license, serving to increase the reach and visibility of the articles. The published material can be seen as explanatory journalism, defined as "an explanation and interpretation of complex events and phenomena placed in social, political, or cultural context," (Forde 2007: 227).

The Conversation Canada was set up as a journalism organization, independent of the academic sector, with a team of professional journalists, several of whom also brought academic expertise. Since the start, it has been led by veteran journalist Scott White, who has served as editor-in-chief for the national press agency, The Canadian Press. However, the launch of *The Conversation* in Canada was met with some institutional wariness from established media in the country, reflecting how journalists have tended to react when actors outside the field have taken on activities traditionally associated with the profession. Only one mainstream newspaper reported on its launch, and that as part of a series of special reports by a journalist

DOI: 10.4324/9781003140399-6

on a foundation fellowship. At the same time, a highly influential report for the federal government on the state of the media included it in a section on "citizen journalism" (Public Policy Forum 2017).

For legacy media, *The Conversation*'s funding model and its close affiliation with the higher education sector prompted consideration about editorial independence and whether its content was an extension of university communications. Such circumspection speaks to how it contests established conceptions of what is journalism and who is a journalist. From the start, *The Conversation* set out to explore such concepts, recognizing "that past forms and ways of being a journalist need to be disrupted and re-oriented for diverse audiences and changing technologies," (Young and Hermida 2017: para. 7)

Universities as institutions, and scholars as members of those institutions, have a long tradition of being involved in journalism. Scholars have long been featured as knowledgeable experts and authoritative sources in news stories, or as opinion contributors providing analysis and commentary. Shoemaker and Reese (2014) talk about the historical close ties between journalism and academia. They highlight how journalists are part of a social elite that includes educational institutions and thinktanks, often spending time at leading universities through mid-career fellowships. Conversely, media organizations have provided financial support for research projects at universities.

By tradition, however, universities and scholars were kept at arms-length from the practice of journalism itself, with their contributions to news mediated by the newsroom and subject to its prevailing norms and practices. Scholars were "house guests" in the newsroom, and the boundaries between who belonged and who was an outsider were clearly delineated. In this sense, scholars' engagement with journalism was subject to mediatization, described by Rowe as "the process by which such knowledge is fashioned or influenced by media imperatives, anticipating topics, approaches, explanations, arguments, interpretations, predictions, recommendations, and so on" (Rowe 2017: 230).

This chapter argues that the coverage of COVID-19 by *The Conversation Canada* points to the growing impact of academia as an institution, and academics as individuals, in journalism. It builds on previous studies pointing to how peripheral actors were benefitting from the economic challenges facing commercial media (Ferrucci and Nelson 2019; Hermida and Young 2019b). The advent and spread of the coronavirus dominated the media in 2020 and continued to do so into 2021. Interest in news about the pandemic increased in its initial months as people turned to trusted sources of news to make sense of a life-altering event on the scale of the virus (Fletcher et al. 2020). *The Conversation Canada* was no exception. Shortly after the WHO declared a global pandemic in March 2020, *The Conversation Canada* saw increased audience interest in articles addressing COVID-19 for the month of April, doubling page views compared to the same period a year earlier (see also, Bélair-Gagnon, this volume). These numbers reflect both rising interest from scholars looking to contribute articles exploring the multiple facets of the pandemic and increasing audience interest.

The increase in readership came alongside tough times in legacy media in Canada. In the first year of the pandemic from March 2020 to March 2021, 67 news outlets were temporarily or permanently shut down across Canada, including 29 community newspapers (Lindgren, Wechsler and Wong 2021). Amidst a flurry of consolidation and cuts, 49 newspapers and magazines cancelled some or all of their print editions. Media outlets sought to reduce staff costs as they struggled to cope with the financial impact of COVID-19. By March 2021, 182 outlets reported job losses and 3,011 editorial and non-editorial jobs had been either permanently or temporarily cut (Lindgren, Wechsler and Wong 2021).

The media ecosystem in Canada

Similar to other countries with a liberal, largely commercial media system (Hallin and Mancini 2004), Canada is showing signs of market failure in some sectors. It is highly concentrated with four newspaper ownership groups accounting for just over 80% of the market, and a recent trend of consolidation in daily and community newspapers creating "in effect, contiguous regional clusters of newspapers in one area after another" (Winseck 2019: 70). The narrative of decline is the story of the newspaper industry in mature media markets such as Canada, with similar falls in circulation and advertising revenues as other media systems have experienced since the advent of television in the 1950s (Picard 2009).

On top of shrinking circulation, newspaper revenue in Canada fell to CAD$1.1 billion in 2019 from its peak above CAD$4 billion annually between 2006 and 2008 (Winseck 2020). Unions reported losses of 16,500 jobs in the media sector between 2008 to 2016, with half of that number in the print industry (Canadian Media Guild, as cited in Fry 2017). An influential report largely written by a former senior newspaper editor warned of the "financial degradation" of the news industry (Public Policy Forum 2017). A year earlier the same think tank warned, "the inevitable result is poorer journalism, fewer voices contributing to the public debate and a loss of loyal readers, viewers and listeners," (Drohan 2016, 5). A further apocalyptic warning came from prominent media executive Richard Stursberg, who outlined the likely collapse of Canada's major media companies unless the government intervened with support (Stursberg 2019).

Some critics rebuffed talk of crisis and predictions of the end of the Canadian news industry as overblown (Edge 2020; Winseck 2017; Wilkinson & Winseck 2019). However, the narrative of crisis as defined by the plight of the newspaper industry has dominated discourse on the future of journalism and the evolution of media policy, signalling the institutional power of legacy media. The decision of the federal government in 2018 to allocate almost CAD$600 million over five years to support journalism has been criticized for propping up legacy, commercial media institutions at the expense of promoting and supporting new entrants (Delamont 2019; Edge 2020; Millar 2019). Figures suggest that established media organizations have the most to gain, with two of Canada's largest journalism outlets expecting to receive between CAD$6–$10 million in annual support from the fund (Young and Hermida 2020a). Similarly, an initiative to fund local reporters has been reproached for allocating the bulk of its reporters to newspapers, including at major dailies (Scire 2020).

A narrative of crisis by established news organizations has significantly shaped the recent media policies of the Canadian government. Canada is not unique in this given how the media industry as a whole has taken up the notion of crisis (Siles and Boczkowski 2012). However, this understanding of the state of journalism privileges the predicament of legacy news organizations. It tends to oversimplify both the perceived crisis and responses to it, papering over systemic gaps including media ownership, a "dismal" history of innovation in legacy outlets (Toughill 2016; Winseck 2016) and a persistent whiteness within journalism (Callison and Young 2020).

When *The Conversation Canada* launched in English in June 2017, it joined more than 70 journalism startups established in Canada over the past 20 years (Hermida and Young 2020). A French-language counterpart, *La Conversation Canada*, was launched in December 2018. The model for this type of journalism organization was established by former newspaper editor Andrew Jaspan when he launched *The Conversation* in Australia in 2011, based on a simple but novel premise. "Why don't I just turn this university into a giant newsroom?" asked Jaspan. "Why don't I just get all these incredibly smart people within their various faculties to become journalists and write for the public?" (as cited in Rowe 2017: 232). The aim was to address what Jaspan saw as a loss of expertise in newsrooms, lower editorial standards and a loss of trust. "*The Conversation* is a response to this crisis of journalism," wrote Jaspan (2014: 172). He went on to describe it as "a new journalism model that attempts to deliver information based on deep knowledge, codified behaviour, codes of conduct and a commitment to delivering the highest quality content free of commercial, or political, interference or bias," (Jaspan 2014: 17–18).

An academic intervention in journalism

As with many of the new journalism enterprises launched in Canada in the 21st century, *The Conversation Canada* was designed as an intervention in the media landscape. It can be considered as a complex peripheral actor, defined as "an emergent journalism organization that is peripheral on multiple levels, from who creates and produces its content to how it is distributed" (Hermida and Young 2019b: 92). At an individual level, the model disrupts the standard editorial model of journalist-as-gatekeeper and expert-as-source. It puts academics at the center of the journalistic process as all articles are written by scholars who have a proven track record of research and expertise in their field, working with *The Conversation*'s team of professional editors. The editorial team are all paid journalists. Scholars, though, are not paid for their contributions as these are considered as part of their duties as salaried academics.

The number of scholars writing for the site has risen considerably since launching. By June 2019, after two years of operation, 1,558 academics had written at least one article (Hermida and Young 2019b). The number rose to 2,989 by December 2020 according to proprietary analytics from *The Conversation*. While the editorial team sends out calls for contributions to member universities, academics can also take on an additional journalistic role by pitching ideas for articles directly via the website. The homepage invites scholars to "pitch an idea," with a page offering advice on what makes for a good pitch. The skill of pitching a story to an editor is considered fundamental in journalism as it requires "precision in identifying the essential from inessential, the ability to synthesize and to systematize information and the confidence to present it," (de Burgh 2003: 100). As the reach and reputation of *The Conversation Canada* has grown, so has the number of pitches, which rose from 467 in the first year to 2,050 in 2020.

Interestingly, the majority of articles published in 2020, 85%, were the result of ideas pitched by scholars, with the remainder commissioned by the editorial team (White 2021). In some ways, the mix of pitched and commissioned stories replicates the traditional newsroom model, with the university sector as the giant newsroom described by Jaspan (2014). But one key departure from the newsroom model is that scholars retain the final sign-off on an article. Such a practice could be considered a challenge to the autonomy of the editor, tipping the traditional power balance in favour of the writer (Bruns 2017). By placing scholars at the core of the journalistic production process, the editorial model blurs traditional institutional definitions of who is a journalist and offsets the traditional power relationship between editor and contributor.

The *Conversation* model diverges from established media practice by making all its content available for anyone to republish for free. An invisible pixel is used to track republication and page views. Under the terms of use, articles must be republished in their entirety without any changes to the content. Publications can rewrite headlines and add their own images. Notably, the original author must approve any material changes to the body of an article. While *The Conversation Canada* articles cannot be sold by a third-party publisher, they can be used on sites that carry advertising. *The Conversation Canada* revenue model is different from traditional journalism organizations in that its value proposition is rooted in its unpaid reach, with its goal to recycle and republish as much free content across diverse media outlets as possible. As such, *The Conversation* model focuses on maximizing the visibility of articles in a fragmented and distributed media environment, capitalizing on on-site and off-site distribution.

Through the republication model, stories have appeared in legacy national media outlets in Canada, such as the site of the national TV network, Global News, the *National Post* newspaper, and *Maclean's* magazine, as well as in local and regional outlets. Distribution also benefits from the global network of *The Conversation* sites, with articles originally published in Canada appearing in international news outlets such as CNN, *The Washington Post*, Quartz, and the *Daily Mail*. Articles have also surfaced in non-traditional journalism outlets, such as AlterNet, IFLScience, Raw Story, and The Weather Network (Canada). While media outlets in Canada are often dominated by US content, particularly in the entertainment sector, *The Conversation Canada* has significant reach across the border to the south, with the US accounting for one-third of page views (Young and Hermida 2020b).

At an economic level, *The Conversation* is part of a broader shift toward not-for-profit journalism as a way to address the market failure of the commercial news model (Pickard 2017). As a not-for-profit, independent journalism organization, its funding is from non-journalistic sources, similar to the findings of Deuze's global study of startups (2017). But its non-journalistic funding sources are different from other not-for-profits, which rely mostly on philanthropy, foundation grants and individuals (Institute for Nonprofit News 2020; see Konieczna, this volume). Instead, *The Conversation Canada* relies on the higher education sector for most of its funding, with some support from federal research agencies, government subsidies for the media, and foundations.

It also belongs to a growing number of academic journalism initiatives in Canada with higher education affiliations (Hermida and Young 2019a). These outlets are able to access financial or in-kind support through their association with universities or research institutes. The involvement of faculty, often former journalists themselves, opens the way to pursue competitive research funding (Hermida and Young 2019a). Recent examples include the Global Reporting Centre, set up in 2016 at the University of British Columbia, and the Institute for Investigative Journalism, launched in 2018 at Concordia University. They focus on public service journalism produced in collaboration between journalists, scholars and journalism students. Housed at universities, such institutes and centres can receive charitable donations, as well as benefiting from funding and in-kind support such as facilities and administrative support.

Of course, universities have been long involved in the news through journalism schools, particularly in the US, usually providing local news coverage produced by students (Anderson et al. 2011). Such initiatives tend to rely on students who are unpaid but gain practical experience under the supervision and mentorship of experienced professors and professionals. Some prominent initiatives, such as News21 at Arizona State University's Walter Cronkite School of Journalism and Mass Communication, are funded by foundations. What sets apart *The Conversation* in Canada, as well as in the UK and Australia, is that they operate as independent journalism organizations, outside, though mostly funded by, universities. In contrast, *The Conversation US* relies significantly on philanthropy (see Konieczna, this volume).

The Conversation and COVID-19

The coverage of COVID-19 by *The Conversation Canada* offers a case study to investigate the impact of a peripheral actor on the media. As an emergent journalism actor, the organization's experience highlights the value of not-for-profit evidence-based journalism, by providing an outlet for academic experts to reach larger publics, and to counter misinformation about the pandemic. Such expertise also addressed a gap in legacy media reporting in Canada, given the shift towards precarious and impermanent positions and the "decline of stable, reasonably well-paid and well-resourced journalistic work" (Wilkinson and Winseck 2019: 389).

Figures from *The Conversation Canada* show how academics stepped into the gap. From the time the World Health Organization declared a pandemic in March 2020 to the end of the year, articles related to the coronavirus made up more than half of the 1,004 stories published by *The Conversation Canada*. There were 543 articles published about COVID-19, written by 738 academics. The number of pitches and stories related to COVID-19 received by *The Conversation Canada* since the start of the pandemic suggests that academics were motivated to add their expertise to media coverage of the coronavirus. Pitches by scholars to the outlet doubled from a monthly average of 84 in 2019 to 171 in 2020 (White 2021). The model of partnering academics and professional editors effectively creates what Lisa Watts, Chief Executive of *The Conversation* in Australia, described as "a giant newsroom with the very best specialist writers" (quoted in Picard, Bélair-Gagnon and Ranchordás 2016).

As with most other media, The Conversation Canada saw an increase in traffic from readers seeking the most up-to-date information about COVID-19. This demand supported an increase in readership, especially in the early months of the pandemic. There were record page views in three months: April 2020, with 3.76 million views (double the page views in April 2019); May 2020, with 3.85 million views; and October 2020, with 4.4 million views (this latter month involved a combination of factors including US election coverage and COVID-19 content). Overall, COVID-19 articles received just over 13.5 million page views, according to proprietary analytics, accounting for 43% of the 31.3 million total page views recorded between March 1 and December 30 2020. The proprietary analytics only measure articles that include a tracking pixel intended for use by republishers. For various reasons, several major republishers, such as The Canadian Press, MSN and Yahoo, do not use the counter code so the actual number of overall page views is likely to be higher. Page views have limitations as they can be affected by a small number of users viewing multiple pages or by automated bots (Imperva 2020; Krall 2009).

Articles on COVID-19 were published across all site sections, not only Health and Science, but also Politics, Business, Culture, Arts, Education, and Environment, and featuring experts from a wide range of disciplines. COVID-19 articles covered critical race issues, including anti-Asian racism and the disproportionate effects of the pandemic on racialized communities. A new COVID-19 section was created to bring the articles together into one index. An analysis of articles published by *The Conversation Canada* in its COVID-19 section, from March 1 to December 31, 2020, sheds light on the most-viewed stories (see Table 4.1). The authors of the most-viewed COVID-19 articles include experts in medicine, epidemiology, public health and social media.

As all of *The Conversation Canada*'s editors are experienced journalists with backgrounds in traditional media, some with academic backgrounds, editorial decisions were guided by long-standing norms and practices, such as assigning stories in a fast-moving news cycle and editing and publishing them as soon as possible. This involved planning ahead and developing relationships with academics to identify emerging topics such as issues of inequality related to the pandemic.

Timely and relevant stories were often among the most popular, including the latest research on the virus, lockdowns, masks. Articles debunking conspiracy theories, FAQs, Q&As and "how-to" guides also tended to perform well. Over the first 10 months of the pandemic, content shifted as reader interests changed. Coverage started

TABLE 4.1 Ten most-viewed COVID-19 articles from *The Conversation Canada* (March–December 2020)

1	COVID-19 masks FAQs: How can cloth stop a tiny virus? What's the best fabric? Do they protect the wearer?
2	Conspiracy theorists are falsely claiming that the coronavirus pandemic is an elaborate hoax
3	QAnon conspiracy theories about the coronavirus pandemic are a public health threat
4	When will the coronavirus restrictions end in Canada?
5	Drug-resistant superbugs: A global threat intensified by the fight against coronavirus
6	I study viruses: How our team isolated the new coronavirus to fight the global pandemic
7	Why it's not OK to take small social risks during the COVID-19 pandemic
8	How the ancient Israelites dealt with epidemics — the Bible tells of prophecy and rituals
9	Coronavirus FAQs: Can people without symptoms spread COVID-19? How long does it live on surfaces? What cleaning products kill the virus?
10	Dangers of a sedentary COVID-19 lockdown: Inactivity can take a toll on health in just two weeks

with answering basic questions, including "What is the coronavirus?" Then, it addressed new behaviours: Should I wear a mask and, if so, what kind? As the pandemic wore on, coverage turned to the devastating impact: Loss of life, school and business closures and "COVID fatigue." The year ended on a hopeful note with news of vaccines.

Science and health issues lend themselves to the format of explanatory journalism, given that the complexities and nuances of science journalism do not translate well into the traditional news pyramid format (Forde 2007). The popularity of COVID-19 articles that offered practical information on the nature of the virus, social distancing, duration of lockdowns, and hoaxes indicate an appetite for "news you can use", a form of news that is often prominent in science journalism on health and medicine (Dunwoody 2014). The reach of these stories suggests they are an effective way for academic experts to translate complex scientific information about COVID-19 for a non-academic audience.

Some 300 media outlets across Canada and around the world republished articles on COVID-19, accounting for just under 50% of page views for pandemic articles. The top 50 republishers were analyzed by page views, and coded as legacy/professional journalism organizations, peripheral journalistic actors and non-journalism organizations (Hermida and Young 2019b). The results showed that 29 of the top 50 were professional media organizations (58%), with 17 peripheral actors (34%) and four non-journalism organizations (8%). The figures are largely consistent with a previous study of *The Conversation Canada* republishers, which found that mainstream outlets accounted for two-thirds of the top 50 republishers, with peripheral journalistic organizations making up just under a third (Hermida and Young 2019b).

Mainstream media outlets in Canada that picked up COVID-19 articles included the TV network, Global News, and newspapers such as the *National Post, Winnipeg Free Press, London Free Press*, and *Halifax Chronicle Herald*. The top international republishers included CNN, Salon, and *U.S. News & World Report*. There were also a number of digital-only, community-focused media outlets in Canada, including a network of local Ontario websites. Peripheral journalistic organizations included specialist sites such as The Weather Network (Canada), AlterNet, and Phys.org, as well as the aggregator Flipboard.

The World Economic Forum was one of the four non-journalism republishers. Aside from the WEF, the other three were university news sites, notably McMaster University's Brighter World website, which highlights research news. By republishing articles from McMaster's researchers, and then promoting those articles on social media, the university was able to support access to this information, resulting in several of the most-viewed COVID-19 articles on *The Conversation Canada*. The reach of university news sites raises interesting research questions about the role of the higher education sector in the media, including whether such content would be considered journalism or corporate communications.

Conclusion

A decade after launching in Australia in 2011, *The Conversation* is one of the most prominent examples of the involvement of the higher education sector, and individual academics, in journalism. More than 100 journalists are employed in its various newsrooms worldwide, with articles published across the network of *Conversation* sites reaching more than 30 million users monthly (Ketchell 2021). The model supports the development of novel infrastructures for the production, publication and propagation of journalism by actors on the periphery of journalism. As such, *The Conversation Canada* is a complex peripheral actor that operates "across individual, organizational, and network levels, and is active across multiple domains of the journalistic process" (Hermida and Young 2019b: 93).

The role and impact of peripheral actors is a burgeoning area of research given the range of people and organizations taking on journalistic activities, as this volume shows. The involvement of the higher education sector in journalism forms part of what Eldridge has described as "a pushback against an idea that 'journalism' rests solely with the traditional media field" (Eldridge 2018: 184). In Canada, the experience of *The Conversation* suggests some pushback from traditional media. Its launch in 2017 barely merited a mention in legacy media, while the influential Public Policy Forum 2017 report on the state of the media was rather dismissive of the organization as citizen journalism.

Since then, articles from *The Conversation Canada* have been placed across media outlets in the country and internationally. Indeed, during the pandemic, there was a healthy appetite for COVID-19 expertise with publishers making up almost 50% of page views. However, the numbers disguise a disinclination by some leading media to publish articles from *The Conversation Canada*, even during the pandemic.

A third of the outlets picking up COVID-19 articles were regional or local publications, which suggests that *The Conversation Canada* COVID-19 coverage was uniquely useful to their newsrooms. We suggest that their motives for using the content included the perceived importance of COVID content, the distinctive expertise and ease of access to articles, as well as financial imperatives given the challenges faced by this part of the journalism sector. Leading news outlets, including the national TV network Global News, and the newspapers, the *National Post* and *Toronto Star*, also picked up articles.

Absent, though, were the public service broadcaster, the Canadian Broadcasting Corporation (CBC), and *The Globe and Mail*, widely considered as Canada's national newspaper of record. Both outlets have dedicated opinion sections and opinion editors, suggesting there may be some institutional resistance to republishing articles written by experts who were not commissioned or edited in house. Moreover, academics retain final sign-off on all articles in *The Conversation* model, rather than an op-ed editor. Such an approach contests the gatekeeping role of opinion editors in deciding how articles are framed, written, and by whom.

The model of *The Conversation* challenges journalism's professional identities, historic practices, and commercial orientation (Rowe 2017). Journalism's ideology and its traditional orientation to knowledge claims with the journalist as an objective, neutral outsider (Deuze 2005) is destabilized as the journalists producing the articles are scholars, working with experienced journalists as editors. It offers an alternative business model, where most of the funding comes from the university sector but operates as an editorially independent, standalone journalism organization. It disrupts traditional notions of exclusivity and control by making its articles available to republish for free under Creative Commons, meaning they appear in both core and peripheral journalism outlets, from legacy news organizations to niche science websites (Hermida and Young 2019b).

The success and resilience of *The Conversation*, not just in Canada but also globally, led the *Columbia Journalism Review* to note that it "may tell us a bit about where nonprofit media is headed" (Schiffrin 2020: para. 1). The growth of its contributors, stories and readership during the pandemic took place against heightened financial pressures on the media, with headlines in Canada about a "mass extinction" event (Bernhard 2020). The hunger for news and information about the coronavirus from the public did little to shore up a shaky news business that had not recovered from the 2008 financial crash.

While *The Conversation Canada* has been able to count on significant financial resources, a business model that is largely based on annual renewal of membership "has sustainability challenges embedded in it" (Young and Hermida 2020b: 129). Universities in Canada and globally are assessing the short and long-term impact of COVID-19 on budgets. As in other countries, the higher education sector in Canada has taken a financial hit, with a decline in tuition fees and the loss of revenue from ancillary services such as residences, food services, and parking (Ansari 2020).

For now, the ability of *The Conversation* to raise the visibility, profile and impact of scholars and their host institutions has proved to be an attractive proposition to its university funders. The pandemic has made it possible to capitalize on the expertise of scholars, at a time when scientists and health experts enjoyed much higher levels of trust than news organizations and governments (Nielsen et al. 2020). As Beth Daley, the editor of *The Conversation US*, explained, "We have a direct line to the front lines of solving – or trying to solve – COVID-19, and our researchers are willing to share that with the public in real time" (quoted in Schiffrin 2020: para. 16).

The role of universities in journalism in Canada is still relatively modest considering the size and scale of the media conglomerates that dominate online news readership (Public Policy Forum 2017). That said, the higher education sector is seen as one of the new avenues to support journalism. In a follow-up to its influential 2017 report, the Public Policy Forum noted that "examples such as *The Conversation* highlight the roles that post-secondary institutions can play in strengthening journalism and local news" (Public Policy Forum 2018: 19). A decade after it first started in Australia, *The Conversation* model has demonstrated one way that the higher education sector can intervene in the media and help counter the market failure of commercial news, capitalizing on the unique position of universities as trusted generators of expert information.

Acknowledgement

This research was supported by the Social Sciences and Humanities Research Council of Canada and by The Conversation Media Group.

Notes

1 Alfred Hermida and Mary Lynn Young are the co-founders of *The Conversation Canada* and serve on its board of directors. They do not work for, consult, or receive any revenue from participation in *The Conversation Canada* or any related organization that would benefit from this chapter. Lisa Varano is the Audience Development Editor at *The Conversation Canada*.

References

Anderson, C. W., Tom Glaisyer, Jason Smith, and Marika Rothfeld. 2011. "Shaping 21st Century Journalism. Leveraging a 'Teaching Hospital Model' in Journalism Education." New American Foundation. October 27. https://www.newamerica.org/oti/policy-papers/shaping-21st-century-journalism/.

Ansari, Sadiya. 2020. "Can Canada's Universities Survive COVID?" *Maclean's*, September 18. https://www.macleans.ca/education/can-canadas-universities-survive-covid/.

Bernhard, Daniel. 2020. "How to Save the Canadian Media Industry From Mass Extinction." *The Hill Times*, April 1. https://www.hilltimes.com/2020/04/01/how-to-save-the-canadian-media-industry-from-mass-extinction/241674.

Bruns, Axel. 2017. "Das Modell The Conversation: 'Academic Rigour, Journalistic Flair'". In *Perspektiven der Wissenschaftskommunikation im Digitalen Zeitalter*, edited by Peter Weingart,

Holger Wormer, Andreas Wenninger and Reinhard F. Hüttl, pp. 78–79. Weilerswist: Velbrück Wissenschaft.

Callison, Candis, and Mary Lynn Young. 2020. *Reckoning: Journalism's Limits and Possibilities.* Oxford: Oxford University Press.

Delamont, Kiernan. 2019. "Canadian Media Is Getting A Bailout. Its Freelancers Aren't." *Canadaland,* July 9. https://www.canadaland.com/no-media-bailout-for-canadian-freelancers/.

de Burgh, Hugo. 2003. "Skills Are Not Enough: The Case of Journalism as an Academic Discipline." *Journalism,* 4 (1), 95–112.

Deuze, Mark. 2005. "What is Journalism? Professional Identity and Ideology of Journalists Reconsidered." *Journalism,* 6 (4): 442–464.

Deuze, Mark. 2017. "Considering a Possible Future for Digital Journalism." *Mediterranean Journal of Communication,* 8 (1), 9–18.

Drohan, Madelaine. 2016. "*Does Serious Journalism Have a Future in Canada?*" Ottawa: Public Policy Forum. https://ppforum.ca/wp-content/uploads/2018/03/PM-Fellow_March_11_EN_1.pdf.

Dunwoody, Sharon. 2014. "Science Journalism." In *Routledge Handbook of Public Communication of Science and Technology,* 2nd ed., edited by Massimiano Buuchi and Brian Trench, pp. 27–39. Abingdon: Routledge.

Edge, Marc. 2020. "Diverging Data in a Canadian Media Bailout." Paper accepted for presentation to the Association for Education in Journalism and Mass Communication Convention (Virtual), August 6–8. http://www.marcedge.com/diverging.pdf.

Eldridge, Scott. A. 2018. *Online Journalism From the Periphery: Interloper Media and the Journalistic Field.* Abingdon: Routledge.

Ferrucci, Patrick, and Jacob L. Nelson. 2019. "The New Advertisers: How Foundation Funding Impacts Journalism." *Media and Communication* 7 (4): 45–55.

Fletcher, Richard, Antonis Kalogeropoulos, Felix. M. Simon, Rasmus. K. Nielsen, 2020. "Information Inequality in the UK Coronavirus Communications Crisis." Reuters Institute for the Study of Journalism, University of Oxford.

Forde, Kathy Roberts. 2007. "Discovering the Explanatory Report in American Newspapers." *Journalism Practice* 1 (2): 227–244.

Fry, Hedy (Chair). 2017. "Disruption: Change and Churning in Canada's Media Landscape." Report of the Standing Committee on Canadian Heritage. Ottawa: House of Commons. https://www.ourcommons.ca/DocumentViewer/en/42-1/CHPC/report-6/.

Gans, Herbert. 2003. *Democracy and the News.* New York: Oxford University Press.

Hallin, Daniel C., and Paolo Mancini. 2004. *Comparing Media Systems: Three Models of Media and Politics.* Cambridge: Cambridge University Press.

Hermida, Alfred, and Mary Lynn Young. 2019a. "Transition or Transformation? The Precarity of Responses to Journalism Market Failure." The Future of Journalism Conference, Cardiff, Wales. September 11–13.

Hermida, Alfred, and Mary Lynn Young. 2019b. "From Peripheral to Integral? A Digital-Born Journalism Not For Profit in a Time of Crises." *Media and Communication* 7 (4): 92–102.

Hermida, Alfred, and Mary Lynn Young. 2020. "Founders, Journalism Startups and Saving the Media." International Communications Association Annual Conference, Gold Coast, Australia, May 21–25, 2020.

Holton, Avery. E., and Valérie Bélair-Gagnon. 2018. "Strangers to the Game? Interlopers, Intralopers, and Shifting News Production." *Media and Communication* 6 (4): 70–78.

Imperva. 2020. "Bad Bot Report 2020: Bad Bots Strike Back." Imperva. https://www.imperva.com/resources/resource-library/reports/2020-Bad-Bot-Report/.

Institute for Nonprofit News. 2020. "INN Index 2020: The State of Nonprofit News." Institute for Nonprofit News. https://inn.org/inn-index-2020/.

Jaspan, Andrew. 2014. "A Brief Journey in Search of Trusted Information." In *A Love of Ideas*, edited by Helen Sykes, pp. 165–175. Sydney, Australia: Future Leaders.

Ketchell, Misha. 2021. "The Conversation story: celebrating 10 years of news from experts." The Conversation, March 23. https://theconversation.com/the-conversation-story-celebra ting-10-years-of-news-from-experts-157593.

Krall, Jay. 2009. "Using Social metrics to Evaluate the Impact of Online Healthcare Communications." *Journal of Communication in Healthcare* 2 (4): 387–394.

Lindgren, April, Steph Wechsler, and Christina Wong. 2021. "COVID-19 Media Impact Map for Canada: Fact Sheet." Local News Research Project, Ryerson University. https://localnewsresearchproject.ca/covid-19-media-impact-map-for-canada/.

Millar, Erin, 2019. "How to Save the News Bailout." The Discourse, July 14. https://the discourse.ca/media/how-to-save-the-news-bailout.

Nielsen, Rasmus Kleis, Richard Fletcher, Nic Newman, J. Scott Brennen and Philip N. Howard. 2020. "Navigating the 'Infodemic': How People in Six Countries Access and Rate News and Information about Coronavirus." Reuters Institute for the Study of Journalism, University of Oxford. https://reutersinstitute.politics.ox.ac.uk/infodemic-how-people-six-countries-access-and-rate-news-and-information-about-coronavirus.

Picard, Robert. 2009. "Tremors, Structural Damage and Some Casualties, but No Cataclysm." Paper presented to the U.S. Federal Trade Commission workshop, From Town Crier to Bloggers: How Will Journalism Survive the Internet Age? Washington, DC, December 1–2.

Picard, Robert, Valérie Bélair-Gagnon, and Sofia Ranchordás. 2016. "The Impact of Charity And Tax Law/Regulation on Not-For-Profit News Organizations." Reuters Institute for the Study of Journalism, University of Oxford, and the Information Society Project, Yale Law School, Yale University. https://reutersinstitute.politics.ox.ac.uk/our-research/impact-charity-and-tax-lawregulation-not-profit-news-organizations.

Pickard, Victor. 2017. "Can Charity Save Journalism From Market Failure?" *The Conversation*, April 27. http://theconversation.com/can-charity-save-journalism-from-market-failure-75833.

Public Policy Forum. 2017. "The Shattered Mirror: News, Democracy and Trust in the Digital Age." Ottawa: Public Policy Forum. https://shatteredmirror.ca/.

Public Policy Forum. 2018. "What the Saskatchewan Roughriders Can Teach Canadian Journalism." Ottawa: Public Policy Forum.https://ppforum.ca/publications/roughriders-and-journalism/.

Rowe, David, 2017. "The University as a 'Giant News-room': The Uses of Academic Knowledge Revisited." *Culture Unbound* 9 (3): 228–239.

Schiffrin, Anya. 2020. "The Conversation thrives during the pandemic." Columbia Journalism Review, June 12. https://www.cjr.org/the_profile/the-conversation-covid-19.php.

Scire, Sarah. 2020. "In Canada, a Government Program to Support Local News Tries to Determine Who's Most Deserving." Nieman Journalism Lab, May 8. https://www.niema nlab.org/2020/05/in-canada-a-government-program-to-support-local-news-tries-to-determine-whos-most-deserving/.

Siles, Ignacio, and Pablo J.Boczkowski. J. 2012. "Making Sense of the Newspaper Crisis: A Critical Assessment of Existing Research and an Agenda for Future Work." *New Media & Society*, 14 (8): 1375–1394.

Shoemaker, Pamela J., and Stephen D. Reese. 2014. *Mediating the message in the 21ˢᵗ century: A media sociology perspective.* New York: Routledge.

Stursberg, Richard (2019) *The Tangled Garden.* Toronto: Lorimer.

Toughill, Kelly. 2016. "Status of Canadian Legacy Media." Research Memo. Canadian Media's Innovation Deficit. Workshop and Event, November 4. Vancouver, BC.

White, Scott. 2021. "CEO's Report." Internal Report [unpublished] Board of Directors meeting, Academic Journalism Society, January 20.

Wilkinson, Sabrina, and Dwayne Winseck. 2019. "Crisis or Transformation? Debates over Journalistic Work in Canada." *Canadian Journal of Communication* 44 (3), 373–395.

Winseck, Dwayne. 2016. "Media and Internet Concentration in Canada Report 1984–2015." Canadian Media Concentration Research Project, Carleton University, November 22. http://www.cmcrp.org/media- and-internet-concentration-in-canada-report-1984-2015/.

Winseck, Dwayne. 2017. "Shattered Mirror, Stunted Vision and Squandered Opportunities." Mediamorphis, February 9. https://dwmw.wordpress.com/2017/02/09/shattered-mirror-stuntedvision-and-a-squandered-opportunities/.

Winseck, Dwayne. 2019. "Media and Internet Concentration in Canada, 1984–2018." Digital Media and Internet Industries in Canada. Canadian Media Concentration Research Project, Carleton University, December 13. doi:10.22215/cmcrp/2019.2.

Winseck, Dwayne. 2020. "Growth and Upheaval in the Network Media Economy in Canada, 1984–2019." Digital Media and Internet Industries in Canada. Canadian Cancer Society, November 16. doi:10.22215/cmcrp/2020.1.

Young, Mary Lynn, and Alfred Hermida. 2017. "It's Time to Start The Conversation in Canada." The Conversation Canada. February 24. https://theconversation.com/its-time-to-start-the-conversation-in-canada-79877.

Young, Mary Lynn, and Alfred Hermida. 2020a. "Who Benefits? Winners and Losers in Canada's Media Policy." International Communications Association Annual Conference, Gold Coast, Australia (Virtual), May 21–25, 2020.

Young, Mary Lynn and Alfred Hermida. 2020b. "The Conversation Canada: A Case Study of a Not for Profit Journalism in a Time of Commercial Media Decline." In *Citizenship in a Connected Canada: A Research and Policy Agenda*, edited by Elizabeth Dubois and Florian Martin-Bariteau, pp. 19–133. Ottawa, ON: University of Ottawa Press.

PART II

The new funders and organizers

5

AUDIENCES AS A DISCURSIVE INSTITUTION?

How audience expectations disrupt the journalistic field

Sandra Banjac

The relationship between journalists and audiences has always been a dynamic one, shifting throughout history with journalism's various developments. For example, while public journalism had a deliberative aim of facilitating a conversation with audiences, citizen journalism used a more radical participatory approach where audiences themselves were invited to become reporters and an active part of news production (Anderson 2011). Undoubtedly, one of the biggest shifts in the journalist-audience relationship has been brought about by digital technologies, which have stoked a relationship that has been one of both "dependence and disdain" with journalists on the one hand seeking to maintain control of the boundaries around their profession while at the same time recognizing that without dialoguing with audiences and meeting their needs, journalism may cease to exist (Holton, Lewis, and Coddington 2016).

Prior to the digital age, journalists often had a "vague image of the audience" (Gans 2004: 229), or a distorted and stereotypical idea of them as "disinterested, sensation-seeking and unintelligent" (Donsbach 1981: 56). Relying on such "gut feelings" to imagine their audiences as recipients, and to decide from a safe distance what their audiences ought to know, allowed journalists to reinforce their enduring normative function as autonomous gatekeepers and informers of the passive, recipient, and dependent "public" (Lewis and Westlund 2015: 26). However, digital and participatory technologies have allowed audiences to more explicitly express their needs and wants, likes and dislikes, and approvals and disapprovals of the journalism they consume, thus challenging and somewhat flattening the hierarchy between journalists and audiences (Craft, Vos, and Wolfgang 2016; Nelson 2021). Increasingly, audiences are able to express their expectations of journalists through digital means and, in doing so, they alter journalists' role orientations (Hanusch and Tandoc 2019).

Audiences have gone from being conceptualized as passive-monolithic, "public spheres" to active-dispersed "public sphericules" with idiosyncratic news consumption preferences and practices (Gitlin 1998). In 2007, Weaver et al. (2007)

DOI: 10.4324/9781003140399-8

had already noted that the fragmentation and splintering of the media market, and therefore audiences, meant that the role of disseminating news to the broadest possible audience decreased in relevance. Since then, journalists have been encouraged to define their audience more narrowly in order to create a more meaningful and collaborative connection with them (Nelson 2018a). More than ever before, "journalists must confront the matter of what to do with their audiences" (Holton, Lewis, and Coddington 2016: 850).

These changes in the journalist-audience relationship raise the question, to what extent have audiences become a force within the journalistic field, capable of provoking change to journalism's institutional identity? Drawing on discussions from role theory, field theory and discursive institutionalism, this chapter asks, how do audiences as discursive communities become a part of journalism's discursive field or even act as discursive institutions themselves?

Role expectations

To study audience expectations is to explore what audiences believe and feel the roles of journalists in society are or should be, and further, to explore what audiences find meaningful and valuable in journalism. According to role theory, a *role* refers to characteristic behaviours of a person holding a position in society, while an *expectation* is a reaction to these characteristic behaviors and can emerge in response to observed behaviour or role performance in others (Biddle 1979). Roles are understood as generated by the expectations one has of themselves (how you conceive of your own roles) as well as the expectations others have for you (how others' expectations shape the way you conceive of your own roles). For example, to act as a watchdog is a role that journalists have revered throughout journalism's history, and characteristic behaviours associated with this role (e.g., exposing abuses of power) are considered crucial for journalists (Vos 2016). At the same time, the importance of the watchdog role has been reinforced by audiences too, in their expectations of journalists' diverse roles (Vos, Eichholz, and Karaliova 2019). Such expectations, or reactions, can be expressed in three distinct ways:

1. *prescriptive expectations* convey approval, encouragement or a request for a specific behaviour – a person expresses what they think the roles of another *should* be (journalists should be watchdogs);
2. *descriptive expectations* convey assumption or objective statements about a specific behaviour – a person expresses what they *believe* the roles of another to be (journalists are watchdogs), and
3. *cathectic expectations* convey an affective or emotional response to a specific behaviour – a person expresses how they *feel* about the roles of another (I like or do not like journalists being watchdogs) (Biddle 1979).

That roles and expectations are concepts intrinsically related is evident in a number of definitions put forward by role theorists. Örtqvist and Wincent (2006: 399) do this in arguing: "a role originates from the expectations about behaviour for a position in a social structure," and that "expectations define what behavioural requirements or limitations are ascribed to the role either by the person filling that role or by others associated with the role." In other words, a role is a role when it fulfils the requirements or limitations imposed by those occupying that role on themselves (e.g., journalists) or by someone who is in some way connected to the role (e.g., fellow journalists, editors, sources etc.).

To see where these influences have an effect on journalism, it is important to clarify what is meant by "behaviour" in reference to roles. Role conceptions by definition are covert expectations one holds for themselves that guide one's internal idea of self (e.g., I expect myself to act as a watchdog) (Biddle 1979). Journalistic role scholars have therefore traditionally defined "role conceptions" to indicate how journalists understand their normative roles in society, which once enacted and made visible in news products become "role performance". In this vein, scholars have been concerned with examining levels of congruence between role conceptions and their performance, with studies finding both gaps and alignment (c.f. Mellado and Van Dalen 2013; Carpenter, Boehmer, and Fico 2016; van Dalen, de Vreese, and Albæk 2012). More recently, Hanitzsch and Vos (2017) reconceptualized this conception-performance relationship, in arguing that journalism is a discursive institution or field, where journalistic roles are discursively constructed at the attitudinal level (normative, cognitive) and become discursive acts when performed (practiced, narrated). Specifically, role orientations consist of "normative roles" constructed in response to the imposed expectations deemed socially desirable, and "cognitive roles," or values and beliefs, that journalists aspire towards. Role performance refers to the way roles are "enacted" or "practiced" and become tangible behaviour, in the way journalists justify their role actions or produce news, as well as to journalists' "narration" of roles or what they say they do (Hanitzsch and Vos 2017: 123–127).

This foundation allows us to turn our attention towards audiences in general, and how their expectations affect journalism specifically. While expectations are said to generate roles, the reverse happens as well; discursively constructed and performed roles can shape expectations. What audiences expect from journalists is at least in part based on their observing and consuming journalistic products (news) and being aware of journalists' narrations of their roles. That is to say, audiences' expectations of journalists are arguably based largely on what they have been implicitly or explicitly told they should or should not expect from journalists. As audiences have started featuring more prominently in journalists' every day work practices, due to technological affordances that allow them to do so, scholars have turned towards asking what it is that audiences expect from journalists to see how closely these reflect the normative role conceptions held by journalists. Studies have explored this question both quantitatively by exploring levels of congruence between journalistic roles and the extent to which audiences deem these roles to be important, and qualitatively by exploring what audiences deem to be good or valuable journalism.

Audience expectations

Studies exploring levels of congruence between journalistic role conceptions and audiences' expectations have revealed mixed results, showing congruence varies both across and within national contexts. For example, in the US both audiences and journalists believed reporting things "as they are" and educating the public were important journalistic roles, while supporting government policy and conveying political leadership in a positive light was seen by both as least important (Vos, Eichholz, and Karaliova 2019). At the same time, while US journalists believed interpretive roles (e.g., investigating claims and analysing problems) were more important, audiences expected journalists to focus on being disseminators (e.g., reporting quickly) (Willnat, Weaver, and Wilhoit 2019). Similar examples of (in)congruence can be found in Israel where journalists placed more importance on the verification of facts and interpretation of news, while audiences expected neutrality and having their interests accounted for (Tsfati, Meyers, and Peri 2006). In Singapore, audiences expect journalists to "serve the public, the nation, and the government," revealing incongruity between these expectations and existing journalistic role conception typologies (Tandoc and Duffy 2016: 3350). Audiences and journalists in Germany generally agreed on the importance of journalists disseminating correct information and explaining complex issues (Heise et al. 2013; Schmidt and Loosen 2015). They also agreed on reporting things as they are. However, journalists believed they should attract a large audience, while audiences expected journalists to motivate public participation (Loosen, Reimer, and Hölig 2020), incorporate opinions, enable user-generated content, and facilitate online conversations (Schmidt and Loosen 2015). What these studies point to is a more significant shift in the role-expectation relationship with a greater demand for journalism to include participatory opportunities.

Qualitative studies of audience expectations have shown that audiences expect journalism to not only be useful, but also valuable and enjoyable, by enabling participation or actively including audiences' knowledge and wisdom in the news, by representing audiences' perspectives and concerns, and by presenting the news in captivating ways (Costera Meijer 2013). When it comes to local news, audiences expect journalists to promote social integration and cohesion, offer inspirational and optimistic storytelling to counter negative news, represent diverse voices and ethnic groups, offer understanding through humour and empathy, and foster collective memory and a sense of belonging in the community (Costera Meijer 2010).

Another significant development in audiences' news consumption is their growing news avoidance. Audiences have been found to avoid news because they perceive it to be negative, biased, driven by political and economic interests, or irrelevant (c.f. Skovsgaard and Andersen 2020). While news avoidance is not an expectation per se, it could be understood as a reaction to journalism's failure to meet audiences' changing expectations. Some of these avoidance motivations, at least, we can understand as emotional reactions to or observations of journalism, in which case they become cathectic or descriptive expectations, respectively (Biddle 1979).

What this work begins to show is that, often, audience expectations of journalists differ from the institutional roles that journalists discursively construct and express, showing it is important to take a bottom-up approach and to consider audience expectations as a way to re-evaluate journalism's well-established, normative roles (Eldridge and Steel 2016). Likewise, audience expectations may be conveyed not only as a series of normative "*shoulds*" but also descriptive beliefs about and emotional preferences of the journalism they encounter. That audiences have and express expectations is a given, however, the question posed here is to what extent and how may these expectations shape the way journalists discursively de- and re-construct their roles in response to these expectations?

Audiences as discursive communities: Expectation orientation and performance

In our modern societies, journalism contends with multiple actors in an effort to maintain its societal legitimacy, fending off new and potentially disruptive entrants to its field, one that consists of its own rules and logics (Benson and Neveu 2005). Aside from new journalistic actors, audiences expressing their expectations of journalists through various feedback mechanisms, ranging from social media sharing to commenting and feedback spaces, have also become regular guests within the journalistic field. Much in the ways traditional journalists have discursively resisted interloper media's claims of in-group belonging by evoking "a familiar lexicon of idealised roles and functions" that allow journalists' to reinforce their professional identity (Eldridge 2014, 3), audiences' direct interventions have long been resisted by a journalistic field that felt assured of its ideas about the audience (Conboy and Eldridge 2017, 166). We see this distance begin to shift in a digital age, though not completely. Within the in-group of traditional journalism, digital journalists as a sub-group have also discursively differentiated themselves from others both within (print journalists) and outside (citizen journalists) the field (Ferrucci, Taylor and Alaimo, 2020; Ferrucci and Vos 2017).

A key way in which journalists have struggled over and attempted to maintain societal authority and legitimacy has been through their shared, collective discourse on journalistic roles. Discursive institutionalism refers to substantive (cognition) and interactive (communication) processes in which institutions are constructed and changed or maintained through ideas discursively conveyed and exchanged among interacting actors or members of an institution (Schmidt 2010). Journalists discursively define and reproduce the desirable norms, values, practices, and narratives that continually stabilize journalistic identity and preserve journalism's indispensable authority in society, and in doing so, they define the parameters of who belongs to the institution of journalism, and why (Hanitzsch and Vos 2018). It is through discourse that roles become formalized as institutional norms (Vos 2016). However, communicative discourse capable of (re)defining institutions can involve both top-down processes coming from institutional leaders (e.g., journalists), and bottom-up interactions from civil society and citizens (e.g., audiences) (Schmidt 2010). The interactive nature of discursive institutionalism reflects symbolic interactionist perspectives in role theory, where roles and expectations are symbolically and discursively constructed and modified based on the changing social conditions and the dynamic and shifting interaction between actors within a particular role relationship (Merton 1957). In considering audience expectations, the question that follows is to what extent and how might the discursive construction and performance of audience expectations prompt journalists to engage in the "discursive (re)creation, (re)interpretation, appropriation, and contestation" of journalistic identity (Hanitzsch and Vos 2017: 121).

We can unpack this by understanding how audience expectations can be both covert and overt. At the substantive level *covert expectations* are cognitive and normative ideas; that is, norms, beliefs and preferences that are discursively constructed and live in the mind of a person (Biddle 1979; Schmidt 2010). As such, covert expectations provide audiences with cognitive and normative *expectation orientations* towards what journalism is or should be, insofar that expectations can be both aspirational, or needs- and interest-driven (cognitive ideas), and driven by a sense of what is appropriate (normative ideas) (Schmidt 2010; Hanitzsch and Vos 2017). At the interactive level, *overt expectations* emerge once the audience expectation is enunciated (spoken) or inscribed (written). Once discursively articulated, they become demands (norms), assessments (preferences), and assertions (descriptions) (Biddle 1979); in other words, an outward performance. Whether these articulated expectations are enacted through self-reports or digital news feedback (e.g., comments, web analytics), they become discursive acts and narrations of what the audience expects of journalists and, thus, emerge as *expectation performance*.

Undoubtedly, the digital turn and its accompanying technological affordances have made these expectation performances all the more apparent. Audiences now have greater opportunity to express their expectations, interactively and visibly providing journalists with detailed insight into what is expected of them. More than ever before journalists are also expected to acknowledge and account for these expectations in the work they do (see Bélair-Gagnon, this volume). This also brings about the potential that audiences' expectation performance becomes a source of disruption to journalistic identity and, moreover, to the boundaries of the journalistic field. We can see audiences as new entrants to the field, in the ways they can actively disrupt journalistic capital, including the various norms and practices that imbue journalism with societal legitimacy (Vos, Eichholz, and Karaliova 2019).

Audience feedback mechanisms as discursive acts

Audiences perform their expectations directly or indirectly through various feedback mechanisms. In their comments on news stories, audiences have been found to express convincing criticism of journalists' reporting practices, thereby demonstrating their entree into the field. Commenters' disapproval of now-defunct Gawker media's insensitive and gratuitous coverage of a person's sexual orientation resulted in that story's removal, demonstrating "the increasingly important roles of audiences in journalism's ongoing boundary work" (Tandoc and Jenkins 2018: 582–583). Elsewhere, we see that in their comments audiences rely on distinct rhetorical strategies to assert their legitimacy (that their comments are worthy of attention) and authority (that they deserve to be listened to), acting as proto-professionals shaping the field (Kananovich and Perreault 2021). Indeed, by "recycling professional language, adopting the basic stances of the profession, and approximating a professional style of writing" audiences speak as insiders, positioning themselves within the journalistic field and demonstrating their right to "engage in boundary work" (Kananovich and Perreault 2021: 332). That audiences both criticize and mimic journalists' work bears a resemblance to previous boundary-challenging dynamics shaking up journalism. Audiences' boundary-work reflects in many ways interloper medias' strategies to both align themselves to journalism's orthodoxy by espousing its ideals and roles, while maintaining their heterodoxy to the field by being contrarian to journalists who they perceive as having become complacent in their commitment to the public service role (Eldridge 2018: 212).

Audience metrics, or aggregated data of audiences' interactions with online news (e.g., clicking, liking, time spent consuming etc.), have also become a key indicator of audience expectations (see Bélair-Gagnon, this volume). The motivations behind audiences interacting with news have been questioned, showing that more often than not, audiences are reluctant to like or comment in fear of others' reactions (Costera Meijer and Groot Kormelink 2014). The significance of a click is also debatable, as argued by Groot Kormelink and Costera Meijer (2017) who found that audiences are motivated to click and, more importantly, to not click on a news item by a vast number of cognitive, affective, and pragmatic consideration that complicate the assumption that clicks equal interest. Nevertheless, audiences' clicks have become a part of:

> sophisticated, data-intensive audience information systems that allow media firms and advertisers to determine not only who has consumed which pieces of content but also predict future content preferences, tailor content for particular individuals, and gather behavioral responses to content exposure.
>
> *(Lewis and Westlund 2015: 26)*

In doing so, media organizations have become more consumer-centric, seeing their audiences as commercialized commodities. Indeed, journalists' reliance on web-analytics has led to a shift in how they think about their roles and work routines, especially in newsrooms with a stronger market-orientation (Hanusch 2017). As journalism becomes more market-oriented or driven by a market logic, journalists are more likely to address their audiences as "consumers" by responding to their wants, rather than "citizens" by responding to their needs, which follows the public interest logic (Ferrucci 2020; Hanitzsch 2007); this only emphasizes the audiences' largesse in shaping the institution of journalism.

Attention to different forms of audience feedback has also been found to affect journalists' orientation towards audiences. While reading reader comments was a predictor for an increase in both the citizen and consumer orientation, relying on web analytics steered journalists towards the consumer orientation (Hanusch and Tandoc 2019). Meaning, the more journalists rely on web-analytics the more market-oriented they will be in how they perceive their audiences and, as a result, how they might adapt their roles and routines to react to the audiences' expectations. Greater interaction with audiences has also prompted journalists to make space for roles that respond to their growing influence and journalism's concern with economic survival. This includes the role of marketing the news, by delivering news directly to their audiences via social media, but also having greater concern with the demands of the consumer audience (Tandoc and Vos 2016). That web analytics have provided journalists with more granular information on audiences' news consumption patterns and preferences, should have improved the relationship between audiences and journalists; on the contrary, audiences continue to express disdain for journalism and consume less news (Nelson 2021; Duffy, Ling, and Tandoc 2018).

From this discussion we can see that audiences have engaged in discursively constructing and performing their expectations through various digital means, and in return how journalists have increasingly responded to these expectations by becoming more market-oriented, and adapting their work routines and roles to reflect these changes. This discussion highlights two further arguments: That journalists have to some extent conformed to their audience expectations, and that these expectation-responses have primarily stemmed from the economic pole of journalism's field, where audiences are addressed as an economic force.

Conforming to audience expectations: Merely the economic profane?

Whether through comments or web analytics we see that audiences have relative power in shaping journalistic roles. That journalists have adopted a greater market orientation towards their audiences is a sign of behavioural conformity, or role conformity, to new sets of expectations and considerations of journalism's changing economic reality. Role conformity refers to a shift in behaviour that is set off by an expectation held either by the role-incumbents (journalists), or senders (audiences) (Biddle 1979, see also, Snoek 1966). Depending on where the impetus to conform is coming from, conformity can manifest in different ways. To conform to expectations that one has of themselves is a marker of internal "consistency" (Biddle 1979: 172); e.g., journalists behaving consistently with their own (changing) expectations for self. To conform to expectations that others hold of you, however, suggests "compliance" (Biddle 1979: 172); e.g., journalists shifting their behaviour to comply with audiences' expectations. Depending on the power audiences have over journalists, compliance may happen out of necessity, as a forced response to pressures journalists have little control over, such as economic constraints. At the same time, compliance to others' expectations can arguably over time become a form of consistency, as journalists internalize audience expectations into their own journalistic norms because they believe it benefits journalism. For this discussion, if audiences were to persistently expect journalists to engage with them more, and if journalists eventually began to accept this expectation as a valid norm and value to aspire towards, journalists' conformance to this expectation would become consistent with their role conceptions. That is, something that may have initially been an act of role-compliance becomes role-consistency. In this process of conforming, journalists may be asked to engage in various adaptive role processes, including role negotiation, internalization, and normalization (Hanitzsch and Vos 2017:123–127).

From the previous section, we could argue that journalism adopting a stronger market orientation, and journalists negotiating new journalistic roles (Tandoc and Vos 2016), is a sign that some expectations have been internalized and have become consistent with journalists' own self-expectations or role conceptions. Alternatively, and more cynically, journalists' new role negotiations could be understood as evidence of "instrumental conformity" (Biddle 1986); a view that journalists conform because they perceive audiences as powerful and in a position to sanction journalists' non-compliance by turning elsewhere, with the risk of non-conforming having direct economic consequences for journalism.

The benefits and consequences to either consistency or compliance to audience expectations can have an effect on journalists' ability to maintain their capital, both in symbolic and cultural terms (e.g., their status, and recognition), but also economically (Willig 2013; Hovden 2008). Two key forms of journalistic capital in relation to audiences' power in these dynamics are legitimacy and revenue, for, "it is the audience who judges the legitimacy of the journalistic field and it is the audience's attention that is monetized in the form of subscription and advertising revenue" (Vos, Eichholz, and Karaliova 2019: 1009). This tension between maintaining legitimacy and gaining revenue that journalism carefully balances, relates to the opposition between economic forces that are external or heteronomous to the journalistic field (economic capital) and the cultural uniqueness or autonomy of the field (cultural capital) (Benson and Neveu 2005). The two poles represent a constant struggle and negotiation between the cultural "sacred", journalists maintaining autonomy over its unique professional roles and claims to societal legitimacy, and the economic "profane", journalism's ability to convert their cultural capital into audience attention and thus revenue, thereby amassing economic capital, while simultaneously resisting actors who impose economic pressures, including audiences who represent a significant economic force from outside of the field.

That audiences have prompted a greater market orientation within the journalistic field suggests that audiences, located on the economic-profane pole, have at least to some extent succeeded in using their economic capital to modify journalists' cultural capital by prompting journalists to renegotiate their journalistic roles. This influence is seen in journalism's reliance on web-analytics as a tool to increase economic capital vis-à-vis the marketization of news to consumer-audiences, and the use of audience feedback expressed through comments primarily for journalistic benefit. To that end, there is evidence that audience expectations, performed via metrics versus reader comments, have been absorbed into journalism's core ideology differently and to varying degrees. When it comes to web analytics, journalists rely on metrics to monitor audience behaviour with stories, which informs their editorial decision-making processes (e.g., story selection, placement, headlines) (Tandoc 2015). Journalists also evaluate headlines as more or less newsworthy depending on whether they show positive or negative analytics data based on audiences' engagement, and as a result, rank the stories higher or lower on the news site (Lamot and Van Aelst 2020).

With regard to comments, journalists find the commenting sections underneath news articles to have a positive effect on their working practices and the profession as a whole when they can use the commenting space to gain new contacts, get follow-up story leads and ideas, gain new sources, source new information, especially from audiences who have expertise on the topic being reported on, and even create a sense of community provided that journalists can moderate comment quality (Ferrucci and Wolfgang 2021; Graham and Wright 2015; Robinson 2010). Journalists also resisted absorbing reader comments into their work practices and norms, perceiving them as reflective of an audience that is irrational and disparate, offering contradictory opinions, low-quality engagement and contribution, which made it difficult to imagine audiences or understand what they wanted (Duffy, Ling, and Tandoc 2018; Bergström and Wadbring 2015).

Audiences, on the other hand, have expressed mixed feelings about the comments section and the idea of participation. They used the commenting function to criticize journalists' reporting practices and ethics, seeing themselves as legitimate and authoritative contributors to journalism (Kananovich and Perreault 2021). However, the more journalists included citizen comments in their reporting, the more audiences also expected journalists to moderate the inclusion of such contributions and rely on these only when they enhance reporting (Karlsson, Clerwall, and Nord 2017). Audiences are also more likely to support the presence of reader comments because they find them interesting, rather than seeing these as a source of high-quality information (Bergström and Wadbring 2015).

Considering both forms of feedback, Duffy, Ling, and Tandoc (2018) found that, although web analytics and comments have been internalized and accepted as part of journalists' established news practices, they were internalized only insofar that they supported journalistic (claims to) autonomy. Journalists claimed autonomy by maintaining control over the structure and packaging of a story, perceiving analytics only in relation to income (clicks equal ad sales) and not journalistic decision-making, maintaining control over how and when journalists respond to reader comments, and maintaining that journalistic norms always trump audience feedback in making news selection decisions. Tandoc (2015), however, found that conceiving of audiences firstly as a form of economic capital led journalists to then see them as a form of symbolic capital, which then led journalists to make editorial adjustments based on analytics. That is, audiences gain symbolic capital because in consuming the news they find relevant or of interest legitimizes the news organisation that fulfils these expectations and responsibilities of serving the public, which in turn provides the news organisation with further symbolic capital (authority, reputation). At the same time, journalists claim to more easily resist reader comments than absorb them as autonomous journalistic practice, precisely because they add little to no commercial value (Duffy, Ling, and Tandoc 2018). Journalists also prefer to moderate comments themselves rather than allow an external institution to do so because it allows them to maintain autonomy and limit external interference (Ferrucci and Wolfgang 2021). As Duffy and colleagues (2018: 1143) conclude: "When it can be aggregated into an impersonal statistic that can contribute to economic capital it is internalized: as long as it is seen as a single personal comment which does not, it is not."

Conclusion

The discussions presented in this chapter suggest that audiences hold expectation orientations, or norms, beliefs, and preferences, and enact these. That is, audiences discursively construct and perform their expectations through various feedback mechanisms, and do so in ways similar to how journalists discursively construct and perform their own institutional role identities. As discursive communities, audiences have therefore become a considerable presence and force within journalism's discursive field. Where journalists may have previously been reluctant to integrate such expectations into their work practices, and allow these to modify their roles, scholarship indicates journalists have slowly conformed to these expectations, albeit to varying degrees and levels of internalization. Of the key forms of audience feedback, web analytics data appear to have had a far greater impact on journalism than reader comments. On the one hand, it seems that web analytics data have become an integral part of journalism, and that journalists' changing role identities are consistent with their changing self-expectations in light of conforming to their audiences' expectations. However, on the other hand, journalists seem to have conformed to these aggregated expectations in somewhat self-serving ways, insofar as it enables journalism's economic survival while simultaneously claiming autonomy to such forces. In journalism's effort to maintain the boundaries of the journalistic field and remain resistant to heterogeneous forces, audiences as the economic profane are relegated to the periphery and their expectations provoke seemingly reluctant role-adaptation. That is, in as far as journalists' discursive claims but also changing work practices suggest at least, audience expectations have provoked in journalists a kind of instrumental conformity or role-compliance driven by economic pressures, rather than an internalized role-consistency driven by a recognition of audiences as journalism's valued (or welcome) member. As such, audiences can be understood as an unwelcome entrant to journalism's discursive field. However, audiences and their expectations are unlikely to disappear any time soon, and as they gain momentum, they may potentially develop to become a discursive institution in their own right.

References

Anderson, C. W. 2011. "Deliberative, agonistic, and algorithmic audiences: Journalism's vision of its public in an age of audience transparency." *International Journal of Communication* 5 (19): 529–547.

Benson, Rodney, and Erik Neveu. 2005. "Introduction: Field Theory as a Work in Progress." In *Bourdieu and the Journalistic Field*, edited by Rodney Benson and Erik Neveu, pp. 1–25. Cambridge: Polity Press.

Bergström, Annika, and Ingela Wadbring. 2015. "Beneficial yet crappy: Journalists and audiences on obstacles and opportunities in reader comments." *European Journal of Communication* 30 (2): 137–151.

Biddle, Bruce. 1979. *Role Theory: Expectations, Identities and Behaviors*. New York: Academic Press.

Biddle, Bruce. 1986. "Recent Development in Role Theory." *Annual Review of Sociology* 12: 67–92.

Carpenter, Serena, Jan Boehmer, and Frederick Fico. 2016. "The Measurement of Journalistic Role Enactments: A Study of Organizational Constraints and Support in For-Profit and Nonprofit Journalism." *Journalism & Mass Communication Quarterly* 93 (3): 587–608.

Conboy, Martin, and Scott Eldridge II. 2017. "Journalism and Public Discourse." In *The Routledge Handbook of Language and Media*, edited by Colleen Cotter and Daniel Perrin, pp. 164–177. London: Routledge.

Costera Meijer, Irene. 2010. "Democratizing Journalism?" *Journalism Studies* 11 (3): 327–342.

Costera Meijer, Irene. 2013. "Valuable journalism: A search for quality from the vantage point of the user." *Journalism* 14 (6): 754–770.

Costera Meijer, Irene, and Tim Groot Kormelink. 2014. "Checking, Sharing, Clicking and Linking." *Digital Journalism* 3 (5): 664–679.

Craft, Stephanie, Tim P. Vos, and David J. Wolfgang. 2016. "Reader comments as press criticism: Implications for the journalistic field." *Journalism* 17 (6): 677–693.

Donsbach, Wolfgang. 1981. "Legitimacy through competence rather than value judgements: The concept of journalistic professionalization reconsidered." *Gazette* 27 (1): 47–67.

Duffy, Andrew, Rich Ling, and Edson C. Tandoc Jr. 2018. "The people have spoken (the bastards?) Finding a legitimate place for feedback in the journalistic field." *Journalism Practice* 12 (9): 1130–1147.

Eldridge, Scott A. 2018. *Online Journalism from the Periphery: Interloper Media and the Journalistic Field*. London: Routledge.

Eldridge, Scott A. 2014. "Boundary Maintenance and Interloper Media Reaction: Differentiating between journalism's discursive enforcement processes." *Journalism Studies* 15 (1): 1–16.

Eldridge, Scott A., and John Steel. 2016. "Normative expectations." *Journalism Studies* 17 (7): 817–826.

Ferrucci, Patrick (2020). It is in the numbers: How market orientation impacts journalists' use of news metrics. *Journalism* 21 (2): 244–261.

Ferrucci, Patrick, Ross Taylor, and Kathleen I. Alaimo. 2020. "On the boundaries: Professional photojournalists navigating identity in an age of technological democratization." *Digital Journalism* 8 (3): 367–385.

Ferrucci, Patrick, and J. David Wolfgang. 2021. "Inside or out? Perceptions of how Differing Types of Comment Moderation Impact Practice." *Journalism Studies* 22 (8): 1010–1027.

Ferrucci, Patrick, & Tim P. Vos. 2017. "Who's in, who's out? Constructing the identity of digital journalists." *Digital Journalism* 5 (7): 868–883.

Gans, Herbert J. 2004. *Deciding What's News: A Study of CBS Evening News, NBC Nightly News, Newsweek, and Time*. Chicago: Northwestern University Press.

Gitlin, Todd. 1998. "Public sphere or public sphericules?" In *Media, Ritual, and Identity*, edited by Tamar Liebes and James Curran, pp. 168–174. London: Routledge.

Graham, Todd, and Scott Wright. 2015. "A tale of two stories from 'below the line' comment fields at the *Guardian*." *The International Journal of Press/Politics* 20 (3): 317–338.

Groot Kormelink, Tim, and Irene Costera Meijer. 2018. "What clicks actually mean: Exploring digital news user practices." *Journalism* 19 (5): 668–683.

Hanitzsch, Thomas. 2007. "Deconstructing Journalism Culture: Toward a Universal Theory." *Communication Theory* 17 (4): 367–385.

Hanitzsch, Thomas, and Tim P. Vos. 2017. "Journalistic Roles and the Struggle Over Institutional Identity: The Discursive Constitution of Journalism." *Communication Theory* 27 (2): 115–135.

Hanitzsch, Thomas, and Tim P. Vos. 2018. "Journalism beyond democracy: A new look into journalistic roles in political and everyday life." *Journalism* 19 (2): 146–164.

Hanusch, Folker. (2017). "Web analytics and the functional differentiation of journalism cultures: individual, organizational and platform-specific influences on newswork." *Information, Communication & Society* 20 (10): 1571–1586.

Hanusch, Folker, and Edson C. Tandoc. 2019. "Comments, analytics, and social media: The impact of audience feedback on journalists' market orientation." *Journalism* 20 (6): 695–713.

Heise, Nele, Wiebke Loosen, Julius Reimer, and Jan-Hinrik Schmidt. 2013. "Including the Audience." *Journalism Studies* 15 (4): 411–430.

Holton, Avery E., Seth C. Lewis, and Mark Coddington. 2016. "Interacting with Audiences." *Journalism Studies* 17 (7): 849–859.

Hovden, Jan Fredrik. 2008. "Profane and Sacred: A study of the Norwegian Journalistic Field." PhD diss., University of Bergen.

Kananovich, Volha, and Gregory Perreault. 2021. "Audience as Journalistic Boundary Worker: The Rhetorical Use of Comments to Critique Media Practice, Assert Legitimacy and Claim Authority." *Journalism Studies* 22 (3): 322–341.

Karlsson, Michael, Christer Clerwall, and Lars Nord. 2018. "The public doesn't miss the public. Views from the people: Why news by the people?" *Journalism* 19 (5): 577–594.

Lamot, Kenza, and Peter Van Aelst. 2020. "Beaten by Chartbeat? An experimental study on the effect of real-time audience analytics on journalists' news judgment." *Journalism Studies* 21 (4): 477–493.

Lewis, Seth C., and Oscar Westlund. 2015. "Actors, Actants, Audiences, and Activities in Cross-Media News Work." *Digital Journalism* 3 (1): 19–37.

Loosen, Wiebke, Julius Reimer, and Sascha Hölig. 2020. "What Journalists Want and What They Ought to Do (In)Congruences Between Journalists' Role Conceptions and Audiences' Expectations." *Journalism Studies* 21 (12): 1744–1774.

Mellado, Claudia, and Arjen Van Dalen. 2013. "Between Rhetoric and Practice." *Journalism Studies* 15 (6): 859–878.

Merton, Robert K. 1957. "The Role-Set: Problems in Sociological Theory." *The British Journal of Sociology* 8 (2): 106–120.

Nelson, Jacob L. 2018. "And Deliver Us to Segmentation." *Journalism Practice* 12 (2): 204–219.

Nelson, J. L. 2021. *Imagined Audiences: How Journalists Perceive and Pursue the Public*. New York: Oxford University Press.

Örtqvist, Daniel, and Joakim Wincent. 2006. "Prominent consequences of role stress: A meta-analytic review." *International Journal of Stress Management* 13 (4): 399–422.

Robinson, Sue. 2010. "Traditionalists vs. Convergers: Textual Privilege, Boundary Work, and the Journalist—Audience Relationship in the Commenting Policies of Online News Sites." *Convergence* 16 (1): 125–143.

Schmidt, Vivien A. 2010. "Taking ideas and discourse seriously: explaining change through discursive institutionalism as the fourth 'new institutionalism'." *European Political Science Review* 2 (1): 1–25.

Schmidt, Jan-Hinrik., and Wiebke Loosen. 2015. "Both Sides of the Story." *Digital Journalism* 3 (2): 259–278.

Skovsgaard, Morten, & Kim Andersen. 2020. "Conceptualizing News Avoidance: Towards a Shared Understanding of Different Causes and Potential Solutions." *Journalism Studies* 21 (4): 459–476.

Snoek, J. Diedrick. 1966. "Role strain in diversified role sets." *American Journal of Sociology* 71 (4): 363–372.

Tandoc Jr., Edson C. 2015. "Why web analytics click: Factors affecting the ways journalists use audience metrics." *Journalism Studies* 16 (6): 782–799.

Tandoc, Edson C., and Joy Jenkins. 2018. "Out of bounds? How Gawker's outing a married man fits into the boundaries of journalism." *New Media & Society* 20 (2): 581–598.

Tandoc Jr., Edson C., and Tim P. Vos. 2016. "The journalist is marketing the news." *Journalism Practice* 10 (8): 950–966.

Tandoc Jr., Edson C., and Andrew Duffy. 2016. "Keeping up with the audiences: Journalistic role expectations in Singapore." *International Journal of Communication* 10 (21): 3338–3358.

Tsfati, Yariv, Oren Meyers, and Yoram Peri. 2006. "What is good journalism? Comparing Israeli public and journalists' perspectives." *Journalism* 7 (2): 152–173.

van Dalen, Arjen, Claes H. de Vreese, and Erik Albæk. 2012. "Different roles, different content? A four-country comparison of the role conceptions and reporting style of political journalists." *Journalism* 13 (7): 903–922.

Vos, Tim P. 2016. "Historical perspectives on journalistic roles." In *Journalistic Role Performance*, edited by Claudia Mellado, Lea Hellmueller, Wolfgang Donsbach, pp. 59–77. New York: Routledge.

Vos, Tim P., Martin Eichholz, and Tatsiana Karaliova. 2019. "Audiences and Journalistic Capital: Roles of journalism." *Journalism Studies* 20 (7): 1009–1027.

Weaver, David H., Randal A. Beam, Bonnie Brownlee, Paul S. Voakes, and G. Cleveland Wilhoit. 2007. *The American Journalist in the 21th Century: US News People at the Dawn of a New Millennium.* New York: Routledge.

Willig, Ida. 2013. "Newsroom ethnography in a field perspective." *Journalism* 14 (3): 372–387.

Willnat, Lars, David H. Weaver, and G. Cleveland Wilhoit. 2019. "The American journalist in the digital age: How journalists and the public think about journalism in the United States." *Journalism Studies* 20 (3): 423–441.

6

FOUNDATIONS AND JOURNALISM

A new business model, a new set of logics

Magda Konieczna

Foundations have long been involved in the field of journalism. This is particularly the case in the United States, a country where a strong culture of philanthropy sits alongside a skepticism of government support for news. Throughout much of the 20th century, American foundations funded public broadcasting and journalism schools. This influence has grown as challenges to the traditional news business model have made it clear that the market can no longer support the journalism necessary for democracy to function (and perhaps it never did; see, e.g., Pickard 2019). As a result, and in response to the financial crisis in news in particular, the last 15 or 20 years have seen foundations' influence grow significantly. Today, more and more news organizations, the vast majority of them nonprofit, and largely but not only in the United States, rely on what has so far been a deepening pot of foundation money.

This support is often portrayed as a common-sense and benevolent social force. And it's true that foundations have done plenty of good, in the journalism world and beyond. At the same time, foundation funding, like any other source of support for journalism, has had an imprint on the field, strengthening it in some ways but also applying external pressure for change. And there's a global inequality at play, too. The United States eclipses other countries in terms of philanthropy, around journalism and around other causes as well, in part because it is itself a more unequal society. This chapter explores the growth and development of foundation funding for news, how it benefits journalism, and the challenges associated with it – examining also, where relevant, the nature and evolution of the (largely) nonprofit newsrooms that are the recipients of the money.

Who are foundation funders? A snapshot of the field

Foundation support for American public broadcasting goes back to the 1950s, when the Ford Foundation contributed to starting educational television in the US

DOI: 10.4324/9781003140399-9

The Carnegie Corporation helped build that into PBS (Public Broadcasting Service) on television in the 1960s, and NPR (National Public Radio) in 1970.[1] Over the latter part of the 20th century, a handful of other foundation-reliant news organizations appeared, including the Center for Investigative Reporting, founded in 1977, and the Center for Public Integrity, in 1989. These were supported by the Ford and MacArthur foundations, as well as the Knight Foundation, which for a long time was one of the few foundations interested in journalistic production outside of public broadcasting (Westphal 2009).

Foundation funding for news changed dramatically in the United States with the financial crash of 2008. The American news media in particular was hit hard because of its disproportionate reliance on advertising revenue, which all but dried up during the crisis (Santhanam and Rosenstiel 2011). Within a short period in 2009, the *Rocky Mountain News* closed and the *Seattle Post-Intelligencer* went online-only, the first major newspaper to do so. The *San Francisco Chronicle* teetered on the brink of bankruptcy, and *The New York Times* needed to secure a $250-million loan from Mexican billionaire Carlos Slim (Westphal 2009). In response to journalism's financial woes, journalists around the country, many of them newly unemployed, began to launch news nonprofits in earnest (Konieczna 2018). In 2009, journalists from 27 of these organizations got together to start what is now called the Institute for Nonprofit News, a professional body that encourages sharing resources and best practices. By the end of 2020, INN had grown to almost 300 members, the vast majority of them heavily reliant on foundation money. Still, that sector has been working to diversify its revenue sources. In 2019, for the first time, foundation funding accounted for less than half of the money in the nonprofit news sector, with 40% coming from audiences, according to a survey of INN members (McLellan and Holcomb 2019). In other words, while foundations and news nonprofits remain inextricably linked, that relationship continues to evolve.

The clearest data on the size of the field comes from Media Impact Funders, a major affinity group. Their figures show that foundations have spent more than $20 billion on media worldwide since 2009. Of that, almost $17 billion was spent in the US. Grants for projects related to journalism, news and information totaled $2.7 billion; grants for investigative journalism specifically have come to just under $500 million of that. The data also tells us that the amount of money in the field has been steadily increasing.

The foundations funding journalism range from large, national or international entities, to small community foundations. They tend to have public-service missions dedicated to journalism and democracy, or to other causes that they hope they can affect by funding reporting projects or newsrooms.

The Knight Foundation is one of few focused specifically on journalism. In that capacity, it has spent almost $250 million in the last decade, according to the Media Impact Funders data. That has included significant grants to universities, as well as money to many of the most prominent news nonprofits. The other top funders, including the Ford Foundation, the Gates Foundation, the MacArthur Foundation,

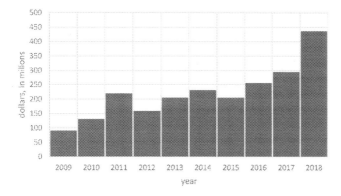

FIGURE 6.1 Growth in foundation funding for journalism, news and information in the US, as reported by Media Impact Funders[2]

and the Foundation to Promote Open Society, support a broad range of causes. For many of them, funding journalism is a way of influencing the other causes they focus on, including improving health outcomes and promoting democracy. Indeed, there remains a tension in the field around whether journalism is something that should be supported for its own sake, or whether it is part of a larger ambition to support a robust civil society.

In addition to these large, national and often international players, smaller regional foundations support journalism around the country. Community foundations have also become a source of news funding and support, contributing 5% of all foundation funding for journalism in the US since 2009 (Armour-Jones 2019) largely based on the understanding that a more informed community can "better hold power to account, advocate for broad community needs and create more representative government" (Armour-Jones 2019: 8). Among the more prominent relationships is the Philadelphia Foundation's ownership of the Lenfest Institute, which in turn owns *The Philadelphia Inquirer*, an arrangement that garnered much attention when it was set up in 2016 (Wang 2016).

In 2020, a number of new funders entered the field with money to educate the public on COVID-19. In particular, Google committed $250 million worth of ads to help disseminate information about the novel coronavirus, immediately propelling it to the top of Media Impact Funders' list in the journalism, news and information category (Pichai 2020). That Google is not a foundation only illustrates how the lines between commercial and nonprofit news and information are blurring. That blurriness has increasingly included foundation willingness to fund commercial news organizations. Report for America, for instance, uses grant money to pay half the salary of reporters placed in newsrooms around the country, in essence leveraging foundation funds to subsidize the work of both nonprofit and commercial newsrooms. The Lenfest Institute for Journalism has made a name for itself by giving grants to both nonprofit and for-profit news projects, including the *Philadelphia Inquirer*, which it owns. This kind of blurry relationship is increasingly common around the world as well, with, for instance, the Canadian government subsidizing positions in largely commercial newsrooms (Scire 2020).

Foundations change the logics of news

On the surface, foundations' role in the field of journalism is to offer funding. However, foundations don't merely act as a financial cushion. Rather, as with all of the institutions in this book, foundations are changing journalism from the outside, in this case, by modifying the logics of news production.

Throughout the 20th century, about three-quarters of news revenue in the United States came from advertising (Santhanam and Rosenstiel 2011), compared to slightly more than half, on average, at news organizations around the world. That structure means journalism operates in a dual product marketplace. News organizations make some amount of money selling content to audiences. To succeed in this marketplace, they need to produce something that audience members are willing to pay for. The more significant revenue source, though, comes from selling space to advertisers. To succeed in that marketplace, news organizations need to promise advertisers exposure for what they're selling. This means that they need to bring in an audience large enough, and affluent enough, that advertisers are willing to pay for access to that audience.

Scholars and critics have long raised concerns that advertisers affect journalism directly, by threatening to pull out support over particular stories, and indirectly, by pegging journalism to a capitalist system in the first place (e.g., Herman and Chomsky 2002). In relying on advertising, news organizations are incentivized to increase eyeballs on the page. That is particularly true in online environments where social media metrics, often posted real-time in prominent places in the newsroom, further prioritize commercial pressures (see Banjac, this volume; Bélair-Gagnon, this volume). This kind of hyper-awareness leads journalists to internalize a sense of what does well, for instance, on Facebook, resulting in newsroom practices that see audiences as "apolitical entertainment seekers rather than engaged citizens of a democratic society" (Pickard 2019: 79). Pickard argues that this leads to incentives that are misaligned with the goals of democracy, and contributes to the spread of misinformation and disinformation by prioritizing the content that gets most clicks and spreads most quickly. Saliently, he adds that "(p)erhaps the real question is why we ever expected anything different to emerge from such a commercialized, profit-driven system" (Pickard 2019: 134).

The challenges around ad funding for news came to a head when the advertising market all but fell apart in the first decade of the 21st century. Until then, many saw the impact of advertising as an unfortunate but necessary compromise in exchange for a robust revenue stream that supported a range of important journalistic work.

Foundation funding may initially look like a simple replacement for advertising revenue. When we look deeper, though, we see that swapping out one revenue source for another has larger implications. Specifically, the dual-product relationship described above means that advertisers support news incidentally: by buying ad space to reach audience members, advertisers are, almost inadvertently, funding journalism (Baker 1994). Foundations, on the other hand, fund journalism *directly*, precisely because of what journalism is and what it does. That's evident when we look at foundations' own descriptions of their work. For instance, the Knight Foundation notes on its "about" page that "We believe an informed citizenry is essential for representative democracy to function effectively." Similarly, in the description of its Creativity and Free Expression program, the Ford Foundation writes that: "Our work explores how cultural narratives affect and shape our reality, and how the arts, journalism, and film can contribute to fairer and more just societies." We can see here that the goal of these funders is explicitly to have an impact on society – whereas the goal of advertisers is, ostensibly, to sell more products.

We might wonder whether this distinction matters. Revenue is revenue, after all, and it's something that news organizations are looking for in ever more creative ways as the traditional models continue to suffer. As we will see below, changing the source of funding realigns incentives for doing journalism in interesting ways that have the potential to significantly change how journalism is done. The closer we look, the more apparent it is that while foundations do relieve, at least to a degree, market pressures on news, they replace them with a new set of pressures. I discuss these challenges and criticisms below.

The challenges of foundation funding

Foundations often focus on supporting the production of quality journalism, making them better aligned with the ambitions of journalists and news media than are advertisers, whose goal is to sell their products or services. Still, one advantage of advertising support is transparency. Corporations buy ads to draw attention to what they're trying to sell. That means that there's no secrecy around who advertisers are and that journalism's responsibility to advertisers ends the moment an ad appears in print (or online, or on the airwaves). Foundations, on the other hand, fund journalism to help push forward an agenda. At its best, this agenda is about democracy and quality journalism. Even in these cases, though, the influence can be complex. And while some foundations and news organizations pledge transparency, that's not inherently built into the system, which can lead to a complex set of influences that can be difficult to unravel (see Bice (2017) for an example of the kind of work sometimes needed to get to the bottom of these relationships).

As a result, many critics are concerned that foundations might seek to influence news content. This kind of influence is familiar to news organizations, in part because of their long relationship with advertisers, but also with other societal actors such as political entities that often try to exert influence. The history of these struggles has led to what is referred to as the firewall between news and advertising divisions. This history of course does not necessarily mean the relationship is easy to manage; financially struggling news organizations may be tempted to accept money even with strings attached, especially when it means the difference between surviving to report for another day and shutting down operations. Indeed, in one study, 60% of funders surveyed said they'd given money for specific stories or investigations, where influence can potentially be more easily exerted, rather than for more general coverage (Rosenstiel et al. 2016)

Still, perhaps more complex and challenging is foundation influence behind the scenes. In interviews with staff at nonprofit newsrooms and the foundations that fund them, Ferrucci and Nelson found that foundations influence behind-the-scenes decision-making in ways that contribute to how news content is produced, for instance by promoting projects connected to engagement (Ferrucci and Nelson 2019). They conclude that this relationship leads journalists to cede authority to foundations, which exist outside of the boundaries of journalism. Ultimately, they find that foundations often have different goals from the newsrooms they're supporting. Foundations are often working to solve problems in news as a whole, making them more interested in experimentation and innovation than are the news organizations they fund, which might just be struggling to survive for one more year. Others (Scott, Bunce, and Wright 2019: 2043) have pointed out that this impact on "non-editorial activities" serves to push the boundaries of journalism by encouraging journalists to engage in non-editorial tasks as well as producing longer-form news stories in select coverage areas.

As we'll see below, these tensions are clearest when the traditional norms of journalism are in conflict with foundation practices.

Transparency, influence, and accountability

Advertising support of journalism is, inherently, transparent (for the most part, at least; see Li, this volume). While we might not know about the work advertisers are doing behind the scenes to influence content, we need only to look at a publication to see who is funding it, with the possible exception of some forms of native advertising. Foundations are not always transparent in this way. Anonymous donations, for instance, are not uncommon in the foundation world. Some organizations have tried to mitigate that. To join the Institute for Nonprofit News, news organizations need to publish a list of all donors that give more than $5,000 in a single year, and must not get more than 15% of their revenue from anonymous sources (Institute for Nonprofit News: n.d.). Still, these workarounds suggest a clash between operations of foundations and of news, with its often-stated commitment to openness and transparency. And, transparency rules like the ones implemented by INN only get us so far. It takes a particularly sophisticated and motivated audience member to seek out and understand the nature of even transparent funding relationships.

Of particular concern are ideologically driven organizations that present their work as nonpartisan. Wisconsin Watchdog, for instance, called itself a nonprofit, non-partisan news organization, using much of the same language as any other recent news startup. And yet, a data hack revealed it had been funded by the Bradley Foundation as part of a concerted effort to build a conservative infrastructure around the country (Bice 2017).[3] A number of organizations have been explicitly linked to conservative money in this way; a number of others surely also have problematic relationships that remain obscured by secretive financial arrangements. Still, it is worth noting that these organizations are a tiny minority of news nonprofits: one report found that 99% of those surveyed disclosed the source of at least some of their funding (Rosenstiel et al. 2016).

The lack of transparency becomes especially problematic, however, when we acknowledge that foundations might be supporting journalism to promote their own interests (see Ihlebæk and Figenschou, this volume). At their normative best, foundation funders aim to support quality journalism that improves the nature of our democracy. Still, as Benson points out, "we must acknowledge the possibility that foundations are just as capable of non-democratic 'media capture' on behalf of their own interests as they are of fostering civic benefits for society as a whole" (2018: 1060).

On one extreme, we have the foundations described above that go to great lengths to obscure their involvement in individual news organizations (see, e.g., Bice 2017). No research exists yet on the kind of content that comes out of these projects, and without knowing who is funding these projects in the first place, there is no way to tell whether these relationships enable foundations to pursue their own interests. We can only assume that this may be one reason for anonymously funding news projects.

On the other end of the spectrum, we see foundations that are open about their support. This alleviates some of the concerns raised above. Still, one study found that half of funders sampled said they made grants to news organizations on issues on which they were trying to change public policy or behavior (Rosenstiel et al. 2016), which means that even in transparent relationships, we see news organizations ceding some of their news judgment to foundations in ways that grant them influence. Even if foundations don't directly interfere with the content, and even if these are causes that we might agree with, the potential to promote topics that satisfy foundation interests is clear. Indeed, this is widely regarded as within the purview of foundation funders. We should note as well that this can exceed the impact advertisers have on news content. When Ferrucci and Nelson refer to foundations as "the new advertisers," they point out that the firewall that was designed to insulate journalism from advertising doesn't exist when it comes to foundations (Ferrucci and Nelson 2019). This means that these relationships are, for the moment, often still *ad hoc*, though as foundation funding for journalism becomes more common it seems likely that a set of norms will emerge, as it did with advertisers.

While comprehensive research on this question is hard to come by, we do have some instructive examples. For instance, the New York City public television station WNET returned a $3.5 million grant for a series about the sustainability of public pension funds when it turned out that the funder had been dedicating himself to persuading municipalities to cut pension funds. Importantly, the series took a similar tone, though the foundation issued a statement saying it did not seek to affect content (Jensen 2014). In the end, it is hard to tell whether the foundation was seeking influence or merely more coverage and whether WNET's coverage was affected by the involvement of the foundation. Certainly the potential exists for undue influence, and for the perception of influence, and we lack the mechanisms to determine whether that's happening.

As I noted above, foundations can also influence non-editorial decisions in ways that are particularly interesting. Nelson (2018) for instance details how this happens in the audience engagement industry. Entities such as Hearken offer persuasive, and often highly relevant, arguments about why journalists should focus more on engaging their audiences. In response, foundations have offered funding to support news organizations' participation in these projects (Bilton 2018). This focus on engagement has the potential to revolutionize the news industry in a range of ways (see also, Nelson and Wenzel, this volume). Still, as Nelson (2018) points out, we've seen little concrete evidence that these projects do improve engagement or increase revenue. In other words, as foundations push for audience engagement, they direct newsroom efforts and resources, without proof that these approaches work. Of course, building a more engaged and diverse newsroom is laudable. Nevertheless, it shows us the ways in which foundations are pushing for change in the news industry, and their incredible power to do so despite the relatively untested nature of these efforts.

Concerns about the lack of transparency and the ability of foundations to promote their own interests are exacerbated by the lack of accountability measures. This is, of course, also an issue with advertisers, which have no inherent responsibility to audiences, but which sometimes withdraw funding from controversial spots when public outcry pushes them to do so. Still, advertisers aren't inherently involved in the process of building democracy like foundations are. Put this way, we can see why government support for news makes so much sense.

Of course, the public service orientation of many foundations offers an alignment with democratic goals, and can lead them to design accountability measures. Indeed, foundations answer to a board, produce annual reports, and ultimately are responsible to the IRS to make good on their missions (though the degree of enforcement is unclear). On the other hand, foundations often engage in what Creech and Nadler call "civic policymaking" (2018: 183). Viewed this way, it becomes apparent why the lack of built-in accountability measures is problematic.

The role of impact

Determining the impact of foundation funding is technically called "measurement and evaluation," a term that's well known to anyone working in the foundation world. The idea of measuring and evaluating impact sits less comfortably, though, with journalists, and is one of the major points of contention between foundations pushing the boundaries of journalism, and the field they're affecting.

To be certain, journalists have long been concerned with the impact of their work (see: Browne 2019; Ettema and Glasser 1998). The journalistic principle of independence, though, has traditionally interfered with expressing that concern out loud, in particular in the US tradition of objective reporting. As a result, journalists have tended to talk about their work in a hands-off way. Ettema and Glasser conducted an extensive study of investigative journalists in the 1990s and found that most refused to discuss the impact of their reporting. Instead, they "underst-[oo]d their power, as well as their responsibility, to be limited to telling a story" (Ettema and Glasser 1998: 82). Put another way, the rhetoric of high-modern journalism requires journalists to disseminate the truth without regard for consequences, either negative or positive (Browne 2019).

The public journalism movement of the 1990s aimed to change that. Merritt and McCombs (2004), for instance, argued that journalists are in fact driven by a set of values, and openness about that would help to close the gap between how journalism operates and its democratic impact. Public journalism came and went as an agenda, but journalists' thinking about impact has continued to evolve (Ferrucci 2017). At the International Consortium of Investigative Journalists, staff consider the potential impact of a project before committing to taking it on (Konieczna and Powers 2017), and the Bureau of Investigative Journalism recently created the position of impact editor to make sure its work has ripples in the real world (Schmidt 2019). Both talk about their increased interest in impact as something that's simply their responsibility as good journalists; BIJ's new impact editor told Nieman Lab that she was frustrated with mainstream journalism: "no matter what you write, no matter how much of a splash it makes, it doesn't always make a change" (Schmidt 2019: n.p.).

Given how journalists' own concerns about impact have grown in parallel to foundations' involvement in news, it is difficult to precisely define the footprint of foundations on the notion of impact. Still, foundation reporting requirements, designed to ensure that money is being spent wisely, illuminate the ways in which they have sought to highlight the "investments" and "returns" of their work (Tofel 2013: 2) as measurement and evaluation has taken "a strong foothold in journalism" (Keller and Abelson 2015: 9). All of this makes journalists uncomfortable because it blurs the line between journalism and advocacy (Pitt and Green-Barber 2017). These new relationships can be uncomfortable for funders, too, as they are more used to supporting service-oriented projects whose impact is easier to measure; inoculations are easy to count, while measuring the impact of media or journalism is more complex (Pitt and Green-Barber 2017).

When will foundation funds dry up?

Around 2009 and 2010, when we started to see dramatic challenges in the news business model and a corresponding explosive growth in news nonprofits, one of the most cited concerns was that there wasn't enough foundation money out there to replace what was being lost. Others phrased the concern in a different way: foundations were willing to offer seed money, they noted, but weren't planning to fund journalism in perpetuity. This concern translated into a need for news organizations to find a path to sustainability, which, in this argument, meant success in the marketplace without relying on foundations.

In turn, many news nonprofits have succeeded in securing funding outside of foundation grants. As I noted above, nonprofit newsrooms responding to the annual survey conducted by the Institute for Nonprofit News reported that in 2019 for the first time more than half their revenue came from sources other than foundations (McLellan and Holcomb 2019). Analysts have noted in particular the success of the *Texas Tribune* in generating revenue from events, *MinnPost* in earning advertising revenue, and, in Europe, *De Correspondent* in securing donations from audience members. This doesn't mean foundation funds are shrinking: rather, as Figure 6.1 shows, total funding in the sector is growing, and is being spread around to a growing number of organizations. Still, foundation money remains a drop in the bucket compared to the revenue that has been lost. Benson estimates that foundation funds amount to one-tenth of the lost revenue, or about half of one percent of existing revenue across the field of journalism (Benson 2017).

Even as foundation funding for media continues to grow, the uncertainty about how much money is available puts particular emphasis on the question of what gets funded. Foundations prioritize certain types of coverage, which may or may not be in line with the kind of coverage news organizations were producing previously. The major concern here is that foundations will offer funds for reporting on their pet causes, essentially removing from news organizations the role of deciding what's news in the first place. This was the case when WNET got a grant to produce a series on public pensions from an organization linked to advocacy on the topic. While the station stood by its reporting and said there had been no undue influence, it returned the grant because of the negative perception. This kind of influence, perceived or real, becomes particularly problematic when there isn't enough money to support all the worthwhile projects.

Foundations are embedded in capitalism

Of course, foundation funding is only one option to help fill the gap as the news business model struggles. Some scholars (e.g., Pickard 2019) have focused on framing news as a public good with positive externalities. From a critical political economy perspective, they argue that we need robust government funding for journalism. (Indeed, in many countries outside the US, this argument has been more successful, which is why we see better funded public broadcasters there.) Seen this way, we might argue that foundations uphold a capitalist order. Benson references Joan Roelofs (1987) to argue that foundations support corporate interests by keeping the opposition fragmented, supporting "forms of activism that do not seriously challenge the power structure", resulting from grant language that "stops short of systemic critique" (Benson 2018: 1067–1068).

This includes the way in which foundations and other external players work to push innovation as a market-oriented solution to journalism's crisis/es, at the cost of promoting other, more democratically oriented solutions (Creech and Nadler 2018). Indeed, while this chapter focuses on how foundations fund journalism, the more prominent and more journalistically focused ones also conduct research and produce reports that reflect their particular approach to rebuilding the field of journalism, one that is often squarely focused on innovation within the marketplace (Creech and Nadler 2018).

These concerns are heightened when we examine the close links between foundations and the business world. Benson (2018) found, for instance, that between a quarter and a half of foundation board members were business leaders, and a fifth of board members came from finance. Members had more cultural capital than did board members of commercial news organizations; on average, members had two degrees, and 80% of those degrees in Benson's sample came from Ivy League or other highly selective universities. Benson expresses concern that this makes it challenging for foundations and news nonprofits to offer a critique of journalism, noting that it "does not preclude an oppositional or alternative stance for nonprofit media, but it certainly makes it more difficult to achieve" (Benson 2018:1067). He concludes that:

> Foundation-supported nonprofit news media are thus deeply incorporated into the U.S. hyper-commercialized system of news production and circulation, in which most of the public is provided a steady menu of infotainment and sponsored content, while a small sector of in-depth (limited) critical news remains largely within the provinces of high cultural capital elites.
>
> *(Benson 2018: 1073)*

Indeed, this concern about journalism that is targeted to elites is ingrained in the nonprofit news sector. Still, it's not entirely clear whether foundations are the problem here, or the antidote. It's likely they're both. On the one hand, as noted above, the foundation world is inherently an elite one. On the other, though, if we consider other likely sources of news revenue, it becomes clear that with advertising in decline and governments, at least in the US, unlikely to step in, audience donations or subscriptions are the remaining obvious source. Money from audiences can also prove problematic in the ways in which it could lead to journalism that prioritizes appealing to those with the ability to pay.

Looking ahead

As this chapter has made clear, foundations, with their public service missions and their concerns about journalism and democracy, have done plenty of good in the news sphere (with the notable exception of those partisan foundations that secretly fund organizations purporting to produce non-partisan news but which in reality act more like political players). It is equally clear, I think, that foundations aren't just replacing lost advertising revenue. In a lot of ways, it makes much more sense for a foundation to support journalism than it does for an advertiser. With their public-service missions, foundations support journalism *directly,* because of what it does, rather than indirectly, as a way of promoting their own messages, as advertisers do.

Still, there is plenty to be wary of here. Most relevant to the discussion at hand is the way in which foundations push the boundaries of journalism. This can take the form of influencing content, though the threat of this kind of influence dates back to the relationship between newsrooms and advertisers, meaning news organizations are better prepared to head it off. The bigger concern here is the non-editorial influence. Even when it seems benign or benevolent, we need to acknowledge that it represents an external force on journalism from entities that can be hard for audience members to track, even in cases where foundations behave transparently. The further lack of obvious accountability mechanisms should make us give these relationships a second look. The most significant impact here is, I think, that foundation funding in the news sector undercuts more radical critiques of journalism by suggesting that private capital can, and even *should*, fund our way out of this crisis.

Notes

1   Note that while Americans refer to PBS and NPR as public broadcasters, very little of their funding comes from government sources. These entities receive $3 per capita per year from government sources, putting the US at the bottom of developed countries in this respect. In comparison, Canada, also on the low end of the spectrum, spends $31 per capita; on the higher end, Norway spends $175 (Benson, Powers, and Neff 2017). Indeed, low levels of government support are a large part of the reason foundations play such a big role in American journalism.
2   Note Data is sourced from foundation tax returns, websites, self-reporting, and other public information collected by Candid, which tracks the financials of nonprofits and foundations.
3   Note that Wisconsin Watchdog, along with its parent organization Watchdog.org, have been subsumed into The Center Square. This kind of acquisition and reorganization appears to be common at news nonprofits with partisan links, perhaps a reflection of the fact that the field remains unsettled.

References

Armour-Jones, Sarah. 2019. *"Journalism Grantmaking."* *Media Impact Funders*. Philadelphia: Media Impact Funders.

Baker, C. Edwin. 1994. *Advertising and a Democratic Press*. Princeton, NJ: Princeton University Press.

Benson, Rodney. 2018. "Can Foundations Solve the Journalism Crisis?" *Journalism* 19 (8): 1059–1077.

Benson, Rodney, Matthew Powers, and Timothy Neff. 2017. "Public Media Autonomy and Accountability: Best and Worst Policy Practices in 12 Leading Democracies." *International Journal of Communication* 11: 1–22.

Bice, Daniel. 2017. "Hacked Records Show Bradley Foundation Taking Its Conservative Wisconsin Model National." *Milwaukee Journal Sentinel*, May 5.

Bilton, Ricardo. 2018. "A New $650K Grant Will Help Pay for Newsrooms to Adopt Tools like Hearken and GroundSource." *Nieman Lab*, January 23. https://www.niemanlab.org/2018/01/a-new-650k-grant-will-help-pay-for-newsrooms-to-adopt-tools-like-hearken-and-groundsource/.

Browne, Harry. 2019. "Philanthropy-Supported Journalism." In *International Encyclopedia of Journalism Studies*. Hoboken, NJ: John Wiley & Sons, Inc.

Creech, Brian, and Anthony M. Nadler. 2018. "Post-Industrial Fog: Reconsidering Innovation in Visions of Journalism's Future." *Journalism* 19 (2): 182–199.

Ettema, James S., and Theodore L. Glasser. 1998. *Custodians of Conscience: Investigative Journalism and Public Virtue*. New York: Columbia University Press.

Ferrucci, Patrick. 2017. "Exploring public service journalism: Digitally native news nonprofits and engagement." *Journalism & Mass Communication Quarterly* 94 (1): 355–370.

Ferrucci, Patrick, and Jacob L. Nelson. 2019. "The New Advertisers: How Foundation Funding Impacts Journalism." *Media and Communication* 7 (4): 45–55.

Herman, Edward S., and Noam Chomsky. 2002. *Manufacturing Consent: The Political Economy of the Mass Media*. New York: Pantheon.

Institute for Nonprofit News. (n.d.) "Become a Member." https://inn.org/for-members/become-a-member/.

Jensen, Elizabeth. 2014. "WNET to Return $3.5 Million Grant for Pension Series." *The New York Times*, February 14.

Keller, Michael, and Brian Abelson. 2015. "NewsLynx: A Tool for Newsroom Impact Measurement." Tow Center for Digital Journalism, June 4.

Konieczna, Magda. 2018. *Journalism Without Profit: Making News When the Market Fails*. New York: Oxford University Press.

Konieczna, Magda. 2020. "Entrepreneurship versus Philanthropy: Can the Market Fund Innovation in the News Sector?" *Journal of Media Business Studies* 17 (2): 132–147.

Konieczna, Magda, and Elia Powers. 2017. "What Can Nonprofit Journalists Actually Do for Democracy?" *Journalism Studies* 18 (12): 1542–1558.

McLellan, Michele, and Jesse Holcomb. 2019. "INN Index 2019." Institute for Nonprofit News. https://inn.org/research/inn-index/inn-index-2019/.

Merritt, Davis, and Maxwell E. McCombs. 2004. *The Two W's of Journalism: The Why and What of Public Affairs Reporting*. Mahwah, NJ: Lawrence Erlbaum Associates.

Nelson, Jacob L. 2018. "The Audience Engagement Industry Struggles with Measuring Success." *Columbia Journalism Review*, April 30.

Pichai, Sundar. 2020. "COVID-19: $800+ million to support small businesses and crisis response." *The Keyword*, March 27. https://www.blog.google/inside-google/company-announcements/commitment-support-small-businesses-and-crisis-response-covid-19/.

Pickard, Victor. 2019. *Democracy Without Journalism? Confronting the Misinformation Society*. New York: Oxford University Press.

Pitt, Fergus, and Lindsay Green-Barber. 2017. "The Case for Media Impact." Tow Center for Digital Journalism.

Roelofs, Joan. 1987. "Foundations and Social Change Organizations: The Mask of Pluralism." *Critical Sociology* 14 (3): 31–72.

Rosenstiel, Tom, William Buzenberg, Marjorie Connelly, and Kevin Loker. 2016. "Charting New Ground: The Ethical Terrain of Nonprofit Journalism." American Press Institute. https://www.americanpressinstitute.org/publications/reports/nonprofit-news/.

Santhanam, Laura Houston, and Tom Rosenstiel. 2011. "Why U.S. Newspapers Suffer More than Others." Pew Research Center's Journalism Project, March 20.

Schmidt, Christine. 2019. "Meet the Impact Editor: The Bureau of Investigative Journalism Is Now Paying Someone to Ensure Its Journalism Makes a Difference." *Nieman Lab*, September 11.

Scire, Sarah. 2020. "In Canada, a Government Program to Support Local News Tries to Determine Who's Most Deserving." *Nieman Lab*, May 8.

Scott, Martin, Mel Bunce, and Kate Wright. 2019. "Foundation Funding and the Boundaries of Journalism." *Journalism Studies* 20 (14): 2034–2052.

Tofel, Richard J. 2013. "Non-Profit Journalism: Issues Around Impact." ProPublica. http://s3.amazonaws.com/propublica/assets/about/LFA_ProPublica-white-paper_2.1.pdf.

Wang, Shan. 2016. "Can Philly's New Institute for Journalism in New Media Live up to the Enormous Hopes Pinned on It?" Nieman Lab, January 22.

Westphal, David. 2009. "Philanthropic Foundations: Growing Funders of the News." University of Southern California. https://cpb-us-e1.wpmucdn.com/sites.usc.edu/dist/2/672/files/2015/07/PhilanthropicFoundations.pdf.

7

JOURNALISM IS NOT A ONE-WAY STREET

Recognizing multi-directional dynamics

Stefan Baack, David Cheruiyot and Raul Ferrer-Conill[1]

Introduction

One of the main occupations of journalism scholarship is to study how journalism, as a profession and institution, is changing and evolving. An established tradition clarifies that journalism is changing, at least in part, because external stressors are influencing the field (Shoemaker and Reese 2014; Singer 2003). In recent years, a new strand of literature has used various metaphors trying to grasp the notion that "outsiders" are "infiltrating" journalism and exerting change (Bélair-Gagnon and Holton 2018; Eldridge 2018). This very book evokes the metaphors of "barbarians" breaching the institutional gates of journalism. Elsewhere in our research (Cheruiyot, Baack, and Ferrer-Conill 2019), we also adopted the widely-used metaphor of "peripheral actors" to investigate how non-journalistic actors perform practices central to data journalism.

While important, the dominance of approaches that study how outsiders exert pressure within journalism creates two blind spots. First, the idea that "barbarians" influence journalism over-simplifies real-world interdependencies and limits our ability to grasp public communication's changing dynamics more broadly. It highlights only the influence journalism experiences from external forces, but usually does not consider the influence that journalism exerts outwardly toward NGOs or technology companies, for example (see Ferrucci, this volume). Second, the locative metaphor of periphery vs center often overlooks the more literal, geographical dichotomy of the center and periphery concerning both journalistic practice and journalism scholarship. The focus and attention to Western news organizations as the centerstage of the journalistic field implicitly turns all that is non-Western into peripheral actors of journalistic production. It also speaks to the proclivity in journalism studies to define journalistic practice within the terms of Western democratic systems (Carey 2010; Josephi 2012; Zelizer 2012), and the persistent notion that journalism in the US is self-contained (Vos 2017).

DOI: 10.4324/9781003140399-10

This chapter aims to address the two aforementioned blind spots by advocating for a research agenda that actively explores the multi-directional interdependencies between journalists and peripheral actors while expanding our view toward wider geographical realities. In particular, we want to show the value of studying how "classic" conceptions of professional journalism shape the self-understandings and profiles of peripheral actors. This is an invitation for journalism studies to more thoroughly investigate multi-directional influences and acknowledge that, while journalism is our object of study, sometimes there is value in understanding how others shape it and are shaped by it outside our field. Lifting the disciplinary blinders could help us see the important influences that journalism has on other fields, beyond its "democratic function" (Kovach and Rosenstiel 2007; Zelizer 2012). Asking more prominently how particular practices and self-understandings of journalism in different contexts shape peripheral actors would allow us to better understand its value and relevance in various contexts.

We approach this discussion first by highlighting how the "periphery vs center" narrative has created a form of "otherism" that by definition demarcates between the what, who, and where of journalism. Our theoretical discussion engages with the notion of institutional autonomy and the institution-as-routine as an analytical lens. Next, we build our argument around three empirical examples taken from previous and ongoing research by the authors from around the world. We do not see these examples as an exhaustive list of areas in which multi-directional exchanges occur, but rather use them to highlight what we might overlook if our empirical work only looks at journalism itself: namely, how certain imaginaries about journalism shape other actors, which might in turn affect the self-perception and practices of journalists and provide us with valuable insights into journalism's role in society. What our examples have in common is a focus on non-journalistic organizations that have a clear connection to journalism, thanks to overlapping aspirations that in some of these cases lead to direct collaborations with journalists. As we hope to illustrate, grasping journalism's role in society requires us to look beyond journalism itself.

"Otherism" and journalism's relationship with others

While old and new actors at the periphery of journalism have an influence on journalism, some of these actors may also reinforce traditional journalistic practices and identities rather than change or expand them (see Hermida, Varano, and Young, this volume). At the same time, while adjacent fields and actors influence journalism, it is also true that journalism is influencing how non-journalistic actors understand and perform their own roles. The main problem with a "one-directional" study of journalism is to overlook or underestimate the importance of those and similar interdependencies. For a field so preoccupied with studying journalism's role in society, not looking at how journalism influences neighbouring fields is a glaring blind spot.

Journalism studies' one-directional problem

Journalism studies has been preoccupied with drawing boundaries across institutional lines (Bélair-Gagnon and Holton 2018; Carlson and Lewis 2015), the implicit consensus being that those boundaries have blurred (Darbo and Skjerdal 2019; Domingo and Le Cam 2014; Lewis 2012). Studies on the transgression of those blurred boundaries often focus on the one-directional influence created during the "holy ritual" of news production (Tuchman 1972). Our early fascination with the mechanisms that inform journalism practice set in motion a valuable yet one-sided strand of literature that tried to understand the inward influences on journalism. Some of the most established models, such as the hierarchy of influences (Shoemaker and Reese 2014) or media systems (Hallin and Mancini 2004) proposed one-directional elaborate structures that could explain the shape of media content through various macro, meso, and micro layers of influence.

We believe the instinct to frame journalism as it relates to non-journalism stems from two major developments. First, our field's inherent need to demarcate its own jurisdiction, trying to make sense of what is and what is not journalism, and this process tends to replicate professional journalists' self-proclaimed norms and institutional autonomy. This is not a unique feature of our field but rather a hallmark of institutional approaches across fields. Journalism as an institution can be understood as "an organizationally bound enterprise with routinized practices, subject to varying factors and forces in the environment" that is "shaped by external forces but also capable of agency within a collective space that has negotiated boundaries, legitimacy, and an internal logic" (Lowrey 2018: 125). This signals to external forces moving inward but omits the outward forces that journalism impact. As Wahl-Jorgensen (2014: 2588) concluded, "the journalistic field and the field of scholarship on journalism exist in a complex interdependent relationship", with scholars often falling into a pattern of conducting "back-up boundary work, supporting the endeavor of the field they studied and thus seeking to ensure its continued viability". Moreover, the dominating interest in capturing change "within" journalism invokes the necessity to locate the source of change, internal or external. The apparent outcome of this is the creation of false binaries that perpetuate vaguely defined "otherisms" by which we recognize our object of study.

The second development that contributed to a focus on "outside" influences on journalism is the fact that journalism is historically a Western construct and that the centers of power for journalistic production reside in the US and Europe. This center is reinforced through its professional and institutional dominance in terms of, among others, acquired professional values and norms (Hanitzsch 2007; Waisbord 2013), technologies and news paradigms (Høyer and Pöttker 2005), education and training models (Josephi 2007), or the democracy-infused hegemonic model of practice (Kovach and Rosenstiel 2007; Nerone 2012).

As it is the tradition in our field, most of these studies and models focus on Western structures, even though some have been updated to encompass broader realities (Hallin and Mancini 2012; Reese 2007). We are not the only ones to point to the Anglo-American slant showing that "theoretical approaches and frameworks developed in the context of Western democracies dominate (digital) journalism scholarship, even if often they are found to be inadequate" (Tandoc, Hess, Eldridge, and Westlund 2020: 302) and important efforts are being put into place to address the issue of diversity in journalism scholarship (see Tandoc, Jenkins, Thomas, and Westlund, 2021). Even after these global inclusivity efforts, the dominance of Western epistemologies within our field is often not matched by an equal epistemic resistance from the periphery, mostly because of entrenched power inequalities (Demeter 2020). Scholars within and beyond the media and communication discipline (see, for example, Cushion 2008, Demeter 2019) have consistently shown through empirical evidence that the odds are stacked against peripheral nations in academia when it comes to publishing and citation practices.

Such "otherism" in the global exchange of journalism is a result of "self-containedness" of the West, mostly the US, and the accompanying sense in which the center is considered to be the *giver* (see for example, Vos 2017: 55) and the periphery as the *taker* of the journalistic model of practice. As such, peripheralization inevitably emerges as a marker of distinctions in both geographic and professional terms, often at risk of "pigeon-holing" peripheral scholarship (Cheruiyot and Ferrer-Conill 2021).

What this leaves out is that despite journalism priding itself on its institutional autonomy to operate and assert its authority (Sjøvaag 2020), it is only a "semi-independent" (Bennett and Livingston 2003) institution that is inevitably forced to interact with neighboring institutions. While this is hardly a new argument, our call is to acknowledge and highlight the multi-directional dynamics between journalism and the "others."

Theorizing the periphery

Peripheral actors can be seen as occupying an insider-outsider position, an arrangement that most often implies they are viewed from the proximity to or distance from the field of journalism. Journalism is, therefore, a frame of reference in defining the practices, norms, values or institutions that they establish in the periphery, for example, by acquiring storytelling techniques and formats employed by legacy news media. On the one hand, peripheral actors' entry into journalism as "outsiders" means that they also carry unique attributes that are non-traditional and deploy their own logic in news production. Yet peripheral actors are not "owners of the soil" and therefore are not necessarily committed to traditional journalism's norms and rules (Holton and Bélair-Gagnon 2018: 72).

There is an interdependency established through the peripheral position in the sense that non-traditional actors' practices lie in a continuum of practices or values that are journalism-like and others that tend to be removed from the professional "core" (cf. Baack 2018). Thus, in journalism research, a variety of metaphors have become important descriptors of this relationship, for example, "interlopers" (Eldridge 2019) to show the cooperative or uncooperative nature of these actors toward journalism, or "intralopers"/ "strangers" (Holton and Bélair-Gagnon 2018) to show how these news producers are little understood in comparison to professional journalists. Journalism studies is not short of such metaphors as means of demarcating boundaries between "non-professionals", "semi-professionals" and "professionals" (Örnebring 2013). Some metaphors, like "barbarians" (Agarwal and Barthel 2015), go to the extent of disregarding their strong colonial connotations.

However, what's more important are the implications of these relationships between professional journalists and peripheral actors. Studies that focus on peripheral actors show a strong culture of interdependencies emerging despite existing tensions between these actors and professional news organizations. These interdependencies are manifested through "entanglements" (Baack 2018) or "fusions" (Lewis and Usher 2013) that are expanding news ecologies (Heinrich, 2011). Baack (2018), for example, shows that overlapping skills and complementary ambitions between civic technologists and data journalists result in entanglements based on "interlocking practices" (Baack 2018: 673). Similarly, Usher (2019) argues there is a "fusion" of skills and expertise when journalists and "hackers" work together.

Thus, we argue that, existing research on peripheral actors shows, implicitly, that the resulting relationship between journalists and others is multi-directional: Journalism takes (e.g. skills, technologies, formats), but it gives as well. Civic technology organizations, for example, co-opt journalistic discourses in the promotion of data literacy and the utilization of freedom-of-information laws in countries with weak data/information dissemination cultures, as we showed in our previous empirical work (Cheruiyot and Ferrer-Conill 2018). Other examples are nonprofits and humanitarian organizations that consider journalism's capacity for impact (its reach) and its authority (legitimacy and trust) as effective values toward promoting their public service or humanitarian missions. Consequently, these NGOs are explicit about "doing journalism" like legacy news media (Konieczna 2018; Wright, Scott, and Bunce 2018). In their practices, these non-traditional producers adopt the "logic of journalism" (Konieczna 2018: 22) in ways we argue best exemplify multi-directional exchanges in institutional and professional journalism. There are several real-world cases showing how journalism shapes non-journalistic actors.

Three cases: How journalism shapes peripheral actors

Based on the discussion above, we argue that research has not ignored, but has underplayed the continuous outward influence of journalism towards other actors relevant for public communication. In the following, we will present three cases from our own empirical work where we focus on the influence that journalism has on peripheral actors: how journalistic practices are imitated, or how imaginaries about journalism influence these actors own practices and self-understanding.

Chequeado: Extracting and pushing journalistic practice

Chequeado is Latin America's most popular fact-checking platform. The site provides in-depth articles fact-checking current affairs events, confirming or debunking information distributed by politicians, the media, or social media. According to their manifesto, their main task is "to provide a new value to truth and raise the costs of lies" ("Acerca de Chequeado" n.d.). Based in Argentina and established in 2010, the site identifies itself as a non-partisan and not-for-profit project fighting against disinformation.

A remarkable aspect of Chequeado is that clear outsiders of journalism founded it: physicist Julio Aranovich, political economist José Alberto Bekinschtein, and chemist Roberto Lugo. Despite their non-journalistic backgrounds and the site positioning itself as an alternative source of information based on facts and data, the mission of the project is undoubtedly familiar to any journalism scholar: "to improve the quality of the public debate to strengthen democracy in Argentina and the world" ("Acerca de Chequeado" n.d.). The current staff of Chequeado come from a wide range of backgrounds, both with and without journalistic profiles; as one example, it is led by lawyer Laura Zommer, a managing board member of the International Fact-Checking Network. In this aspect, Chequeado is an excellent example of the multi-directional dynamics between the periphery and the core of journalism because it is run by so-called outsiders who are inspired by journalistic values, taking up this ambition in part as a reaction to what they and Chequeado's founders see as something lacking in the news media. Moreover, their practice is meant to both have an impact on news outlets including by teaching fact-checking practices to other organizations. The advocacy for facts and truth is such a basic precept of both fact-checking organizations and watchdog journalism that what we normally would consider the organization at the periphery of journalism (Chequeado) challenges and reinforces what we would consider the core of journalism (watchdog journalism).

The site highlights stories that are currently gaining public attention and dissects the narrative by qualifying the story's degrees of facticity and veracity. These topics are then approached through various narrative formats, from addressing simple falsehoods and myths on social media to deep dives into specific debates on current affairs. While Chequeado's articles approach topics in relation to what has been said or stated in other fora, the site's presentation remarkably resembles that of a digital newspaper. While not necessarily a journalistic endeavour, Chequeado acknowledges their attempt to explore new ways to convey content and information to the public, while also communicating in a way that engages and involves citizens. However, this is not the only aim of the project. They have also set two other goals: First, to innovate and "experiment with the way in which journalism and the formats and tools to receive and distribute the best facts and data to the people". And, second, to educate citizens, "journalists and communicators in exercise and formation" ("Acerca de Chequeado" n.d.).

When explaining the characteristics of their content, Chequeado clearly adopts both journalistic lingo (such as objectivity and truth) and practices (such as verification and transparency) to support their fact-checking methods. The entire framework of the practice is extracted from a view of journalism as a discipline of verification, based on the essence that facts and data can illuminate the truth. It is clear through their mission statement that Chequeado believes that transparency and respect for the public is the guiding principle in aid of their democratic duty, a belief not far from what traditional Western legacy news organizations would hold dear.

At the same time, and while not explicitly saying so, the nature of Chequeado raises doubts about the current state of journalism in the region. First, its main targets are journalists and media organizations. Second, its objective is to foster innovation in how journalism is practiced, and its stated goal in doing so is to educate journalists on how to accurately fact-check stories and present data. This is a familiar pattern we see across fact-checking organizations: adopting journalistic values, questioning whether current news organizations are fulfilling their duties, and proposing to improve journalism. In its assessment of news media, it approves of and adopts the aspirational norms and values, judges and rejects the current application of those norms and values, and wants to influence and improve those changes. And this is a goal it is arguably accomplishing, as Chequeado's method of verification has been adopted by at least twenty media organizations across fourteen countries in Latin America.

Mozilla: Stabilizing identity with mission-compatible journalism

Mozilla is rooted in open source culture and best known for the development of the Firefox web browser. While it had more direct connections to journalism in the past, most notably with the Knight-Mozilla News Technology Partnership (Lewis and Usher 2016), Mozilla's role as a peripheral actor to journalism might be less obvious today. However, recent changes to the so-called "Mozilla Manifesto" (Mozilla n.d.), a document outlining the core values and goals of the organization, have created pathways for new connections. Originally created in 2007 with a focus on openness, security and privacy, the manifesto was updated in 2018 to "address the quality of people's experiences online", which included a commitment to diversity, "civil discourse", "reasoned argument", and "verifiable facts" (Baker 2018).

Even though journalism is not explicitly mentioned, Mozilla's shift created a degree of overlap between supporting a particular idea of "Manifesto-compatible" journalism and supporting Mozilla's own mission. There are clear connections between the values added to the manifesto in 2018 and typical associations with traditional Western notions of journalism as a provider of objective facts that enables and facilitates political deliberation (cf. Hanitzsch and Vos 2018). More generally, the updated manifesto meant that advancing Mozilla's mission and advancing actors' ability to fulfill Manifesto-compatible societal functions are now more intermeshed. There are numerous ways Mozilla's own goals lead to support or direct collaboration with journalism. Here, we will highlight a more recent example: the "Firefox Better Web with Scroll" initiative to support alternatives to advertising as the dominant business model for online content.

Scroll[2] is a US-based service that offers a monthly subscription in exchange for an ad-free experience on partner websites from its network, e.g. BuzzFeed or *The Atlantic*. Partners are rewarded with revenue by Scroll based on the amount of time users spent on their website. Scroll claims that the reward per person is higher compared to ads, creating an incentive for media companies to depend less on advertisements. Mozilla collaborated with Scroll by offering a browser extension for Firefox that further reduces advertisements on these partner websites, further blocks tracking, and offers additional services like audio for articles.

The project allowed Mozilla to address several issues at once. First, it provided a service that helped Scroll's partner websites. These partner websites generally provide credible informative content that can be seen as core to political deliberation, which in turn supports the values outlined in Mozilla's updated manifesto. Second, the project supported a revenue model that rewards time spent on websites over clicks. As the project homepage stresses, it is "rewarding quality and privacy – not ads" (Mozilla 2021), thereby suggesting to help not just to move away from ad-driven business models, but also to mitigate their negative implications. Many problems central to Mozilla's own mission are seen as negative side-effects of online advertisement: privacy-invasive surveillance, misinformation, and discriminatory algorithms. Finally, the project had the potential to create a new subscription-based revenue stream for Mozilla, which is searching for new sources of revenue.[3]

This example illustrates how supporting journalism aligns with Mozilla's mission because particular ideals of journalistic practice are considered to support the values outlined in the Mozilla Manifesto: fighting disinformation, caring about privacy and security, and so forth. More pointedly, the example shows that Mozilla is not trying to replicate journalism, it seeks to complement this vision of journalism by investing into technologies and business models that support this idea of journalism. The existence of journalists and organizations that identify with "traditional" Western values in journalism thereby shapes Mozilla's practices and strategic decision-making.

Supporting a particular idea of journalism that can thrive outside of ad-driven business models also helps Mozilla to differentiate itself from big tech companies such as Google or Facebook (see Russell and Vos, this volume). Google, Facebook, and others also support journalism in various ways, but not in ways that would fundamentally lower news publishers' dependency on the ad-driven commercial ecosystems on which they thrive. Mozilla thereby acts as a distinct, alternative partner to journalists.

At the same time, the example of "Firefox Better Web with Scroll" illustrates that practically aligning Mozilla's mission-driven focus with its need to secure new streams of revenue is difficult and, more generally, it shows how difficult it can be to align interests of peripheral actors and journalists practically. Mozilla is implicitly trying to push journalism in a direction that supports its values, i.e. the values outlined in the Mozilla Manifesto, and to also benefit from that shift with revenue-generating services: a journalism that is less dependent on privacy-invasive business models and rewards "quality" more than "misleading click-bait". Yet while subscription-based models such as the one supported by Mozilla in this example have the potential to introduce different business logics that support more "quality content" in line with Mozilla's manifesto, there is no guarantee that they will be successful in doing so.

Moreover, while the project tries to avoid creating barriers to content by giving an ad-free version of Scroll partner websites that can also be accessed for free with ads (and the tracking of users that comes with it), it might incentivize media organizations to more heavily rely on subscriptions as barriers to access "higher quality content", leaving people that cannot afford such subscriptions with more limited and less privacy-friendly versions of news websites. Still, the example shows how visions of journalism that we might describe as "traditional Western" shape Mozilla's identity and practices for both mission-based and financial reasons.

Open Up: Journalism as a necessary building block of its mission

Open Up is a civic technology organization based in South Africa that promotes civic engagement through citizens' active involvement in data creation, interpretation, and distribution. Initially named "Code for South Africa", as part of the "Code for All" global network, Open Up broke away from the larger network in 2017 and was rebranded as an open data nonprofit. Its operations focus on data accessibility and transparency by developing applications to ease access to data (see examples below) and training citizens and journalists in data-driven practices.

Its mission is rooted mainly in a public service ideal. The government, civil society, and citizens are jointly seen as essential in expanding open data practices. The free flow of information between state and civil society actors on the one hand, and citizens on the other, is considered necessary for public accountability. Under that view, Open Up argues that governments hold the key to providing data (e.g., census reports or local government budgets), and should guarantee the free and unhindered right to information. For Open Up, citizens can only participate in initiatives to promote public accountability if they can freely access data from public institutions and interpret and understand these data. Further, Open Up sees news media's access to the citizenry as crucial in that the news media can serve as a "dissemination partner" for the services the organization provides.

Among Open Up's early initiatives was a data liberation project to create a searchable database of all government gazettes (official records of government declarations) in South Africa called Open Gazettes. Open Up undertook the project with Code for Africa, the African Networks of Centers for Investigative Reporting (ANCIR), Indigo Trust (a charity), and the Southern African Legal Information Institute (a nonprofit law project). The final database produced by this project was publicly accessible to journalists and citizens. Open Up sees its role as facilitative in promoting the use of the database, for example, through establishing a help desk to provide technical support to investigative journalists and civil society organizations undertaking public accountability projects.

Further, to promote public accountability through this project, Open Up collaborated with the South African government to design a web-based tool for accessing all municipal authorities' financial records in South Africa. The "Municipal Money" tool provided easy access to data, analysis and visualization. In the same way, Wazi Map, another web-based tool, aggregates census, election, and crime data in South Africa. Wazi Map is particularly relevant here because it was developed with journalists in mind and in close collaboration with Media Monitoring Africa, a media watchdog based in South Africa. Wazi Map evolved into a continental data journalism project that became a resource for journalists in Nigeria and Kenya for reporting on elections (Wazimap 2018).

Open Up's practices emphasize citizen participation as a broader mission to increase access and circulation of information. However, it considers public and independent organizations central to its larger goal to promote data literacy and expand information sources for news organizations. It is important to emphasize that the relationship between Open Up and legacy news media is less clear on the surface because of the nonprofit's strong civic goals and its operations that focus less on disseminating information. Open Up is explicit about its role in empowering news organizations towards better storytelling while at the same time opening up databases for citizens' scrutiny. The organization considers that when legacy news media have access to accurate data, for example, government records through Open Gazette, their capacity for truth-telling would be enhanced. This contribution to news production would be auxiliary in providing complete and accurate data towards supporting public accountability. We consider Open Up's work to be in line with the concept of "implicit interlopers", or peripheral actors that are not necessarily adversarial to traditional journalism, but push traditional practice limits (Holton and Bélair-Gagnon 2018).

We see Open Up's operations edging towards reinvigorating civic-oriented practices and playing a watchdog role in the broader news ecosystem by providing citizens with data and expertise to scrutinize information (in the media or government's hands) themselves. Partly, such civic-oriented goals echo the public service ideal that most civic journalism attains to uphold, which essentially goes against the "everything goes" strategies adopted by some profit-driven journalism (see for example, Konieczna 2018). The organization develops and expands data practices to "open up" the information ecosystem to the public, who could either engage in information production themselves or scrutinize news production, thus challenging journalistic authority. However, actors including the news media and the government, are considered collaborators in promoting public accountability. Similar to the example of Mozilla above, traditional visions of journalism are an essential component of Open Up's larger vision in that they promote accountability, transparency, and the use of public information for civic participation.

Conclusion: (Re-)Articulating journalism's relationship with the periphery

In this chapter, we have argued that while the relationship between peripheral actors and journalism is predominantly studied from the external influences on the internal mechanics of journalism, this approach tends to forget the important outward influences of journalism. Similarly, we proposed that looking at the relationship between the core of journalism and the periphery in geographic terms perpetuates the idea that

Western journalism lies at the core and non-Western expressions of journalism are the "others". Our goal has been to embrace the dynamics between journalism and its peripheral actors more fully by putting a stronger empirical emphasis on the practices and identities of actors affected in various ways by journalism. Studying the multi-directional dynamics between journalism and others not only allows us to "demystify" these "barbarians at the gates," but also help us see that journalism is not this feeble institution that suffers from the influence of others. The profession exerts its influence on others, and this can lead to a shared and strengthened idea of what journalism is and what role it has in society.

The examples discussed here are a testimony to that multi-directional relationship. In the case of Chequeado, a group of non-journalists guided by journalism's ideals, created a fact-checking operation. They aimed to fulfil and inform what they thought the media failed to provide the Latin American public. A traditional look at Chequeado emphasizes its attempts to "influence" news media as a peripheral actor might have missed the foundational influence that journalism had over the fact-checking organization in shaping its vision and mission. Moreover, the fact that the managing team comprises editors and journalists only highlights the multi-directional dynamics of this relationship.

In the case of Mozilla, we see in its manifesto an overlap between supporting its own mission as an organization, and supporting particular visions of journalism more broadly, that mirror very traditional ideas of objective watchdog journalism common in Western societies. This provides insights into how actors such as Mozilla see their position in society, and suggests new avenues to study the impact of journalism. Actors such as Mozilla strengthen journalists that identify with the vision of journalism it supports, which in this particular case contributes to a reinforcement of traditional values of professional journalism in the West.

In Open Up's case, we see its operations primarily aligned to the idea of civic journalism. Indeed, legacy news media have experimented with forms of civic-oriented journalism as a means to engage the public in practices such as sourcing (Massey 1998), but often, it is a response to the critique about elitism and commercial-oriented production. It is also important to acknowledge forms of civic-oriented practices that mark journalism as practiced in mostly non-Western nations, such as South Africa, whose goal is to promote social change (Hanitzsch et al. 2011). Open Up's operations consider citizens as partners in information production and as central for effective public accountability. At the same time, however, it implicitly challenges journalistic authority by providing data, resources, and training to enhance the public's capacity to scrutinize government's records and the news.

Peripheral actors do influence journalism. Their institutional underpinnings interact and shape the evolution of our field in many ways. As we have argued, however, journalism is not a one-way street, and those at the periphery, while exerting their influence, are often heavily influenced by journalism as well. Sometimes, even at a foundational level. Moreover, the examples presented here show similar patterns and developments in different geographic and cultural regions

(US/Europe, Latin America, Africa). This emphasizes that multi-directional dynamics are by no means exclusive to particular regional contexts. The outward influences of journalism on other actors relevant for public communication is a general blind spot in journalism studies that needs to be addressed. In the ebb and flow of journalistic evolution, periphery and center may be closer than we think.

Notes

1 One of the authors is affiliated with the Mozilla Foundation. The Mozilla Foundation gave permission to the author to conduct this research as an independent research project. It did not fund or otherwise support the research, nor did it influence the interviews, the data analysis, or the writing of this chapter.
2 https://scroll.com.
3 The majority of the revenue of the Mozilla Corporation to date comes from setting the default search engine in new Firefox installations, which is Google in most regions.

References

"Acerca de Chequeado". n.d. Chequeado (blog). https://chequeado.com/acerca-de-che queado/.

Agarwal, Sheetal D., and Michael L.Barthel. 2015. "The Friendly Barbarians: Professional Norms and Work Routines of Online Journalists in the United States". *Journalism* 16 (3): 376–391. https://doi.org/10.1177/1464884913511565.

Baack, Stefan. 2018. "Practically Engaged: The Entanglements between Data Journalism and Civic Tech". *Digital Journalism* 6 (6): 673–692. https://doi.org/10.1080/21670811.2017. 1375382.

Baker, Mitchell. 2018. "Mozilla Marks 20th Anniversary with Commitment to Better Human Experiences Online". The Mozilla Blog (blog). https://blog.mozilla.org/ blog/2018/03/29/mozilla-marks-20th-anniversary-commitment-better-human-experiences-online.

Bélair-Gagnon, Valérie, and Avery E.Holton. 2018. "Boundary Work, Interloper Media, and Analytics in Newsrooms: An Analysis of the Roles of Web Analytics Companies in News Production". *Digital Journalism* 6 (4): 492–508. https://doi.org/10.1080/21670811. 2018.1445001.

Bennett, W. Lance, and Steven Livingston. 2003. "Editors" Introduction: A Semi-Independent Press: Government Control and Journalistic Autonomy in the Political Construction of News". *Political Communication* 20 (4): 359–362. https://doi.org/10.1080/ 10584600390244086.

Carey, James. 2010. "Where Journalism Education Went Wrong". 11 August. https:// lindadaniele.wordpress.com/2010/08/11/carey-where-journalism-education-went-wrong/.

Carlson, Matt, and Seth CLewis. 2015. *Boundaries of Journalism: Professionalism, Practices and Participation.* New York, NY: Routledge.

Cheruiyot, David, Stefan Baack, and Raul Ferrer-Conill. 2019. "Data Journalism Beyond Legacy Media: The Case of African and European Civic Technology Organizations". *Digital Journalism* 7 (9): 1215–1229. https://doi.org/10.1080/21670811.2019.1591166.

Cheruiyot, David, and Raul Ferrer-Conill. 2018. "'Fact-Checking Africa': Epistemologies, Data and the Expansion of Journalistic Discourse". *Digital Journalism* 6 (8): 964–975. https:// doi.org/10.1080/21670811.2018.1493940.

Cheruiyot, David and Raul Ferrer-Conill. 2021. "Pathway outta pigeonhole? De-contextualizing Majority World Countries." *Media, Culture & Society* 43 (1): 189–197. https://doi.org/10.1177/0163443720960907.

Cushion, Stephen. 2008. "Truly International?" *Journalism Practice* 2 (2): 280–293. doi:10.1080/17512780801999477.

Darbo, Karoline Nerdalen, and Terje Skjerdal. 2019. "Blurred Boundaries: Citizens Journalists versus Conventional Journalists in Hong Kong". *Global Media and China* 4 (1): 111–124. https://doi.org/10.1177/2059436419834633.

Demeter, Marton. 2019. "The Winner Takes It All: International Inequality in Communication and Media Studies Today." *Journalism & Mass Communication Quarterly* 96 (1): 37–59. doi:10.1177/1077699018792270.

Demeter, Marton. 2020. *Academic Knowledge Production and the Global South: Questioning Inequality and under-Representation*. Basingstoke: Palgrave Macmillan.

Domingo, David, and Florence Le Cam. 2014. "Journalism In Dispersion: Exploring the Blurring Boundaries of Newsmaking through a Controversy". *Digital Journalism* 2 (3): 310–321. https://doi.org/10.1080/21670811.2014.897832.

Eldridge, Scott A. 2019. "Where Do We Draw the Line? Interlopers, (Ant)Agonists, and an Unbounded Journalistic Field". *Media and Communication* 7 (4): 8–18. https://doi.org/10.17645/mac.v7i4.2295.

Eldridge, Scott A. 2018. *Online Journalism from the Periphery: Interloper Media and the Journalistic Field*. London; New York, NY: Routledge.

Hallin, Daniel C, and Paolo Mancini. 2004. *Comparing Media Systems: Three Models of Media and Politics*. Cambridge, UK: Cambridge University Press.

Hallin, Daniel C., and Paolo Mancini, eds. 2012. *Comparing Media Systems beyond the Western World*. Communication, Society and Politics. Cambridge; New York: Cambridge University Press.

Hanitzsch, Thomas. 2007. "Deconstructing Journalism Culture: Toward a Universal Theory". *Communication Theory* 17 (4): 367–385. https://doi.org/10.1111/j.1468-2885.2007.00303.x.

Hanitzsch, Thomas, and Tim P. Vos. 2018. "Journalism beyond Democracy: A New Look into Journalistic Roles in Political and Everyday Life". *Journalism* 19 (2): 146–164. https://doi.org/10.1177/1464884916673386.

Hanitzsch, Thomas, Folker Hanusch, Claudia Mellado, et al. 2011. "Mapping Journalism Cultures Across Nations; A comparative study of 18 countries". *Journalism Studies* 12 (3): 273–293.

Heinrich, Ansgard. 2011. *Network journalism: Journalistic practice in interactive spheres*. New York: Routledge.

Holton, Avery E., and Valérie Bélair-Gagnon. 2018. "Strangers to the Game? Interlopers, Intralopers, and Shifting News Production". *Media and Communication* 6 (4): 70–78. https://doi.org/10.17645/mac.v6i4.1490.

Høyer, Svennik, and Horst Pöttker. 2005. *Diffusion of the News Paradigm, 1850–2000*. Göteborg, Sweden: Nordicom.

Josephi, Beate. 2007. "Internationalizing the Journalistic Professional Model: Imperatives and Impediments". *Global Media and Communication* 3 (3): 300–306. https://doi.org/10.1177/17427665070030030303.

Josephi, Beate. 2012. "How Much Democracy Does Journalism Need?" *Journalism* 14 (4): 474–489. https://doi.org/10.1177/1464884912464172.

Konieczna, Magda. 2018. *Journalism without Profit: Making News When the Market Fails*. New York, NY: Oxford University Press.

Kovach, Bill, and Tom Rosenstiel. 2007. *The Elements of Journalism: What Newspeople Should Know and the Public Should Expect*, 1st ed., New York: Three Rivers Press.

Lewis, Seth C. 2012. "The Tension Between Professional Control and Open Participation: Journalism and Its Boundaries". *Information, Communication & Society* 15 (6): 836–866. https:// doi.org/10.1080/1369118X.2012.674150.

Lewis, Seth C., and Nikki Usher. 2013. "Open Source and Journalism: Toward New Frameworks for Imagining News Innovation". *Media, Culture & Society* 35 (5): 602–619. https:// doi.org/10.1177/0163443713485494.

Lewis, Seth C., and Nikki Usher. 2016. "Trading Zones, Boundary Objects, and the Pursuit of News Innovation A Case Study of Journalists and Programmers". *Convergence: The International Journal of Research into New Media Technologies* 22 (5): 543–560. https://doi. org/10.1177/1354856515623865.

Lowrey, Wilson. 2018. "Journalism as Institution." In *Journalism*, edited by Tim P. Vos, pp. 125–148. Boston: De Gruyter Mouton.

Massey, Brian L. 1998. "Civic Journalism and Nonelite Sourcing: Making Routine Newswork of Community Connectedness." *Journalism & Mass Communication Quarterly* 75 (2): 294–407.

Mozilla. 2021. "Firefox Better Web with Scroll". Wayback Machine Snapshot. 14 January. https://web.archive.org/web/20210114150121/https://firstlook.firefox.com/betterweb/.

Mozilla. n.d. "The Mozilla Manifesto". https://www.mozilla.org/en-US/about/manifesto/.

Nerone, John. 2012. "The Historical Roots of the Normative Model of Journalism". *Journalism* 14 (4): 446–458. https://doi.org/10.1177/1464884912464177.

Örnebring, Henrik. 2013. "Anything You Can Do, I Can Do Better? Professional Journalists on Citizen Journalism in Six European Countries". *International Communication Gazette* 75 (1): 35–53. https://doi.org/10.1177/1748048512461761.

Reese, Stephen D. 2007. "Journalism Research and the Hierarchy of Influences Model: A Global Perspective". *Brazilian Journalism Research* 3 (2): 21–42. https://doi.org/10.25200/ BJR.v3n2.2007.116.

Shoemaker, Pamela J., and Stephen D. Reese. 2014. *Mediating the Message in the 21st Century: A Media Sociology Perspective*. New York, NY: Routledge.

Singer, Jane B. 2003. "Who Are These Guys? The Online Challenge to the Notion of Journalistic Professionalism". *Journalism* 4 (2): 139–163. https://doi.org/10.1177/ 146488490342001.

Sjøvaag, Helle. 2020. "Journalistic Autonomy: Between Structure, Agency and Institution". *Nordicom Review* 34: 155–166. https://doi.org/10.2478/nor-2013-0111.

Tandoc, Edson, Kristy Hess, Scott Eldridge II, and Oscar Westlund. 2020. "Diversifying Diversity in Digital Journalism Studies: Reflexive Research, Reviewing and Publishing." *Digital Journalism* 8 (3): 301–309. doi:10.1080/21670811.2020.1738949.

Tandoc, Edson, Joy Jenkins, Ryan J. Thomas, and Oscar Westlund, eds. 2021. *Critical Incidents in Journalism: Pivotal Moments Reshaping Journalism around the World*. London; New York: Routledge.

Tuchman, Gaye. 1972. "Objectivity as Strategic Ritual: An Examination of Newsmen's Notion of Objectivity". *The American Journal of Sociology* 77 (4): 660–679. https://doi.org/ 10.1086/225193.

Usher, Nikki. 2019. "Hacks, Hackers, and the Expansive Boundaries of Journalism". In *The Routledge Handbook of Developments in Digital Journalism Studies*, edited by Scott A. Eldridge and Bob Franklin, pp. 348–359. London; New York: Routledge.

Vos, Tim P. 2017. "Historical Perspectives on Journalistic Roles". In *Journalistic Role Performance: Concepts, Contexts, and Methods*, pp. 41–59. New York: Routledge.

Wahl-Jorgensen, Karin. 2014. "Is WikiLeaks Challenging the Paradigm of Journalism? Boundary Work and Beyond". *International Journal of Communication* 8: 2581–2592.

Waisbord, Silvio R. 2013. *Reinventing Professionalism: Journalism and News in Global Perspective.* Cambridge: Polity.

Wazimap. 2018. "Why Wazimap? A Brief History". https://wazimap.co.za/about.

Wright, Kate, Martin Scott, and Mel Bunce. 2018. "Foundation-Funded Journalism, Philanthrocapitalism and Tainted Donors". *Journalism Studies* 20 (5): 675–695. https://doi.org/10.1080/1461670X.2017.1417053.

Zelizer, Barbie. 2012. "On the Shelf Life of Democracy in Journalism Scholarship". *Journalism* 14 (4): 459–473. https://doi.org/10.1177/1464884912464179.

8

BEYOND INNOVATION

Pioneer journalism and the re-figuration of journalism

Andreas Hepp and Wiebke Loosen

If journalism is in an era of ongoing transformation, as we keep emphasizing in our research, what sense does it make to keep stating this over and over again? It would then be an unchanging constant, signifying transformation as a permanent condition, whose continual thematization would no longer have any news value. In the journalistic field, there is also frequent talk about how journalism should "innovate" itself and its "products", and that its institutions should support such a process of change. Within this frame "innovation" becomes the unchanging constant: "innovation," then, is the permanent condition of institutional change. The "innovation" discourse seems to fulfil an important purpose: It contributes to a general self-assurance of "innovation's" importance. This discourse acts as a driving force for the initiation and legitimization of processes of institutional change, leading us to believe observers would agree that both journalism and journalism research are primarily concerned with future trends. This implies a particular construction of the past, often in the form of (self) complaints that "innovation" has been drastically overlooked by many media organizations. Comparing both the present construction of the past and an anticipated future often results in a diagnosis that points to the need for a fundamental change in the shape of pressure to innovate: journalism or media organizations would have to do this or that so as not to miss trend x, to meet challenge y.

We would like to oppose this discourse by arguing that it is necessary to be sensitive to differences between such "innovation imperatives" and an analysis of transformation if we want to reflect on institutional change. Taken in this way, our position is not meant to imply that we doubt or even criticize the field's "innovation practices." Rather, our aim is to see "innovation" and the associated change in journalistic organizations in the context of the transformation of journalism as a whole, a context through which we can grasp the conditionality of these perspectives on the field. We cannot overestimate the relevance and power of these constructions and imaginaries of journalism's transformation and its future(s). However,

DOI: 10.4324/9781003140399-11

we argue that our scholarly task is to adequately describe and understand *transformation as structural* change. Within processes of transformation, "social" and "technological" innovations play a role if we understand that "new" practices and technologies become established in a particular field. However, transformation as a structural change is much more comprehensive and, often, what is understood as the "innovation" of today is *not* the driving force for tomorrow's transformations.

This does not mean that we cannot learn from studying the failures of innovation for which journalism criticizes itself.[1] However, the differences between journalism's self-perception and the academic observation of it remains crucial to us, especially in regard to the topics of transformation and innovation. This is the main reason why we have developed the concept of "pioneer journalism" to describe and explain journalism's transformation instead of linking change so closely to "innovation," as while it is already common to describe change and ambition, we continue to shroud the term in quotations to imply the need to approach it from an analytical distance (Evans 2018). This is not to avoid the term "innovation" *per se*, as "innovation speak" (Vinsel 2014a, 2014b) plays an important role in journalism.

In this chapter, we introduce a particular contribution and approach for a scientific analysis as a "second-order observation" of how journalism transforms. Our guiding question is: How do practitioners in the field construct "innovation"? But we must always bear in mind other questions: What (experimental) practices do they perform? What kind of connections to each other do they build in the context of journalism's transformation? What kind of futures do they imagine? And what does all this mean for our understanding of journalistic institutions?

In taking this approach, we start from a premise and also apply a "trick": Our premise is that journalism, as a genuine media phenomenon, changes with the media environment in which it operates *in* and *with* the media technologies journalists appropriate. We see here a co-articulation of journalism's transformation and its media environment. In this sense, the transformation of media in general can be grasped through the transformation of journalism in particular. Our "trick" is studying those actors and those forms of journalism that are already oriented toward the future of journalism, imagining it and experimenting with new forms. We call these forms of journalism "pioneer journalism" and the actors dedicated to these practices "pioneer journalists" (Hepp and Loosen 2021: 577).

In the following, we first introduce pioneer journalism as a concept and unfold its theoretical foundations. We then elaborate on the characteristic elements of pioneer journalism as a figuration. In doing so, we discuss the actor constellations and the trans-organizational dynamics of pioneer journalism. Furthermore, we are concerned with areas of experimentation in pioneer journalism and look at technology and its relation to products, work practices, funding, and audience relationships. We conclude by addressing the question of what we can learn about how these possible transformations from research into pioneer journalism.

Pioneer journalism: The need for a holistic perspective

While the concept of pioneer journalism – as we introduce it in this chapter – is just beginning to establish itself in journalism research (cf. for example Appelgren and Lindén 2020; Heft 2021; Deuze and Witschge 2019; Porlezza 2019; Schmidt and Lawrence 2020), what we understand as the investigation of pioneer journalism has been a subject of journalism research for a much longer period of time.

At its core, this research refers to a certain way of dealing with the transformation of journalism which aims to overcome the "centricity" (Wahl-Jorgensen 2009) on established media organizations and their newsrooms. Mark Deuze and Tamara Witschge (2019) use the metaphor of "beyond journalism" to capture this move away from a preoccupation with newsrooms to journalism as a social practice of (professional) coverage, that is increasingly pursued by actors who are located "beyond" what is traditionally attributed to journalism, its established organizational contexts, and modes of work. Some examples of journalism that go "beyond" include citizen journalism, journalistic start-ups, and cooperatives. Accordingly, "beyond" refers to "entrepreneurial activity" and "bottom-up initiatives" (Deuze and Witschge 2019: 7), which are considered to be incredibly relevant for journalism's transformation. Two reasons for this are that these "beyond actors" can signal developments that may also gain importance on a broader level, and that the (academic) exploration of these journalistic actors, forms, and practices help to paint a much more multifaceted picture of the field. But, only looking at these "peripheral actors" (Holton, Bélair-Gagnon, and Westlund 2019) as they are sometimes called, would also be short-sighted as more established newsrooms rapidly change, becoming more experimental with so-called "in-house innovation labs" (Boyles 2016: 229) in established media companies pursuing similar goals and efforts to drive change. The transformation of journalism must therefore be seen in the *interrelation of* pioneering forms of journalism *beyond* established journalistic organizations and the pioneering efforts *within* them. For this perspective the core/periphery is of less importance as we focus more on the relational aspect (Eldridge 2019), that is, the relationships and connections between pioneering actors in different organizational surroundings and their practices.

However, if we want to understand the *transformation* of journalism as a whole, we need to broaden our view: it is not simply about moving "beyond" the newsroom, it is about moving "beyond innovation": We are dealing with the paradox that we need to overcome the focus on "innovation" whether in the newsroom or in other institutional contexts, when we aim to describe journalism's transformation and the role of "innovations" as part of that change. In this sense, we understand our approach to pioneer journalism as operating "beyond innovation."

In the context of this argument, we can define pioneer journalism as a figuration of actors who experiment with their journalistic practices and imagine possible futures for the field (Hepp 2020: 32f.; Hepp and Loosen 2021: 581f.). Individual pioneer journalists in this overall figuration can be defined by a set of criteria:

1. Pioneer journalists perceive themselves as *forerunners* of their profession and are accepted as such by other members of that profession (but not necessarily all);[2]
2. Within their field, pioneer journalists act as *intermediaries* (Bourdieu 2010: 151, 325, 359); bringing together often disparate (professional) spheres, often advocating in favor of departures beyond their own field;
3. Pioneer journalists are typically embedded within "communities of practice" (Wenger 1999); we can understand these communities as "pioneer communities" (Hepp 2016);
4. Within these communities, selected professional pioneers take on the role of an "organisational elite" (Hitzler and Niederbacher 2010: 22);
5. By virtue of their experimental practices, pioneer journalists play a special role in the development of their profession (e.g. they also act as trainers or consultants, maintain and write blogs);
6. Pioneer journalists typically embody imaginations of possible future scenarios which leads to them becoming a topic in the media's discourse on related change (e.g. in self-reflexive discourses on the future of journalism).

We use the term pioneer journalism to connect the argument that it is especially those pioneer journalists who, through established media companies, start-ups, accelerators, or as individual pioneers, have a lasting influence on the transformation of journalism.

However, one has to be careful and should not adopt a simple linear perspective according to which individual pioneers act as catalysts for "innovations" that then change the breadth of the field. The situation is far more complex: Believing that the impact of pioneer journalists, their projects, and their startups necessarily lead to successful products or companies is too narrow an understanding of how pioneer journalism operates; in fact, their ventures often fail.[3] Nevertheless, pioneer journalism is crucial to journalism's ongoing transformation process: First, the experimental nature of pioneering endeavors opens up a space for new practices and technologies which have the potential to become appropriated more generally. Second, pioneer journalists' visions of the future of the field inspire "ideas" for potential trajectories of change. Research in other fields has already demonstrated that the translation of these kinds of ideas into organizational practice represents a critical moment in any organizational transformation (Fredriksson and Pallas 2017).

This understanding of pioneer journalism is based on the observation that the ways in which journalism is currently undergoing change do not simply "happen," but are also explicitly, avowedly, and more or less purposefully driven by various actors in the field and in the context of a demand for strategic innovation. Part of this development is what we call *the re-figuration of the organizational foundations of journalism* (Hepp and Loosen 2021: 589f; Hepp 2020: 115–143). The most striking indicator of this is the frequent establishment of new media organizations in recent years, "which, as remarkable contrasts to a established places of journalistic production" (Buschow 2018: 363; *own translation*), are increasingly attracting research interest, especially in the form of start-ups (Carlson and Usher 2016; Hess, Köster, and Steiner 2014; Werning 2019). Other examples are cross-organizational, transnational networks of journalists (Heft 2021), as is the figure of the "entrepreneurial journalist" (Singer 2017), which addresses the question of the extent to which the separation between editorial and advertising departments or between journalistic and entrepreneurial activity is constitutive for independent journalism, or whether the merging of the two into a journalistic entrepreneurial spirit is essential for survival under the conditions of digital change (Vos and Singer 2016).

As relevant and insightful as individual studies on these developments may be, a more comprehensive picture of journalism's re-figuration cannot be gained by looking at only one (type of) media organization, one type of actor, or one area of experimentation such as data journalism, constructive journalism, or other "x journalisms" (Loosen et al. 2020). An approach is needed which, in principle, considers the various types of actors oriented towards change or (imagined) future journalistic forms and their interrelationships. From this perspective, the transformation of journalism cannot be grasped with the concepts of "diffusion" (Rogers 2003), nor with the idea that one particular type of actor alone could change journalism (Bleyen et al. 2014; García-Avilés et al. 2019).

Rather, a more complex "holistic perspective" (Hepp and Loosen 2020) is necessary for a robust understanding of journalism's transformation as a process of negotiation taking place at various levels, supported by the dynamics of various "individual" and "supra-individual actors" (Schimank 2010: 327–341). Individual actors can be, for example, single outstanding "entrepreneurial journalists," while "corporate actors" ("established" and "new" media companies or organizations as well as actors promoting innovation processes such as accelerators) and "collective actors" (pioneer communities such as the Hacks/Hackers movement) come into focus as supra-individual actors. It is, therefore, crucial to look at pioneer journalism's overall figuration and its internal dynamics.

In many cases, media technologies (adopted or developed for journalistic and editorial purposes) take on the role of "boundary objects" in these constellations (Star 2010; Bélair-Gagnon and Holton 2018; Jarke and Gerhard 2018; Lewis and Usher 2016). This is to say, that technologies are not simply introduced into (journalistic) organizations as an "innovation" that then spontaneously causes change, they become the "object" on the basis of which changes are negotiated. As we have already said, often, and particularly when it comes to the experimenting practices of pioneering actors, it is not only technologies in their materiality that are the point of reference, but the "imaginations" of the (potential) power of change associated with them (Fredriksson and Pallas 2017). This can be observed particularly well in the current public and academic discourses around AI in journalism, which tend to revolve around opportunities and risks, almost always emphasizing that AI can barely be defined (Beckett 2019).

To facilitate a more holistic perspective a "figurational approach" (Hepp 2020: 100) proves helpful, thanks to its roots in Norbert Elias' (1993) process sociology. Here, the concept of figuration as an analytical means of grasping this process theoretically and describing it empirically is useful because it draws attention to the continuous articulation of figurations in human practice. Figurations are inter-dependent networks of people who share a meaningful orientation in their practice (Elias 1993: 141–143). A newsroom, for example, can be understood as a specific figuration, as can a start-up or a pioneer community. Empirically, each figuration can be described in terms of its constellation of actors (who is part of these figurations and which social roles do they play?), the practices that characterize it along-side their entanglement with media technologies (what characterizes the practices of the figuration?), and the frames of relevance that give a figuration its sense orientation (what are the actors and practices of a figuration oriented towards? Which construction of meaning do they share?) (Hepp 2020: 100–109; for the journalism/audience relationship: Kramp and Loosen 2018). Furthermore, fig-urations do not simply sit alongside each other, but are often interwoven or interlaced with one another through overlapping constellations of actors. However, "figurations of figurations" (Couldry and Hepp 2017: 57) emerge: a figuration (a working group or department, for example) is part of a superordinate figuration (a company). In this sense, pioneer journalism's overall figuration is constituted by various (partial) figurations and individual actors: for example, departments for development and innovation in established media companies, start-ups, pioneer communities, and outstanding individual pioneer journalists.

That said, we do not focus on pioneer journalism as an end in itself, we under-stand this particular figuration as crucial to an investigation into journalism's re-figuration (Hepp 2020: 115; Knoblauch and Löw 2017). In other words, it is about a change in the constellations of actors (which actors are added to individual figura-tions, which disappear? How do their roles change?), of practices intertwined with media technologies (how do practices change with (media) technologies?), and in frames of relevance (how does the orientation of meaning or "self-understanding" change in individual figurations?). The assumption is that this kind of re-figuration cannot only be described from an internal perspective of individual figurations, it is also about the change in the relationships between individual figurations. From this point of view, an investigation into journalism's transformation means a description of the transformation patterns of individual figurations *and* their relationship to one another.

Actor constellation: The trans-organizational dynamics of pioneer journalism

On the basis of the discussion on figurations, the question inevitably arises as to how pioneer journalism's constellation of actors can best be described. Based on a mapping exercise we realized that for Germany (Hepp et al. 2021), and in general, at least on a typological level, for other European countries, the constellation of actors in pioneer journalism can be described by means of the types of actors shown in Table 8.1.

The category "groups of actors", based on the typology developed by Uwe Schimank (2010: 327–341), enables us to describe pioneer journalism's figuration

TABLE 8.1 Groups and types of actors in pioneer journalism

Groups of actors	Types of actors
Individual actors	Freelancers
	Employees
	Founders
Corporate actors	Start-ups
	Established companies
	Spin-offs
	Supporters
Collective actors	Pioneer communities
	Networks
	Projects

along three basic groups of actors: Humans, as individual actors, and corporate actors (i.e. organizations with a formally regulated membership, binding agreements and corresponding structures) and collective actors (which are constituted in particular through a shared identity, a common "we", and a certain orientation in practice) as supra-individual actors. Collective actors are much more fluid than corporate actors, partly temporary in nature (e.g. with projects with team members who come from different departments or organization) and only slightly formalized. Constellations with a project-type character are increasingly coming into view through investigations into pioneer journalism; as entities they have received little attention in journalism research to date, but are likely to gain in importance, considering changing (journalistic) roles and working routines. Of course, there are transitional and hybrid forms between collective and corporate actors (a movement that "becomes" an organization, for example), but this distinction seems helpful for grasping the entire constellation of actors in the realm of pioneer journalism. That said, if we want to look at pioneer journalism's figuration as a whole, it can only be understood in terms of the dynamics between these different actors as exemplified in Figure 8.1.

In what we call pioneer journalism, we are dealing with a complex figuration characterized by an actor constellation in which actors are in more or less close relationships with each other. The crucial point here is to grasp the patterns of their interconnections. It is not just their work that makes individual actors part of the figuration of corporate actors such as start-ups or companies. In addition, individual and corporate actors come together to form various collective actors: in projects in which they cooperate for a certain period of time, in networks for mutual exchange, in pioneer communities in which ideas and imaginations of future journalism are developed and tested in practice. This is also apparent in the "innovation departments" of established media companies, which often represent an interface between organizations and other actors (for example, as a cooperation partner). Similar to accelerators and incubators, they pursue the goal of creating

Individual actors   **Corporate actors**

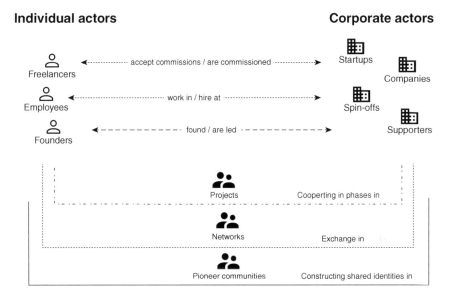

Collective actors

FIGURE 8.1 Pioneer journalism's actor constellation

"spaces of innovation" to develop "new ideas" and thereby break with "old routines". At the same time, they also create something akin to "innovation routines" that sometimes hinder their own goals.

Pioneer journalism is closely intertwined with the way the various actors in the field construct "innovation," the form of journalism from which they want to distance themselves, and the ideas of journalism that they want to contribute to and develop themselves. In this context, the "pioneering" character of pioneer journalism is continuously the subject of a process of negotiation about what (the future of) journalism might look like. It is this overall dynamic which makes up the special role pioneer journalism plays in the re-figuration of the general field. Pioneer journalism's organizational elite is crucial for this process. Such individuals are not only positioned in the center of the field as founders, owners or employees of start-ups, companies, or support organizations. They are also key organizers of networks and pioneer communities, preparing events and forums for exchange.

Areas of experimentation: Technology and its relationship to products, work practices, funding, and audience relationships

We have already spoken about the experimental character of pioneer journalism. But, what exactly are the areas in which this experimentation takes place? To pursue this question, both a broad (reflecting the contexts of journalism's transformation) and a specific (focusing on particular practices and processes) view of current developments in journalism are necessary. From a broad point of view, we can see that journalistic practices and processes are articulated as part of the production of media products and artifacts (including all the preliminary activities required, such as research and verification), their distribution, their use, and their appropriation by audiences (including editorial monitoring of this use). The ways in which this news cycle is organized and financed represent key structural and contextual conditions for the field, and fundamental aspects in influence and journalistic context models (Shoemaker and Reese 2012; Weischenberg 2004).

It is, therefore, no coincidence that these *basic categories of journalism* are also evident when it comes to pioneer journalism's areas of experimentation. Based on our own research in Germany (Hepp et al. 2021), while recognizing studies carried out by others (Bleyen et al. 2014; Buschow and Wellbrock 2020; García-Avilés et al. 2019) that often speak of "areas of innovation,"[4] we distinguish a total of four *areas of experimentation*: products, work practices, funding, and audience relationships (see Table 8.2). Under *products* we include both forms of experimentation in regard to journalistic content and those that primarily relate to the (re-)distribution of content. *Work practices* focus on experimenting with the journalistic organization, in newsrooms or in the working relationships across them. We have described the various forms of experimentation with new ways of creating value as an area of *funding*. And *audience relationship* encompasses pioneering ways of building and shaping the relationship between media professionals and media users, for example, in the development of topics, in research or in the exchange of content. These four areas mark a distinction between experimental practices that can relate to journalistic products, the organizational context (referred to as process innovation in strategic management studies; Evans 2018: 5), and social relationships.

All areas of experimentation relate in varying degrees to (media) technology, which has become an important "boundary object" in the negotiation of change in journalism. Large parts of innovation research in journalism studies tend to argue in the form of *technology adoption research*, that is: to construct technology as the driving force for change (see: Mitchelstein and Boczkowski 2009; Paulussen 2016; Steensen 2011). In doing so, this kind of research reflects primarily on the trend of media differentiation, fueling a view of innovation that is, especially for established media, of particular importance if you want to "be where the people are" (on Facebook, Twitter, Instagram, TikTok, and so on). From a pioneer journalism approach, however, it is inadequate to focus on the respective processes of "diffusion" and "adaptation" of ever new platforms and channels. The crucial point is less about how certain technologies work to "innovate" journalism, and more about what kind of transformation is negotiated by referring to technologies as objects that *represent* the new? We consider technology, therefore, to be transversal across all four fields (see Table 8.2) avoiding a "technology-focused approach to journalism innovation"

TABLE 8.2 Pioneer journalism's areas of experimentation

(Media-) Technology	Products
	Work practices
	Funding
	Audience Relationships

(Lewis and Usher 2013: 603). In the following, we will detail these four areas of examination and their relation to technology. While our arguments are conceptual in their character, we refer to our own research and the research of others to illustrate them.

Products

The spread of "product" or "product innovation" concepts can be considered a special characteristic of the expansion of pioneer journalistic thinking. "Product" can refer to a *container* in which journalistic content is "packaged" or "re-packaged" (a product as a kind of bundle such as a newsletter, a website, or a social media account) and to a particular *content* or *format*. In both cases, experimenting with products means finding and testing new types of journalistic offerings (a product as a new form of journalistic narrative or way of presentation, such as a virtual reality story or constructive journalism).

That said, we should be aware that "product" is an integral part of the "innovation rhetoric": to talk of "products" and "product development" is a way of arguing for change in editorial offices, for example. At this point, media technologies are important because they open up possibilities for the development of new products (e.g. apps) or facilitate work on a new product (e.g. a new content management system that makes it possible to realize different products with one piece of content). So, the technologies are not simply the product themselves, they are a means to construct a new product.

Often the person who will "push" transformation within established media organizations is labelled a "product manager," "product innovation manager", or similar. The aim of introducing these types of positions is to develop "new products" across the "silos" of different departments in organizations. It is important, therefore, to keep in mind that talking about "products", as opposed to "topics," "stories," or "pieces" in editorial offices is still relatively new, or at least unusual, and creates internal tensions; "products", as a concept, places an emphasis on economic-strategic considerations instead of journalistic values. This is also the source of the concern that "the emphasis on technology, product and business innovation might [...] go to the expense of content quality" (Picone and Pauwels 2013: 159).

Work practices

Experimentation with work practices means trying out new *ways of working* (together). This can refer to *individual work stages* or to the entire *organization of the work process*. Here, pioneer journalism is primarily associated with ideas of process orientation, working in teams, and applying "innovation methods."

By way of analogy with "products", one could say that this is about how products can be *conventionally built* and how journalistic work processes in general can be *differently organized*. The resulting change and the expansion of work practices in journalism is not merely a "side consequence" of the introduction of new technologies, but the subject of experimental practices for which such technologies are used. These experimental practices are significantly related to the constellations of actors described above, for example, through the role played by projects, and the formation of (temporary) teams, networks, and innovation departments.

Fostered by the collaboration and the developing professional intimacy between journalists and technologists, the adaptation of certain values or principles can be observed, which Lewis and Usher (2013: 608) refer to as, "journalism as tinkering" and "journalism as iteration" providing a theoretical nod toward open-source culture. Striking, then, is that pioneer journalism strives for more "open," "less hierarchical", "free", and "agile" ways of working. Here, too, one has to be careful not to be taken in by a simple "innovation ideology" present in the field's discourse, and that of academia as well (Kreiss and Brennen 2016). Empirically, however, there is evidence that pioneer journalists often see traditional ways of working as too pre-structured, hierarchical, and inflexible, and this is often a decisive reason for leaving established media organizations (Hepp and Loosen 2021).

Funding

Funding is a pertinent issue in relation to pioneer journalism in two respects. On the one hand, it enables *finance experimentation*, while on the other, it is a central question of how new ideas and concepts can lead to "lasting" *business models*. In both cases, pressure to find economically viable "solutions" weighs on pioneer journalism, and in part runs counter to experimentation.

The search for new sources of income, in turn, is an important factor for established media organizations wanting to get involved in pioneer journalism. With the continuously shrinking advertising market, the decreasing number of subscribers, rising distribution costs for printed newspapers, and an increasing, but still low willingness to pay for news on the internet (Buschow and Wellbrock 2019; Hölig and Hasebrink 2020), some established media organizations are looking for new funding models and are pinning their hopes on pioneer journalism. This manifests in an argument for them to try spin-offs. At the same time, start-up founders face the challenge of developing a sustainable funding model for their ideas and, correspondingly, accelerators and incubators primarily geared toward providing start-ups with a form of feedback and contact networks enable the discovery of just such a business model. Technologies are seen here as an opportunity to open up new sources of income. The "innovative power" of a technology is thus measured by its potential for monetization. The Silicon Valley idea that a commercially successful "disruptive technology" could be identified (Daub 2020: 115–133) has given way to other ideas in pioneer journalism: In particular, it is about being viable against the background of strong economic pressure (see, Russell and Vos, this volume).

In this context, ideas for new models of financing are emerging within the field of pioneer journalism. Ideas here concern, for example, donations for investigation, crowdfunding to develop a particular micropayment for journalistic content such as podcasts or hyperlocal journalism, or membership fees for community-oriented journalism (Hunter 2015, see also Alleyne et al. 2020). In general, it is striking that while pioneers at established media organizations experiment on the "next big product" that might provide financial security for the company, freelance pioneer journalists and many start-ups look for collaborative forms of financing. It is here that the development of cooperatives is seen as an important way of avoiding financial precarity (Fenton et al. 2010).

Audience relationships

Audience relationships do not usually appear in (media economic) typologies of the areas of "innovation" in journalism (Bleyen et al. 2014; Buschow and Wellbrock 2020; García-Avilés et al. 2019). This may or may not be surprising insofar as "the audience" always seems to be considered in "innovation processes" and "product development", although an audience is addressed primarily as "users". After all, one might think that the absence, migration, or desire to gain an audience is a central reason for "innovation" efforts. As a consequence, pioneer journalism is often about trying out *new relationships with users* who are no longer understood as a mass audience, but as participants in the tension between individual users with their own interests and needs and a social community to which pioneer journalism wants to connect.

Various contexts can identify the ways in which attention to audience relationships as a field of experimentation has been rearticulated. One stems from experimentation with new financial models. In those moments where these are designed for community building, they are also about rethinking the relationship with the audience. In essence, this development is also about a general reorientation of the field towards winning over more and more direct-paying audiences. A second, sometimes parallel, development is the increasing orientation towards participation and dialogue in journalistic practice (Kramp and Loosen 2018), reflecting the undisputed transformation of the journalism-audience relationship (Loosen and Schmidt 2012). Media technology is repeatedly conceptualized in a double sense here: On the one hand, "new" media technologies, such as social media platforms, have reconfigured the relationship with the audience; the audience can now communicate "back" in real time (see Banjac, this volume). On the other hand, technology is seen as a tool to reshape the relationship with users and build-up communities through digital technologies (Hansen and Goligoski 2018).

This explains why audience relationships are such an important field of experimentation. If we look specifically at start-ups, they often focus on audience relationships that differ from those of traditional journalism. Because start-ups do not aim at a mass audience that often, this is also evident in the way the term "audience" is employed to refer to users, the community, members, or co-producers (Loosen 2019). As we have already seen with pioneering projects, when a crowdfunding campaign is developed, an audience is involved before a journalistic offer even exists. Pioneer journalism, therefore, stands for an idea of journalism that moves away from an orientation toward the "dispersed audience" of mass media

(Maletzke 1963: 85), including through individual and personal forms of address, and engendering member and community care with exclusive rights (such as commenting on contributions or participating in events). This reorientation in the journalism-audience relationship is also supported by the special importance attached to user centricity and the user-centered development of innovations in the "methods of pioneer journalism" discussed above.

Conclusion: Pioneer journalism and the refiguration of journalism

In what we refer to as pioneer journalism, we are dealing with a complex figuration characterized by a constellation of actors in which individual and supra-individual actors are in relationships of varying intimacy with each other. This directs our attention to three intertwined developments relevant for journalism's re-figuration:

- an expansion of the constellation of actors,
- a transformation in the character of journalism's organizational figurations, and
- a change in work practices and processes.

First, pioneer journalism brought and continues to bring new actors into the field of journalism, thus contributing to an *expansion of the constellation of actors in journalism* as a whole. In the case of corporate actors, this particularly refers to start-ups as well as the accelerators and incubators that support them. In the case of collective actors, this refers above all to the networks, pioneer communities, and projects in which collaboration takes place in phases, in which ideas and experimental forms of collaboration arise. Beginning from pioneer journalism, the constellation of actors in the entire field of journalism has fundamentally changed. We are dealing with new figurations.

Second, pioneer journalism comes with an increasing "fluidity" and diversity of organizational structures and practices of organization; that is, a *transformation in the character of journalism's organizational figurations*. For example, the boundaries of a newsroom can no longer be so clearly defined if it also includes "bought-in" pioneer journalists and if certain projects are realized in cooperation with external actors. Pioneer journalism's overall figuration can be seen as a driving force for transformation within established media organizations' "figurations": Their "pressure to innovate" increases the willingness to engage with pioneering actors, their organizational forms and their ways of working, or at least to take a step toward them and the related imaginaries of how to organize journalistic practices.

Third, we can notice as part of this transformation of organizational figurations a *change in work practices and processes*. This happens especially through the adaptation of "innovation methods" which go hand in hand with certain notions of "user-centricity" and "developing products", yet, it is still unclear how exactly they relate to established understandings of audiences and journalistic offerings.

Overall, it becomes clear that pioneer journalism stands for more fluid, sometimes temporary, structures, including a "projectification" (see Baur, Besio, and Norkus

2018) of journalistic work than that applied to journalism produced in established newsrooms, which must have a comparatively "high-density structure" in order to reliably produce news in the daily routine and always be able to react quickly to special news situations.

Such transformations have remarkably changed what journalism is and how it will be in the future. The process of transformation we are facing is about constructing new forms of journalism that correspond to today's deeply mediatized, individualized, and commercialized society: Various practices, processes, and organizational patterns of pioneer journalism "promote" an orientation toward "products" and "users" and are part of establishing particular models of the self and society within journalism. As other research shows, creative methods and models of organizing work such as "design thinking" are not simply neutral tools but are closely interwoven with ideas of a neoliberal society (Turner and Butler-Wall 2021). Conversely, this does not mean that every application of pioneer journalism's methods is a push in that direction from the outset. But it does mean that we must continuously question what kind of journalism is established by such concepts and methods and where they interfere with the original normative expectations around journalism, even those that most pioneer journalists feel dedicated to. A broader orientation toward the journalist as "entrepreneur" and "brand" and toward the audience as "users" and "consumers" is linked to a particular conception of the self and the role journalism should and does play in society. In shifting from a societal orientation towards user-centricity, journalism might not only become more project-oriented and structurally more fluid, but also more precarious (Deuze and Witschge 2019: 49–65).

Pioneer journalism is fundamental for these transformations because it is through its figurations that experimental products, work practices, forms of funding, and audience relationships can be explored. All this, in turn, is translated back into the everyday practice of established media organizations whose scope for experimentation is much more limited and who must repeatedly measure what they have tried against what is commercially viable. In this sense, pioneer journalism achieves a lot, but one thing it does not do is overcome journalism's "built-in schizophrenia" (Weischenberg 2004: 171) and the tension between its status as a social institution that is supposed to serve the general public while being an industry that follows economic interests. Maybe journalism's biggest challenge is not to keep up with digitalization and media change, but to preserve precisely this "built-in schizophrenia," that is, to maintain this field of tension, and to not abandon it or let it collapse.

In summary, it becomes quite evident that we should not understand pioneer journalism as separate from legacy journalism that could somehow be distinguished from "non-pioneer," "normal," and "routine" journalism. Pioneer journalism is a fundamental part of journalism in general. Anything which is regarded as "pioneering" is continuously negotiated within the overall figuration of journalism and the field's search for "innovation" is nothing more than an expression of this. Pioneer journalism is thus closely related to traditional journalism as the various actors in the field perceive and define it and the journalism from which they want to distinguish themselves, as well as the imaginations of a future journalism they want to introduce and develop. It is this overall dynamic that marks the particular role of pioneer journalism in the refiguration of journalism as a whole.

Notes

1 If we discuss journalism in this general way (as a field, a social domain, or a system) and not explicitly about journalists, it is to make clear that these descriptions claim themselves as systemic evidence for journalism on a general level, even though they may not apply to every journalist.
2 It is also possible to imagine cases in which it is the other way around: the attribution as a forerunner from external sources is there, but in the self-description it is not so clear.
3 The much-heralded "art of failure" has in itself become part of the "innovation narrative" in the field, however, it is typically framed in terms of Silicon Valley: A "failure" is even worth celebrating because this was (or should be) the foundation for a learning experience that results in success (Daub 2020: 134–152).
4 Against the backdrop of interviews with journalists "working in the most innovative outlets" (1) in Spain, García-Avilés et al. (2019: 2) differentiate between four areas of innovation: production, distribution, organization, and commercialization. Bleyen et al. (2014: 35), on the other hand, define five areas on the basis of a literature review from media economics and media management and propose a typology that distinguishes between process-related and product-related innovations, with the former encompassing the areas of business model, production and distribution, and the latter, the areas of consumption & media, inner form, and core.

References

Alleyne, Malene, Camille Canon, Amelia Evans, Yichen Feng, NathanSchneider, and Mara Zepeda. 2020. *Exit to Community. A Community Primer.* Boulder: MedLab, Zebras Unite.

Appelgren, Ester, and Carl-Gustav Lindén. 2020. "Data Journalism as a Service." *Media and Communication* 8 (2): 62. doi:10.17645/mac.v8i2.2757..

Baur, Nina, Cristina Besio, and Maria Norkus. 2018. "Projectification of Science as an Organizational Innovation." In *Innovation society today*, edited by Werner Rammert, Arnold Windeler, Hubert Knoblauch, and Michael Hutter, pp. 341–370. Wiesbaden: Springer VS.

Beckett, Charlie. 2019. *New Powers, New Responsibilities.* London: LSE.

Bélair-Gagnon, Valérie, and Avery E. Holton. 2018. "Boundary Work, Interloper Media, and Analytics in Newsrooms." *Digital Journalism* 6 (4): 492–508. doi:10.1080/21670811.2018.1445001.

Bleyen, Valérie-Anne, Sven Lindmark, Heritiana Ranaivoson, and Pieter Ballon. 2014. "A Typology of Media Innovations". *The Journal of Media Innovations* 1 (1): 28–51. doi:https://doi.org/10.5617/jmi.v1i1.800.

Borger, Merel, Anita van Hoof, Irene Costera Meijer, and José Sanders. 2013. "Constructing Participatory Journalism as a Scholarly Object." *Digital Journalism* 1: 117–134. doi:10.1080/21670811.2012.740267..

Bourdieu, Pierre. 2010. *Distinction*, London, New York: Routledge.

Boyles, Jan Lauren. 2016. "The Isolation of Innovation." *Digital Journalism* 4 (2): 229–246. doi:10.1080/21670811.2015.1022193.

Brown, Tim. 2009. *Change by Design.* New York: Harper Business.

Buschow, Christopher. 2018. *Die Neuordnung des Journalismus*. Wiesbaden: Springer VS.

Buschow, Christopher, and Christian Wellbrock. 2019. *Zahlungsbereitschaft für digitaljournalistische Inhalte*. Düsseldorf: LfM.

Buschow, Christopher, and Christian Wellbrock. 2020. *Die Innovationslandschaft des Journalismus in Deutschland*. Düsseldorf: Landesanstalt für Medien NRW. https://www.ssoar.info/ssoar/handle/document/69718.

Carlson, Matt, and Nikki Usher. 2016. "News Startups as Agents of Innovation." *Digital Journalism* 4 (5), 563–581.

Couldry, Nick, and Andreas Hepp. 2017. *The Mediated Construction of Reality*. Cambridge: Polity Press.

Daub, Adrian. 2020. *What Tech Calls Thinking*. New York: Macmillan.

Deuze, Mark, and Tamara Witschge. 2019. *Beyond Journalism*. Cambridge: Polity.

Eldridge, Scott. A. 2019. "Where Do We Draw the Line? Interlopers, (Ant)agonists, and an Unbounded Journalistic Field." *Media and Communication* 7 (4): 8–18.

Elias, Norbert. 1993. *Was ist Soziologie?* Weinheim: Juventa.

Evans, Sandra K. 2018. "Making Sense of Innovation." *Journalism Studies* 19 (1): 4–24. doi:10.1080/1461670x.2016.1154446..

Fenton, Natalie, Monika Metykova, Justin Schlosberg and Des Freedman. 2010. *Meeting the News Needs of Local Communities*. London: Goldsmiths University of London.

Frederiksen, Dennis Lyth, and Alexander Brem. 2017. "How do entrepreneurs think they create value?" *International Entrepreneurship and Management Journal* 13 (1): 169–189. doi:10.1007/s11365-016-0411-x.

Fredriksson, Magnus, and Josef Pallas. 2017. The localities of Mediatization. In *Dynamics of Mediatization*, edited by Olivier Driessens, Göran Bolin, Andreas Hepp, and Stig Hjarvard, pp. 119–136. London: Palgrave Macmillan. doi:10.1007/978-3-319-62983-4_6.

García-Avilés, Jose Alberto, Miguel Carvajal-Prieto, Félix Arias, and Alicia De Lara-González. 2019. "How Journalists Innovate in the Newsroom." *The Journal of Media Innovations* 5 (1): 1–16.

Hansen, Elizabeth, and Emily Goligoski. 2018. *Guide to Audience Revenue and Engagement*. New York: Columbia University. doi:10.7916/D86T1ZNN/download..

Heft, Annett. 2021. "Transnational Journalism Networks 'From Below'." *Journalism Studies* 22 (4): 454–474. doi:10.1080/1461670x.2021.1882876..

Heidbrink, Henriette. 2020. "Innovationsmethoden im Unternehmerjournalismus." In *Innovation in der Medienproduktion und -distribution – Proceedings der Jahrestagung der Fachgruppe Medienökonomie der DGPUK 2019*, edited by Christian Wellbrock, and Christian Zabel, pp. 37–54. Stuttgart: Deutsche Gesellschaft für Publizistik- und Kommunikationswissenschaft e.V. https://doi.org/10.21241/ssoar.68091.

Hepp, Andreas. 2016. "Pioneer Communities." *Media, Culture & Society* 38 (6): 918–933.

Hepp, Andreas. 2020. *Deep Mediatization*. London: Routledge.

Hepp, Andreas., and Wiebke Loosen. 2020. Neujustierung Holistisch Gedacht – und Gemacht. In *Neujustierung der Journalistik/Journalismusforschung in der digitalen Gesellschaft*, edited by Jonas Schützeneder, Klaus Meier, and Nina Springer, pp. 21–33. Eichstätt: Deutsche Gesellschaft für Publizistik- und Kommunikationswissenschaft e.V. https://doi.org/10.21241/ssoar.70816.

Hepp, Andreas, and Wiebke Loosen. 2021. "Pioneer Journalism." *Journalism* 22 (3): 577–595. https://doi.org/10.1177/1464884919829277.

Hepp, Andreas, Wiebke Loosen, Hendrik Kühn, Paul Solbach, and Leif Kramp. 2021. "Die Figuration des Pionierjournalismus in Deutschland." Communicative Figurations, ZeMKI Working Papers, No. 38: 1–26.

Hess, Thomas, Antonia Köster, and Robert Steiner. 2014. "Journalistic Startups in the Online World." *Management Report* 3: 1–12. http://www.wim.bwl.uni-muenchen.de/download/epub/mreport_2014_3.pdf.

Hitzler, Ronald, and Arne Niederbacher. 2010. *Leben in Szenen*. Wiesbaden: Springer VS.

Hölig, Sascha, and Uwe Hasebrink. 2020. "Reuters Institute Digital News Report 2020." Arbeitspapiere des Hans-Bredow-Instituts, No. 50.

Holton, Avery E., Valérie Bélair-Gagnon, and Oscar Westlund. 2019. "Peripheral Actors in Journalism: Agents of Change in Journalism Culture and Practice." *Media and Communication* 7 (4).

Hunter, Andrea. 2015. "Crowdfunding Independent and Freelance Journalism." *New Media & Society* 17 (2): 272–288. doi:10.1177/1461444814558915.

Jarke, Juliane, and Ulrike Gerhard. 2018. "Using Probes for Sharing (Tacit) Knowing in Participatory Design." *i-com* 17 (2): 137–152. doi:10.1515/icom-2018-0014.

Knoblauch, Hubert, and Martina Löw. 2017. "On the Spatial Re-Figuration of the Social World." *Sociologica* 11 (2): 1–27.

Kramp, Leif, and Wiebke Loosen. 2018. "The Transformation of Journalism." In *Communicative Figurations*, edited by Andreas Hepp, Andreas Breiter, and Uwe Hasebrink, pp. 205–240. London: Palgrave Macmillan.

Kreiss, Daniel, and J. Scott Brennen. 2016. "Normative Models of Digital Journalism." In *The SAGE Handbook of Digital Journalism*, edited by Tamara Witschge, C. W. Anderson, David. Domingo, and Alfred Hermida, pp. 299–314. London: Sage.

Lewis, Seth C., and Nikki Usher. 2013. "Open Source and Journalism." *Media, Culture & Society* 35 (5): 602–619. doi:10.1177/0163443713485494.

Lewis, Seth. C., and Nikki Usher. 2016. "Trading Zones, Boundary Objects, and the Pursuit of News Innovation." *Convergence* 22 (5): 543–560. doi:10.1177/1354856515623865.

Loosen, Wiebke. 2019. "Community Engagement and Social Media Editors. " In *The International Encyclopedia of Journalism Studies*, edited by Tim P. Vos, Folker Hanusch, Dimitra Dimitrakopoulou, Margaretha Geertsema-Sligh, and Annika Sehl. Hoboken, NJ: John Wiley and Sons. doi:10.1002/9781118841570.iejs0251.

Loosen, Wiebke, Laura Ahva, Julius Reimer, Paul Solbach, Mark Deuze, and Lorenz Matzat. 2020. "'X Journalism'". *Journalism*. https://journals.sagepub.com/doi/pdf/10.1177/1464884920950090.

Loosen, Wiebke, and Jan-Hinrik Schmidt. 2012. "(Re-)Discovering the Audience." *Information, Communication & Society* 15 (6): 1–21.

Maletzke, Gerhard. 1963. *Psychologie der Massenkommunikation*. Hamburg: Hans-Bredow-Institut.

Mitchelstein, Eugenia, and Pablo J. Boczkowski. 2009. "Between Tradition and Change." *Journalism* 10 (5): 562–586.

Paulussen, Steve. 2016. "Innovation in the Newsroom." In *The SAGE Handbook of Digital Journalism*, edited by Tamara Witschge, C. W. Anderson, David. Domingo and Alfred Hermida, pp. 92–206. London: Sage.

Peters, Chris, and Tamara Witschge. 2015. "From Grand Narratives of Democracy to Small Expectations of Participation." *Journalism Practice* 9 (1): 19–34. doi:10.1080/17512786.2014.928455..

Picone, Ike, and Caroline Pauwels. 2013. Belgium: Big changes in a Small News Economy. In *State aid for newspapers*, edited by Paul Murschetz, pp. 149–162. Wiesbaden: Springer.

Porlezza, Colin. 2019. "From Participatory Culture to Participatory Fatigue." *Social Media + Society* 5 (3): 1–4. Doi:doi:10.1177/2056305119856684.

Rogers, Everett M. 2003. *Diffusion of Innovations*. New York: Free Press.

Schimank, Uwe. 2010. *Handeln und Strukturen*. Weinheim: Juventa.

Schmidt, Thomas R., and R. Lawrence. 2020. "Engaged Journalism and News Work." *Journalism Practice* 14 (5): 518–536. doi:10.1080/17512786.2020.1731319.

Schwaber, Ken, and Mike Beedle. 2002. *Agile Software Development with Scrum.* Upper Saddle River, NJ: Pearson.

Shoemaker, Pamela J., and Steven D. Reese. 2012. *Mediating the Message.* London: Routledge.

Singer, Jane B. 2017. "Reinventing Journalism as an Entrepreneurial Enterprise." In *Remaking the news*, edited by Pablo. J. Boczkowski and C. W. Anderson, pp. 195–210. Cambridge: MIT Press.

Star, Susan Leigh. 2010. "This Is Not a Boundary Object." *Science, Technology, & Human Values* 35 (5). https://doi.org/10.1177/0162243910377624.

Steensen, Steen. 2011. "Online Journalism and the Promises of New Technology." *Journalism Studies* 12 (3): 311–327. doi:10.1080/1461670x.2010.501151..

Turner, Fred, and A. Butler-Wall. 2021. "Designing for Neoliberalism." In *After the Bauhaus, Before the Internet. A history of Graphic Design Pedagogy*, edited by Geoff Kaplan. Cambridge: MIT Press.

Vinsel, Lee. 2014a. "How to Give Up the I-Word." Part 1. https://culturedigitally.org/2014/09/how-to-give-up-the-i-word-pt-1/.

Vinsel, Lee. 2014b. "How to Give Up the I-Word.". Part 2. https://culturedigitally.org/2014/09/how-to-give-up-the-i-word-pt-2/.

Vos, Tim P., and Jane B. Singer. 2016. "Media Discourse About Entrepreneurial Journalism." *Journalism Practice* 10 (2): 143–159.

Wahl-Jorgensen, Karin. 2009. "News Production, Ethnography and Power." In *Journalism and anthropology*, edited by S. Elizabeth Bird, 21–35. Bloomington: Indiana University Press.

Weischenberg, Siegfried. 2004. *Journalistik: Medienkommunikation: Theorie und Praxis Band 1.* 3rd ed. Wiesbaden: VS Verlag für Sozialwissenschaften.

Wenger, Etienne. 1999. *Communities of Practice.* Cambridge: Cambridge University Press.

Werning, Stefan. 2019. "Start-up Ecosystems Between Affordance Networks, Symbolic Form and Cultural Practice." In *Making Media*, edited by Mark Deuze and Miriam Prenger, pp. 207–219. Amsterdam: Amsterdam University Press.

PART III
The technological institutions

9

INSIDERS TURNED INTERLOPERS

The change agents behind engaged journalism

Jacob L. Nelson and Andrea Wenzel

Many within the news industry have begun to embrace "engagement" as a primary goal. The term has several interpretations that stem from one underlying belief: Journalists better serve their audiences and community members when they explicitly focus on how these groups interact with and respond to the news in the first place (Nelson 2019). The increasing popularity of "engaged journalism" has been accompanied by a growing body of research focused on the various ways in which the term gets conceptualized and subsequently implemented within newsrooms (Bélair-Gagnon, Nelson, and Lewis 2019; Ferrucci 2015; Lawrence, Radcliffe, and Schmidt 2018; Schmidt and Lawrence 2020; Schmidt, Nelson, and Lawrence 2022), as well as the way in which it is received by the public (Curry and Stroud 2021; Stroud, Scacco, and Curry 2016; Tenenboim and Stroud 2020; Wenzel 2020).

One of the most interesting, and under-studied, aspects of engaged journalism is the group of people behind its pursuit. "Engagement" itself means different things to different stakeholders within journalism, and the goals of its advocates consequently tend to vary as well. Some see engagement primarily as a means to increase newsroom revenue, and therefore tend to pursue it with an eye toward their digital audiences. Others, however, see engaged journalism from a more ideological perspective; they believe that one of journalism's biggest failures is that it has perpetuated a disconnect between the people the news gets written *about* and the people the news gets written *for*. This group, therefore, sees the pursuit of engaged journalism as one primarily focused not on improving journalism's monetization of its audience, but instead on building bridges between journalists and the communities they seek to cover. The overarching difference in conceptualizations of "engagement" within journalism leads to differences in execution, which inevitably leads to differences in what the news looks like, as well as whom it is intended to reach.

Complicating this attempt at journalistic transformation even further is the fact that calls for journalism to become more engaged often originate not from people

DOI: 10.4324/9781003140399-13

working within newsrooms, but from those working outside of them. These circumstances raise important questions about the increasing influence of these organizations within journalism discourse and practice: What motivates these engaged journalism advocates to attempt to change what news production looks like? What approaches have they embraced as the most effective for accomplishing their goals? Finally, what do these outsider attempts to transform journalism reveal about the relationship between those who make the news, and those who hope to change it (see Baack, Cheruiyot and Ferrer-Conill, this volume)?

This chapter explores these questions. It reviews previously published studies of engaged journalism that derive from interview data gathered from employees of several well-known organizations in the US focused on pushing newsrooms to embrace engaged journalism's values and practices in order to put forward a novel theoretical lens for understanding the pursuit of engaged journalism and the people behind it. It focuses primarily on the group of people advocating for the conceptualization of engaged journalism that privileges better ties between journalists and community members. At a moment when there is so much focus on transforming journalism's relationship with and approach to the public, we seek to offer a first step toward a better understanding of the journalistic stakeholders attempting these transformations. In taking a comprehensive view of the scholarship focused on engaged journalism, our aim is to contribute a more detailed portrait of these change agents, focusing primarily on their motivations for transforming journalistic practice, and the mechanism by which they hope to do so. In doing so, we hope this chapter offers a useful theoretical tool for future empirical studies not only of engaged journalism, but of other efforts to transform the news as well.

Our overarching argument is that the change agents on the front lines of the pursuit of engaged journalism, those who seeks to strengthen journalists' bonds with the communities they attempt to cover, often comprise people who once worked in traditional news organizations, but subsequently left those positions for ones focused as much (if not more) on *transforming* the news than on producing it. It is within these new quasi-outsider roles that these formerly traditional journalists are each attempting to influence journalistic practice so that community members play a larger role. Their attempts are informed by their own unique motivations and goals, which themselves are shaped by their assumptions about journalism and the public, and what they see as the ideal relationship between the two. Equally important, their attempts to transform journalism are influenced by their prior experiences as working journalists, which have informed their opinions on how best to motivate change within the profession (Ferrucci 2018). These circumstances suggest that advocates for engaged journalism perceive themselves, and hope to persuade others to similarly see them, less as journalism *outsiders* than as former *insiders* turned agents of change. We define these insiders-turned-interlopers as *liminal journalists*.

Adding to the already significant challenge that engaged journalism advocates face is the fact that they find themselves as interlopers not only when it comes to the journalists whose methods and ideals they seek to change, but also when it comes to the community members with whom they seek to build better relationships. Engaged journalism advocates therefore find themselves tasked with both persuading more traditional journalists to embrace their notions of journalism's problems and solutions, as well as persuading community members, many of whom have good reason to be skeptical of reporters, to accept these new efforts by those same reporters to engage with them. The people pursuing engaged journalism find themselves walking a familiar tightrope, one for example walked by public journalism evangelists, that requires careful consideration for how they get perceived by two distinct groups of people: the journalists reporting on communities in ways that may not accurately represent those community members' needs or experiences, and the community members themselves (Corrigan 1999).

To illustrate this argument, we fuse two theoretical frameworks that have been previously used to understand attempts to change news production: Giddens' notion of structuration (1984), which posits that what the social world looks like is not fixed, but is instead mutually reproduced and altered by agents and structures; and Eldridge's notion of interlopers, which refers to "journalistic actors who originate from outside the boundaries of the traditional journalistic field" (Eldridge 2019: 857) and "frequently and overtly challenge journalistic norms" (Holton and Bélair-Gagnon 2018: 73). Combining these two theoretical discussions within journalism studies offers an opportunity to understand how engaged journalism advocates leverage their unique positions outside of newsrooms, yet still within the news media environment, in their attempts to transform journalistic practice, how these advocates' prior professional experiences both enhance and limit these attempts, and finally, how those attempts to do so are ultimately received.

In short, by putting forward this novel theoretical lens through which to understand the ongoing journey of engaged journalism, we hope to show how those behind the pursuit of engaged journalism understand their barriers to success, and how that understanding shapes their attempts to transform the relationship between news media and communities.

The promise of engaged journalism

For decades, the news industry has struggled to overcome dismal financial circumstances. We now find ourselves faced with a severely constricted news media environment, where many outlets have shuttered, and many more have reduced their staff (Hare 2022; McChesney and Pickard 2011; Siles and Boczkowski 2012). "News deserts" of communities or regions with no local news outlets have grown in number (Abernathy 2018; Mathews 2020), while misinformation has exploded (Nelson and Taneja 2018). The result, as has become all-too-apparent during the coronavirus pandemic, is a situation in which people sometimes believe things that they should not, perhaps because they lack a credible alternative source of information that might offer a correction, or perhaps because they, like a majority of the public, do not trust the news in the first place (Brenan 2019; Hopp and Ferrucci 2019).

In response to a news media environment in which journalists lack financial as well as public support, there's a growing call for journalism to improve its relationship with the people that it hopes to reach. This "audience turn" in journalism (Costera Meijer 2020; Costera Meijer and Groot Kormelink 2016) has been accompanied by a variety of steps and initiatives within the profession. For example, many within both journalism practice and research are increasingly focused on audience analytics (see Bélair-Gagnon, this volume), and how these metrics can be used to understand audience interactions with news (Cherubini and Nielsen 2016; Ferrucci 2020; Tandoc and Thomas 2015, 2017).

Journalism's increased focus on its audiences is not only evident by its ongoing efforts to quantify those audiences, but also by the profession's intensifying efforts to more actively interact with them. There has been an ongoing push within the news media environment by a small but growing group of passionate advocates for what is now commonly referred to as *audience engagement* or *engaged journalism* (Batsell 2015; Bélair-Gagnon, Nelson, and Lewis 2019; Ferrucci, Nelson, and Davis 2020; Lawrence, Radcliffe, and Schmidt 2017; Powers 2015; Wenzel 2019). Although these terms are inconsistently defined, they generally refer to the idea that journalists "better serve their audiences when they treat them as active participants – rather than passive recipients – in the news production process" (Nelson 2021: 30). Despite, or perhaps because of, the increased interest in engaged journalism, the term's meaning often takes many forms. Some, for example, conceptualize engagement primarily as a means of corresponding with audiences via social media once an article has already been published, while others conceptualize it as a more explicit effort to bring the public into the news reporting process.

In other words, engagement is often understood as a measure of audience attention *to* news as much as it is understood as the act of improving audience participation *in* news. Nelson (2021) argues that the many understandings of engaged journalism can be divided into two larger categories: *production-oriented* engagement, which includes journalists' attempts to bring the public more actively communicate with and solicit input from the public throughout the news production process; and *reception-oriented* engagement, which includes journalists' attempts to capture and measure audience attention after they have already published the news.

As Wenzel (2022) points out, however, engaged journalism is not solely focused on journalism's relationship with its audiences. In fact, a growing subset of engaged journalists bristle at the term "audience" altogether, which they see as prioritizing news consumers for economic motivations (e.g. more subscription revenue) rather than for civic reasons (e.g. a better informed and empowered public). A growing number of researchers and practitioners who use the term *engagement*, according to Wenzel, are referring to efforts by journalists to interact with their audience and the communities they are working with that, in some fashion, assesses and responds to their information needs and to their interests, and which also involves them in the journalistic process (Wenzel 2022).

The ambiguity surrounding engaged journalism's conceptualization and implementation unsurprisingly leads to complicated questions about the underlying assumptions held by its advocates, as well as the impact of those assumptions on the

way that these advocates ultimately approach the work of journalistic transformation. Yet these assumptions have not been studied as much as its other aspects. To
be sure, there is tremendous value in the studies focused on how attempts to
implement engaged journalism are received within newsrooms (Lawrence et al.
2017; Schmidt and Lawrence 2020), and among communities who comprise the
very people these engagement efforts are intended to reach (Gerson, Chen,
Wenzel, Ball-Rokeach, and Parks 2017; Wenzel, Gerson, Moreno, Son, and
Morrison Hawkins 2018). What remains under-studied is the relationship between
the assumptions, motivations, and approaches that have been embraced by the
people making the case for engaged journalism in the first place. Who are these
people, why are they attempting to alter news production in this way, and how do
the answers to these first two questions shape the way they ultimately attempt to
accomplish their goals?

There are two theories that are most useful for understanding the answers to
these questions: the notion of journalistic interlopers, and structuration. Before
turning to these theories, however, we first provide more context on the subset of
engaged journalism advocates focused on building better bridges between journalists and community members.

Community-centered journalists

Although there exist a variety of organizations focused on making *engagement* a larger
part of news production, this chapter focuses on those (1) that have been previously
researched by scholars seeking to understand journalism's changing approach to the
public, and (2) explicitly pursue the conceptualization of engaged journalism focused
on improving the relationship between journalists and community members. *Resolve
Philly*, for example, is a nonprofit organization in Philadelphia, Pennsylvania, that seeks
to work with newsroom partners in order "to facilitate a range of approaches to
community engagement" (Wenzel 2020: 128). Resolve's mission to elevate community voices and make journalism more cooperative has resulted in, for example, collaborations between journalists and formerly incarcerated citizens. As Wenzel notes
(2020: 128), these sorts of efforts allow *Resolve Philly* "to not only strengthen storytelling network ties between different newsrooms of local journalists and residents, but
also with community organizations."

City Bureau, a nonprofit news organization located in Chicago's South Side, is
similarly focused on making journalism more collaborative. The organization seeks
to produce journalism about the city's South and West Side communities that is
explicitly more inclusive of the residents from these communities as compared to
more traditional journalism. The organization pursues this goal by hosting events
that bring journalists and community members together, by offering journalistic
training, as well as compensation, for community members interested in doing
their own municipal reporting, and by mentoring reporters "to be more conscious
of the ways they think about, report on, and eventually write local news stories"
(Nelson 2021: 13). "Community engagement should be baked into journalism.

Good relationships are about accountability and trust. The opportunity lies in building a two-way learning street between reporters and their community," said Andrea Hart, a founder of *City Bureau* and its former community engagement director (Tinworth 2018, n.p.).

Many other organizations are similarly focused on making journalism more equitable and representative when it comes to the relationship between those who make the news and the communities they seek to cover. These include groups such as *Free Press*, a nonprofit news organization based in Washington, DC that seeks to "give people a voice in the crucial decisions that shape our media" via "activism and advocacy," (About Free Press n.d.), as well as Hearken, an engaged journalism tools and service provider that seeks to equip newsrooms with the tools and knowledge they need to better communicate with and solicit input from the public. Though these organizations may vary in their approaches, they are similarly focused on changing journalism to better reflect and involve the communities they attempt to cover.

Equally important, these organizations tend to present themselves as insiders-turned-outsiders, mostly comprising former professional journalists who have learned from their own experiences and now wish to share their insights with those still working to make the news.

Engaged journalists as journalism interlopers

As journalism has struggled to figure out how best to overcome its severe and ongoing crises, the profession has increasingly turned to outsiders for help. These "strangers to the game" (Holton and Bélair-Gagnon 2018) come in the form of audience analytics providers such as Comscore and Nielsen, which promise to tell news organizations who their audiences comprise in the form of sophisticated and granular audience measurement data (Zamith, Bélair-Gagnon, and Lewis 2020). They also take the form of unconventional news producers, such as ProPublica, Deadspin, and WikiLeaks, who generate news but do so outside of the boundaries of mainstream journalism (Eldridge 2018, 2019; Wahl-Jorgensen 2014). They also take the form of funding sources. As news organizations are able to depend less and less on digital advertising and subscription dollars for support, they find themselves turning instead to foundations, which may have their own notions of which kind of news to fund (Birnbauer 2018; Ferrucci and Nelson 2019; Konieczna 2018; see also Konieczna, this volume).

Though these types of organizations differ in terms of approach, mission, and motivations, they are linked by their outsider position within journalism, as well as by their increasingly powerful influence over the way that journalism gets produced, measured, and monetized. Unsurprisingly, a growing amount of scholarship has therefore focused on these outsiders, which Eldridge refers to as *media interlopers* (Eldridge 2019), which have been defined as "non-traditional journalism actors who may not necessarily be welcomed or defined as journalists and work on the periphery of the profession while directly contributing content or products to the creation and distribution of news" (Holton and Bélair-Gagnon 2018: 72).

Yet, what is missing from the existing literature surrounding journalistic interlopers are studies that focus on a distinct form of interlopers: those who once were journalists and are now working for organizations explicitly focused on transforming the news. As previous research into engaged journalism reveals, many of the people that comprise this group are interlopers who believe they are better able to transform journalism working in these intermediary roles than they were when they worked as more traditional journalists. We define this specific type of interloper as *liminal journalists.*

As the previous section revealed, the people behind engaged journalism's more well-known organizations, including engaged journalism tools and service providers such as Hearken, as well as organizations supporting engaged journalism such as *City Bureau, Resolve Philly*, and *Free Press*, all include people who came from traditional journalism backgrounds. Furthermore, these liminal journalists find themselves in unique positions, where they both collaborate with more conventional news organizations while also attempting to encourage those same organizations to change the way they conceptualize and approach their readers. Applying an interloper framework to the pursuit of engaged journalism thus allows for a greater understanding of the advocates of a more community-focused form of news production.

This framework can be useful for understanding the way that the liminal journalists advocating on behalf of engaged journalism present themselves to the people whose behaviors they hope to change. For example, as Wenzel describes, engaged journalists may draw from and identify with other fields, such as community organizing. Mike Rispoli, the director of *Free Press*, does this when describing how he has utilized his professional background when making the case for engaged journalism to more traditional journalists. When Rispoli was asked "Aren't you a journalist?" during a workshop for journalists in Philadelphia, he identified himself as a "former journalist." He elaborated "that while he still works in the field of journalism, his primary professional identity now was as an organizer" (Wenzel 2020: 125). Wenzel observes that the *City Bureau* co-founder and lab director Darryl Holliday describes his organization's mission similarly: "We want to live right at the intersection of organizing and local news" (Wenzel 2020: 150).

The liminal journalists who comprise engaged journalism's advocates did not begin as outsiders within the profession tasked with ingratiating themselves so that they can change the profession to suit their expertise. Instead, they primarily comprise former journalists, in other words, former insiders, who left their more conventional positions within the profession in hopes that doing so would make it easier for them to transform it. These insiders turned interlopers have embraced their new roles for ideological reasons; they believe that journalism must change to better serve the needs of the public, as well as for practical reasons, they believe this change can only occur if those within the profession are persuaded to embrace it.

Indeed, the reasons that engaged journalism advocates often cite for changing their professional trajectories so that they were less about participating in news production and more about changing its very nature stem from the circumstances they faced working within traditional journalism, and their desire to change them. As Hearken cofounder and former CEO Jennifer Brandel explained in a previously published study:

> One day I never had any power about what news my community would get, and the next day I did, and I thought, "That's awesome!" And then I thought, "That's fucked up!" ... It was amazing to suddenly have permission to do things I was interested in with the assumption that if I was interested, other people would be, too. But it bothered me that I had that power just by being on the inside. (Nelson 2018a: 536)

In short, using the interloper framework thus allows us to explore the motivations and approaches embraced by those who hope to improve journalism's relationship with the public. However, to understand the way in which these interlopers attempt to act on those motivations, as well as the obstacles they face as they execute their approaches, it is necessary to complement this framework with another one, Giddens' notion of structuration, which we turn to next.

A structurational approach to change

Examining those who pursue engaged journalism only reveals one side of the ongoing effort to transform journalism. To understand what this effort means for the profession and the public, as well as its likelihood for success, it is necessary to also examine the traditional journalists who are being asked to change their ways. In other words, as Nelson writes, the transformation of journalism is "a question of agency: How much power do its advocates have to change what news production looks like? And how powerful are the structures obstructing their efforts?" (Nelson 2018a: 532).

There are a variety of theoretical frameworks that have been used by journalism scholars to examine these questions, such as journalistic boundaries (Carlson and Lewis 2015; Ferrer-Conill 2016; Lewis 2012) and Bourdieu's notion of field theory (Benson 2012; Møller Hartley 2018; Tandoc 2019). One theoretical framework used less often within journalism studies but with more frequency within communication studies generally and audience studies specifically is Giddens' notion of *structuration* (Giddens, 1984). This theory posits that "the social world is not fixed, but is instead mutually reproduced and altered by agents and structures through the process of duality" (Nelson 2018a: 532). The structures that comprise the world around us are not all-powerful, nor are those who would seek to tear them down. Instead, the two are constantly engaged in a process by which either the status quo is perpetuated or somehow transformed in what Webster refers to as a "process of duality" (Webster 2011).

Scholars often draw on language as a useful example by which to illustrate this dynamic. All people are born into a society that privileges one specific language over all others. Although any of those born into these circumstances has the ability to forgo that language in favor of another, most embrace it instead. In other words, individuals face a structure that privileges one set of circumstances over another, yet they also play an important role in perpetuating those circumstances. "The result is the reproduction of the social world in which this language is privileged" (Nelson 2018a: 532).

Structuration was not originally used to explain the dynamics within media systems; however, it has since been used by communication and journalism scholars alike to make sense of how circumstances do, or do not, change within the news industry specifically and the media environment more generally (Eide 2014; Nelson 2018a; Schauster 2015; Sjøvaag 2013). For example, when people decide to consume a piece of media, they do not act on their preferences alone. Instead, their behaviors are shaped by a variety of structural circumstances that are so obvious they are often overlooked altogether. These include the amount of time a person has to watch, read, or listen to something, as well as the algorithms powering the recommendation systems that determine, say, which movies are promoted to that person on Netflix or which album is suggested on Spotify. These structures may seem all-powerful, but they are just as much a reaction to people's behaviors as people's behaviors are a reaction to them. If a person becomes a parent, for example, they may seek out an entirely different kind of music than they had been previously listening to (e.g., less indie rock, more Raffi), which will likely change the recommendations they receive.

When scholars use structuration to describe news media production, they frame the agents as the journalists who seek to change the news media environment, and the structures as the large, institutional obstacles in their path. In the pursuit of engaged journalism, these structural obstacles include everything from organizational culture, for example, a newsroom's reluctance to change its ways (Nelson 2018), to the structures that comprise journalism's funding models, including the fact that audience metrics tend to privilege superficial measures of exposure over deeper yet more difficult to capture understandings of attention and engagement (Nelson 2018a). In short, using structuration as a theoretical lens through which to understand the pursuit of engaged journalism "illuminates the barriers that audience engagement advocates face in their quest to transform journalistic practice, but does so without removing the possibility that they might succeed" (Nelson 2018a: 532).

Conclusion

In this chapter, we have fused two theoretical frameworks previously used to understand transformation within journalism, Giddens' notion of structuration and Eldridge's notion of interlopers, in an effort to better understand the ongoing attempt by journalism stakeholders to improve the profession's relationship with the public via more *engaged journalism*. Taken together, these two approaches to journalistic transformation allow the discourse surrounding engaged journalism to become more comprehensive, so that it not only comprises the efforts being pursued and their impact on journalism and the public, but also the motivations and assumptions behind these efforts, as well as the obstacles in their paths. In doing so, they push the conversation surrounding the pursuit of engaged journalism away from the specific interventions that are being advocated, and toward a conversation with more explicit implications for our understanding of how journalism does, or does not, change. In short, the interloper and structuration frameworks provide a theoretical lens by which to understand why and how journalism transformations get pursued, as well as where they might eventually lead.

The uniqueness of engaged journalism advocates positions within their profession creates both opportunities and limitations as they go about attempting to transform journalistic practice. In terms of opportunities first, these advocates do not have to wait to be welcomed into the social circles they must approach to make their case when it comes to the value of engaged journalism. Because the advocates come from journalism, they have already established networks of people to reach out to (see Hermida, Young and Varano, this volume). Furthermore, they can speak to these journalists using the language, or logics, of insiders rather than as interlopers trying to break in. Brandel, for example, can draw on her own experiences working as a journalist in public radio when pitching the necessity of Hearken's offerings, which is likely to be more persuasive when it comes to advocating for journalists to change their ways (Nelson 2018a). At the very least, it perhaps offers these advocates a way in which to plead their case to journalists with a lower risk of offending them, since the implication is that these advocates are attempting to fix journalism based on *their own* experiences, not based on the shortcomings of the journalists they're speaking to.

The last advantage these insiders-turned-interlopers, or liminal journalists, have when it comes to changing journalism is that they know first-hand how traditional journalism works, and therefore likely have a more accurate notion of how they might be most effective in attempting to change it. Unlike consultants, who must first study a firm before assessing its needs and areas for improvement, engaged journalism advocates have arrived at the scene of journalism's crisis already equipped with a set of ideas about how to move forward, as well as a toolkit for how to actually implement them. The close ties between engaged journalism advocates and journalism funders suggests the knowledge held by these insiders turned interlopers has tangible benefits. At a time when money is incredibly limited throughout the news media world, engaged journalism ventures such as *City Bureau*, Hearken, and *Resolve Philly* have been able to raise considerable funds from Knight Foundation, Lenfest, and Democracy Fund. We do not believe this is simply a matter of luck or timing, but also at least partially due to the people behind these ventures having a powerful familiarity with how journalism works, thus allowing them to make a compelling case for how it can and should be improved.

Yet, the liminal journalists approach is not without its limitations. First, although engaged journalism advocates' professional backgrounds open some doors when it comes to access to traditional journalism organizations, others remain closed. In general, engaged journalism advocates focused on bettering the relationship between journalists and community members tend to come from public media and local news, which means they have more access to those sectors of news media than, say, commercial TV or even some legacy newspapers. This perhaps is one reason there appears to be a more noticeable embrace of engaged journalism within public media (Bélair-Gagnon, Zamith, and Holton 2019; Wenzel 2019) than within other types of news organizations, and notably within television news.

The other limitation these insider-turned-interlopers face as they attempt to implement their notion of engaged journalism is that they find themselves tasked with persuading not one but two distinct groups of the value of their efforts. Engaged journalists behind organizations such as *City Bureau, Resolve Philly,* and *Free Press* must first and foremost coax more traditional journalists to acknowledge that journalism has historically done a disservice to large swaths of society, particularly communities of color, and that the solution is for those journalists to more deliberately communicate with and give agency to those community members. Yet they also must persuade those community members who have good reason to be skeptical of outsiders generally and journalists specifically to maintain an open mind when it comes to these efforts. Consequently, the same professional backgrounds of these journalistic interlopers that are perhaps invaluable when it comes to persuading more traditional journalists to consider the merits of engaged journalism may actually be a disadvantage when it comes to making the same argument to community members.

As this chapter suggests, we believe that the future of journalism is not solely a matter of ideas people have about how best to fix the profession, but also a matter of how effectively they are able to persuade both journalistic stakeholders and community members to embrace and subsequently implement those ideas. It is no mystery why the pursuit of engaged journalism is being led by insiders-turned-interlopers: these people know the profession from having worked within it, and now feel they are better able to change it from outside it. What remains unknown is what the outcome will be of their efforts. Understanding their success or failure to transform journalism is not only important for understanding innovation and change within the news media environment, but also for understanding how change happens within any organized field more generally.

The decision by journalists to become engaged journalism advocates and to go from insiders to interlopers is not just a choice made for ideological reasons, but practical and rhetorical ones as well. It seems likely that engaged journalists have embraced the insider-turned-interloper approach at least in part because they believe this approach is likely the most persuasive. Is it? More research should be done to answer this question, as doing so will shed light on how transformation gets pursued, how it unfolds, and how it might, or might not, ultimately succeed.

References

Abernathy, Penelope M. 2018. "The Expanding News Desert." https://www.cislm.org/wp-content/uploads/2018/10/The-Expanding-News-Desert-10_14-Web.pdf.

About Free Press. n.d. https://www.freepress.net/about.

Batsell, Jake. 2015. *Engaged journalism: connecting with digitally empowered news audiences*. New York: Columbia University Press.

Bélair-Gagnon, Valérie, Jacob Nelson and Seth C. Lewis. 2019. "Audience Engagement, Reciprocity, and the Pursuit of Community Connectedness in Public Media Journalism." *Journalism Practice* 13 (5): 558–575.

Bélair-Gagnon, Valérie, Rodrigo Zamith and Avery Holton. 2020. "Role Orientations and Audience Metrics in Newsrooms: An Examination of Journalistic Perceptions and their Drivers." *Digital Journalism* 8 (3): 347–366. https://doi.org/10.1080/21670811.2019.1709521.

Benson, Rodney. 2012. *Shaping Immigration News: A French-American Comparison*. Cambridge: Cambridge University Press.

Birnbauer, Bill 2018. *The Rise of NonProfit Investigative Journalism in the United States*. Milton: Routledge.

Brenan, Megan. 2019. "Americans' Trust in Mass Media Edges Down to 41%." https://news.gallup.com/poll/267047/americans-trust-mass-media-edges-down.aspx.

Carlson, Matt, and Seth C. Lewis. 2015. *Boundaries of Journalism: Professionalism, Practices and Participation*. New York: Routledge.

Cherubini, Federica and Rasmus Kleis Nielsen. 2016. "Editorial Analytics: How News Media are Developing and Using Audience Data and Metrics." *SSRN Electronic Journal*. https://doi.org/10.2139/ssrn.2739328.

Christin, Angèle, & Caitlin Petre. 2020. "Making Peace with Metrics: Relational Work in Online News Production." *Sociologica (Bologna)* 14 (2): 133–156.

Corrigan, Don. 1999. *The Public Journalism Movement in America: Evangelists in the Newsroom*. Westport, CT: Praeger.

Costera Meijer, Irene. 2020. "Understanding the Audience Turn in Journalism: From Quality Discourse to Innovation Discourse as Anchoring Practices 1995–2020." *Journalism Studies* 21 (16): 2326–2342.

Costera Meijer, Irene & Tim Groot Kormelink. 2016. "Revisiting the Audience Turn in Journalism: How a user-based approach changes the meaning of clicks, transparency and citizen participation." In *The Routledge Companion to Digital Journalism Studies* (pp. 345–353). Abingdon: Routledge.

Curry, Alexander L., & Natalie Jomini Stroud. 2021. The effects of journalistic transparency on credibility assessments and engagement intentions. *Journalism* 22 (4): 901–918.

Eide, Martin. 2014. "Accounting for journalism." *Journalism Studies* 15 (5): 679–688.

Eldridge, Scott A. 2018. "Repairing a fractured field: Dynamics of collaboration, normalization and appropriation at intersections of newswork." *Journal of Applied Journalism & Media Studies* 7 (3), 541–559.

Eldridge, Scott A. 2019. "Where Do We Draw the Line? Interlopers, (Ant)agonists, and an Unbounded Journalistic Field." *Media and Communication* 7 (4): 8–18.

Eldridge, Scott A. 2019. "'Thank god for Deadspin': Interlopers, metajournalistic commentary, and fake news through the lens of "journalistic realization." *New Media & Society* 21 (4): 856–878.

Ferrer-Conill, Raul. 2016. "Boundaries of Journalism: professionalism, practices and participation." *Digital Journalism* 4 (3): 401–403.

Ferrucci, Patrick. 2015. "Public journalism no more: The digitally native news nonprofit and public service journalism." *Journalism* 16 (7): 904–919.

Ferrucci, Patrick. 2018. "Mo 'meta' blues: How popular culture can act as metajournalistic discourse." *International Journal of Communication* 12 (2018): 4821–4838.

Ferrucci, Patrick. 2020. "It is in the numbers: How market orientation impacts journalists' use of news metrics." *Journalism* 21 (2): 244–261.

Ferrucci, Patrick and Jacob Nelson. 2019. "The New Advertisers: How Foundation Funding Impacts Journalism." *Media and Communication* 7 (4): 45–55.

Ferrucci, Patrick, Jacob Nelson, and Miles P. Davis. 2020. "From 'Public Journalism' to 'Engaged Journalism': Imagined Audiences and Denigrating Discourse." *International Journal of Communication* 14 (2020). https://ijoc.org/index.php/ijoc/article/view/11955/3010.

Gerson, Daniela, Nien-Tsu Nancy Chen, Andrea Wenzel, Sandra Ball-Rokeach, and Michael Parks. 2017. "From Audience to Reporter: Recruiting and training community members at a participatory news site serving a multiethnic city." *Journalism Practice*, 11 (2–3): 336–354.

Giddens, Anthony. 1984. *The Constitution of Society: Outline of the Theory of Structuration*. Los Angeles: University of California Press.

Hare, Kristen. 2022. "Here are the newsroom layoffs, furloughs and closures caused by the coronaviru." Poynter. February 17. https://www.poynter.org/business-work/2022/here-are-the-newsroom-layoffs-furloughs-and-closures-caused-by-the-coronavirus/.

Holton, Avery E. and Valérie Bélair-Gagnon. 2018. "Strangers to the Game? Interlopers, Intralopers, and Shifting News Production." *Media and Communication* 6 (4): 70–78. https://doi.org/10.17645/mac.v6i4.1490.

Hopp, Toby and Patrick Ferrucci. 2020. "A Spherical Rendering of Deviant Information Resilience." *Journalism & Mass Communication Quarterly* 97 (2): 492–508.

Konieczna, Magda. 2018. *Journalism Without Profit: Making News When the Market Fails*. New York, NY: Oxford University Press.

Lawrence, Regina G., Damian Radcliffe, and Thomas R. Schmidt. 2018. "Practicing Engagement." *Journalism Practice* 12 (10): 1220–1240.

Lewis, Seth C. 2012. "From Journalism to Information: The Transformation of the Knight Foundation and News Innovation." *Mass Communication and Society* 15 (3): 309–334.

Mathews, Nick. 2020. "Life in a news desert: The perceived impact of a newspaper closure on community members." *Journalism*.

McChesney, Robert W. & Victor W. Pickard. 2011. *Will the Last Reporter Please Turn Out the Lights: The Collapse of Journalism and What Can Be Done to Fix It*. New York: New Press.

Møller Hartley, Jannie. 2018. "'It's Something Posh People Do': Digital Distinction in Young People's Cross-Media News Engagement." *Media and Communication*, 6 (2): 46–55.

Nelson, Jacob L. 2018a. "The Elusive Engagement Metric." *Digital Journalism* 6 (4): 528–544.

Nelson, Jacob L. 2018b. "And Deliver Us to Segmentation." *Journalism Practice* 12 (2): 204–219.

Nelson, Jacob L. 2019. "The next media regime: The pursuit of 'audience engagement' in journalism." *Journalism*. https://doi.org/10.1177/1464884919862375.

Nelson, Jacob L. 2021. *Imagined Audiences: How Journalists Perceive and Pursue the Public*. New York: Oxford University Press.

Nelson, Jacob L. & Harsh Taneja. 2018. "The small, disloyal fake news audience: The role of audience availability in fake news consumption." *New Media & Society*, 20 (10): 3720–3737. https://doi.org/10.1177/1461444818758715.

Powers, Elia. 2015. "The Rise of the Engagement Editor and What It Means." MediaShift.

Rosenberry, Jack & Burton St. John. 2010. *Public Journalism 2.0: The Promise and Reality of a Citizen-Engaged Press*. New York: Routledge.

Schauster, Erin. 2015. "The relationship between organizational leaders and advertising ethics: An organizational ethnography." *Journal of Media Ethics*, 30 (3): 150–167.

Schmidt, Thomas R. & Regina G. Lawrence. 2020. "Engaged Journalism and News Work: A Sociotechnical Analysis of Organizational Dynamics and Professional Challenges." *Journalism Practice*, 14 (5): 518–536. https://doi.org/10.1080/17512786.2020.1731319.

Schmidt, Thomas R., Jacob L. Nelson & Regina G. Lawrence. 2022. "Conceptualizing the Active Audience: Rhetoric and Practice in 'Engaged Journalism'." *Journalism*. 23(1): 3–21.

Siles, Ignacio, & Pablo J.Boczkowski. 2012. "Making sense of the newspaper crisis: A critical assessment of existing research and an agenda for future work." *New Media & Society*, 14: 1375–1394. https://doi.org/10.1177/1461444812455148.

Sjøvaag, Helle. 2013. "Journalistic autonomy: Between structure, agency and institution." *Nordicom Review* 34: 155–166.

Stroud, Natalie Jomini, Joshua M. Scacco & Alexander L. Curry. 2016. "The Presence and Use of Interactive Features on News Websites." *Digital Journalism*, 4 (3): 339–358. https://doi.org/10.1080/21670811.2015.1042982.

Tandoc, Edson C. & Ryan J. Thomas. 2015. "The Ethics of Web Analytics: Implications of using audience metrics in news construction." *Digital Journalism* 3(2): 243–258. https://doi.org/10.1080/21670811.2014.909122.

Tandoc, Edson C. & Ryan J. Thomas. 2017. "Is 'doing well' doing any good? How web analytics and social media are bringing about a new journalistic norm." *Parágrafo* 5(2): 30–44.

Tandoc, Edson C. 2019. "Journalism at the Periphery." *Media and Communication* 7(4): 138–143. https://www.cogitatiopress.com/mediaandcommunication/article/view/2626.

Tenenboim, Ori & Natalie Jomini Stroud. 2020. "Enacted Journalism Takes the Stage: How Audiences Respond to Reporting-Based Theater." *Journalism Studies* 21 (6): 713–730. https://doi.org/10.1080/1461670X.2020.1720521.

Tinworth, Adam. 2018. "Andrea Faye Hart: creating a brave space for civic engagement." https://onemanandhisblog.com/2018/10/andrea-faye-hart-creating-a-brave-space-for-civic-engagment/.

Wahl-Jorgensen, Karin. 2014." Is WikiLeaks challenging the paradigm of journalism? Boundary work and beyond." *International Journal of Communication* 8 (1): 2581–2592.

Webster, James G. 2011. "The Duality of Media: A Structurational Theory of Public Attention." *Communication Theory* 21(1): 43–66. https://doi.org/10.1111/j.1468-2885.2010.01375.x.

Wenzel, Andrea. 2019. "Public Media and Marginalized Publics: Online and offline engagement strategies and local storytelling networks." *Digital Journalism* 7 (1):146–163. https://doi.org/10.1080/21670811.2017.1398594.

Wenzel, Andrea. 2019. "Engaged Journalism in Rural Communities." *Journalism Practice* 13 (6): 708–722. https://doi.org/10.1080/17512786.2018.1562360.

Wenzel, Andrea. 2020. *Community-Centered Journalism: Engaging People, Exploring Solutions, and Building Trust.* Urbana: University of Illinois Press.

Wenzel, Andrea. 2022. "Engaged Journalism." In *Encyclopedia of Journalism*. 2nd ed. London: SAGE.

Wenzel, Andrea, Daniela Gerson, Evelyn Moreno, Minhee Son, & Breanna Morrison Hawkins. 2018. "Engaging stigmatized communities through solutions journalism: Residents of South Los Angeles respond." *Journalism*, 19 (5): 649–667. https://doi.org/10.1177/1464884917703125.

Zamith, Rodrigo, Valérie Bélair-Gagnon & Seth C. Lewis. 2020. "Constructing audience quantification: Social influences and the development of norms about audience analytics and metrics." *New Media & Society* 22 (10): 1763–1784. https://doi.org/10.1177/1461444819881735.

10

WEB ANALYTICS IN JOURNALISM

Valérie Bélair-Gagnon

In April 2019, in a plea to embrace web analytics and their metrics in journalism, *the Guardian*'s head of editorial innovation, Chris Moran, wrote a piece in the *Columbia Journalism Review*. In that column, Moran claimed that for as long as he could remember, "journalism metrics in general, and particularly reach metrics – like pageviews and unique users – have been the subject of profound suspicion within the news industry." In Moran's journalistic social circles, the negativity toward web analytics and metrics had intensified (see also Andersson 2013). Across the news industry, journalists have used "bankrupt journalistic culture", "journalists as telemarketers", and "pageviews and unique users as evil" as expressions to describe the disruption on journalism culture and practice that these systems and tools catalyze to track, record, store, and analyze characteristics and behaviors of online audience.

Over the years, as these systems (analytics) and tools (metrics) became part of digital and non-digital journalism, and the business of online communication more generally, they have evolved into a normalized, essential part of news production. As tools not specifically developed for journalism, analytics and metrics are now quintessential for digital newsrooms as they enable journalists to quantify and make sense of online audience behavior (Tandoc 2019). Moreover, news organizations have started incorporating data scientists or product managers into newsrooms to reflect these vast structural changes in the news industry (Ferrer-Conill and Tandoc 2018). However, analytics and the companies offering services providing them reflect larger trends in the ongoing digital disruption of journalism, an industry where we continue to see new entrants. Once seen as the product of evil outsiders, web analytics have embedded themselves in news production and thus are one of many outsider institutions now actively changing journalism. In an effort to explore the role of analytics as an institution changing journalism, this chapter looks at how journalism studies research has portrayed web analytics and its

DOI: 10.4324/9781003140399-14

metrics. With a focus on institutions, this chapter shows that as journalism exists in an era of constant transformation, technological institutions such as web analytics companies have changed the nature of journalism while also threatening the public nature of the journalism in exchange for clicks and market-driven norms.

Web analytics in journalism

Before turning to discussing web analytics specifically, it is worth acknowledging that ways of quantifying audience consumption and interaction are not new. The emergence of these quantification systems and tools can be traced to a long historical need to quantify things, from the birth of statistics in 17th-century Europe, to the accounting of slaves in American plantations, and the rise of Taylorism as a management system in the 1930s (Christin 2020). For news media, the impetus to measure audiences can be found most saliently in the era of market-driven journalism, in the surveys and focus groups carried out by newspapers and television stations in the 1980s (Christin 2020; McManus 1994). With the expansion of computation, the scale and granularity of the data that can be gathered about audiences and their engagement have dramatically increased (Christin 2020). Web analytics and the companies that constitute this institution have grown significantly since the mid-1990s and the rise of the internet. In the 1990s, Accrue, Omniture, and WebSideStory were for-profit company leaders in the field. These early companies provided a service on the web to collect and process data and information, key performance indicators, and used these to promote strategies to optimize online business. Google Analytics, now one of the most widely known companies, emerged later, entering into the analytics game in 2005. This was a year after they acquired Urchin Software Group, which had a web statistics analysis program called Urchin that Google eventually made publicly available. This tool allowed companies and general web users to monitor real-time web traffic, such as through the now commonly used metric of page views (Bélair-Gagnon and Holton 2018).

Such monitoring tools enabled companies operating on the web to create their brand, content, and engagement and to do so while gearing these efforts toward catering to their online audience. By 2011, analytics companies originally aimed toward a more marketing mindset, including Chartbeat and Parse.ly, had become commonplace in news organizations and within the field of journalism. Other companies including Hootsuite, Facebook Insight, and the Twitter activity dashboard have, since, also become central players in digital news production (Bélair-Gagnon and Holton 2018). These companies have subsequently shaped and altered journalism culture and practices. Today, news organizations use analytics to determine which content should be published or placed, among other things (Bélair-Gagnon and Holton 2018; Lee, Lewis, and Powers 2014).

However, news organizations have also built their own proprietary web analytics platforms. For example, the British Broadcasting Corporation (BBC) uses its own proprietary analytics platform to evaluate audience behavioral data. The public broadcaster has used analytics to look at what audiences read, time they spend reading stories, from trending topics and stories, to formats and devices. The broadcaster also relied on "The Science of Engagement" to create data on formats, topics, and story arcs and to assess the impact they have on long-term memory. From the perspective of a public broadcaster that needs to defend its value in society, this approach has led to a qualitative assessment of content performance with the dual goal of serving their audiences and their clients who can see their return on investment, such as with branded content (Lim 2019). At the time, as with all media in Europe, the BBC also had to comply with the General Data Protection Regulation and remain mindful of the information they use from their local audiences as well as be transparent about it about how the data is collected and for what purposes (e.g., slicing and dicing data to target audiences using analytics and their metrics, machine learning, and artificial intelligence). This compliance with data protection, in part, explained why this organization used a proprietary platform as opposed to a non-proprietary one owned by an outside company.

Whether analytics are proprietary or not to newsrooms, journalism studies research has scrutinized the impact such systems and tools have had on journalism culture and practice. Formulated with a focus on changes in journalism as an object of inquiry, this research has looked at changes in the field's core-periphery dynamics, addressing the fluid-yet-established epistemology, practices, norms, and ethics of journalism, and the normative challenges associated with analytics and the attainment of journalistic democratic ideals.

Journalistic influence

Journalism studies has long been fascinated with understanding audiences in news. Early media sociology research looked at how media workers envision their audiences, finding that journalists tend to understand audiences through themselves as well as their family and peers (Tuchman 1978; Gans 1979). Recent research has shifted this focus, highlighting a "reconceptualization of the journalist-audience relationship" including how digital audiences may best contribute to the news (Ferrucci, Nelson, and Davis 2020: 1586; Kim, Lewis, and Watson 2018; see also Nelson and Wenzel, this volume). For example, Robinson suggested that "digital platforms offer a potential wealth of data about readers and their behavior; insights that publishers hope to spin into gold" (Robinson 2019: n.p.). However, Robinson also found that despite this promise, little seemed to have changed from the print era, and that even among journalists who seem open to having greater knowledge about their audiences, the way that they go about producing the news is in practice very similar to a pre-internet era. At the same time, other scholars have conceptualized audiences as prosumers (Bird 2011), activists (Tufekci 2017; Rauch 2007), and labor (Turow and Couldry 2018; Bruns 2008), all suggesting that audiences have become part of journalistic practice, challenging the notions of who is a journalist and what is journalism and for whom.

Analytics and their metrics have challenged the traditional concept of gate-keeping. Historically, gatekeeping comprises complex processes involving journalists, audiences and a constellation of influences and web analytics and metrics complicate this dynamic. Web analytics are changing journalism, both by including web analytics companies within journalistic production processes and in allowing journalists and news organizations new avenues through which they can imagine digital audiences. Combined, these shifts show where web analytics institutions are contributing to changing news agendas. Such reconfigurations may be contributing to justify a shift toward more trendy, clickbait or low-quality content and neglected and stereotyped particular communities in favor of a more sensational and exploitative journalism.

One way of understanding the effect of these institutions on journalism is by seeing web analytics as gatekeepers and, in doing so, to understand them as both a set of social actors (e.g., web analytics companies, social media platforms, and social media editors) and technological actants (e.g., algorithms, post meta data, etc.) deciding what information to include in the news and the activities that they take part into (cf. Lewis and Westlund 2015). As both social actors and technological actants, analytics influence the gatekeeping process on multiple levels of analysis: the routines, individual, organizational, institutional, and system levels (Shoemaker et al. 2001). Gatekeepers make choices and these choices influence the news that reaches audiences. As newer gatekeepers, web analytics have a particular influence on the social, cultural, ethical, and political aspects of news production by letting the information they amass shape the news. They both draw on and join other actors and technological actants, like social media and algorithms, which have, also, empowered audiences in news production and distribution processes, having their own roles in news gatekeeping (Vos and Heinderyckx 2015). For example, web analytics companies construct metrics to measure digital audiences and work with media organizations to personalize their metrics to the goals of these organizations. On the other hand, other metrics developed by these companies, such as reach, have been culturally contested in newsrooms as different interpretations of these metrics have different meanings for different actors and publishers. The validity of metrics can also be contested such as by being gamed; measures such as unique site visitors or reach have been shown to have shortcomings when bots generate illegitimate site traffic such and when some organizations inflate visitor counts (Bélair-Gagnon, Zamith, and Holton 2020: 18). These forms of interactions will be discussed further in the following section.

Analytics as gatekeepers

Over the past decade, studies of web analytics in journalism studies have dramatically increased. These studies have conceptualized web analytics in journalism in multiple ways. Researchers have conceptualized analytics as a mechanism that allows audience feedback to flow into the newsroom (Tandoc 2014; see also: Banjac, this volume). Research has shown how the activities that are part of analytics in journalism are a form of "participative gatekeeping" that facilitates audience influence on news construction processes (Neheli 2018). Scholars have also looked at metrics as tools that facilitate audience quantification (Anderson 2011), and analytics in journalism has been understood as part of the rationalization of audience understandings (Tandoc 2019; Zamith 2018). For example, Tandoc (2014) showed how journalistic uses of web analytics highlight the normalization of technology and emerging ways of working, thus changing the actors and processes of gatekeeping. This section catalogs the intertwined explanatory factors that the literature on web analytics has analyzed in the past decade. This literature focuses on gatekeeping theory's five levels of forces: individual, routines, organization, social institutions, and social system.

Individual

First, individual forces refer to the gatekeeper's personal tastes, though they can't be understood without also understanding the professional routines that shape these individual gatekeeping behaviors. While audience metrics existed before, they were limited (and still are) due to resistance from journalists and editors to utilize them (Ryfe 2012; Deuze 2008). Anderson argued that "journalists' professional self-conception and their paternalistic vision of its audience" has limited the effects of audience measurement technologies (Anderson 2011: 554). Based on qualitative findings, Weblers and colleagues found that "the influence of audience clicks on news selection was denied or strongly nuanced" (2006: 13). "This discrepancy can be explained as a manifestation of the struggle journalists are engaged in to balance audience preferences with their professional judgment," the scholars added (2006: 14; cf. Tandoc and Thomas 2015). Furthermore, research shows that individual journalists' perceptions concerning news metrics significantly influence how they utilize them (Tandoc and Ferrucci 2017). Therefore, web analytics impacts gatekeeping on the individual level in a variety of manners, mostly concerning individual newsworkers' perceptions.

Routines

Second, routine forces in gatekeeping differ from individual forces focused on journalists' and editors' preferences to focus instead on professional journalistic routines or the normative patterns that transcend individual organizations and exist across the journalism field (Shoemaker et al. 2001). With real-time information such as page views or click through rates provided by web analytics, journalists and editors can understand digital news audiences in detail. Research has shown that audience metrics act as gatekeepers of news, with Lee, Lewis, and Powers (2014) demonstrating how audience clicks affected the placement of stories on a webpage. Vu (2014) surveyed American newspaper and news sites editors, finding that editors claim that they are "willing to adjust their editorial decision-making based on web metrics" (Vu 2014: 11), though other studies have found contradictory positions (Zamith 2015). Similarly, Karlsson and Clerwall found that the impact of web analytics in Swedish newsrooms is highly "moderated by journalists and their news judgment" (2013: 73). There is no debate, then, that metrics have catalyzed new routines and affected traditional ones in terms of news production processes.

Organizational

Third, organizational forces also affect the work of journalists. Scholars argued that the organizational environment contributes to the adoption and implementation of news analytics in organizations. MacGregor (2007) showed that news and brand values may push journalists toward considering audience behaviors, as a counter-weight to market pressures for organizations to grow audience members, thus relying less on journalistic gut feeling or "instinct" and individual preferences. Cheribini and Nielsen (2015) found that digital news organizations are developing different forms of editorial analytics tailored to their goals, priorities, and situations. These vary from rudimentary to generic approaches:

> (1) in being aligned with the editorial priorities and organisational imperatives (whether commercial, non-profit, or public service) of specific news organisa-tions, (2) in informing both short-term day-to-day decisions and longer-term strategic development, and (3) in continually evolving to keep pace with a changing media environment.
>
> *(Cheribini and Nielsen 2015: 7)*

Institutional culture has had a heavy impact on the conceptualization of metrics in newsrooms. Bunce's (2015) study of African foreign correspondents demonstrated that based on readership rates, news directors praised and/or criticized journalists. Ferrer-Conill and Tandoc (2018) showed how audience-oriented editors whose work focus is on different types of metrics have increasingly populated newsrooms, claiming that they act as intermediaries to help journalists balance between informa-tion obtained by metrics and journalistic intuition in the editorial process (see also Bélair-Gagnon and Holton 2019). They noted that there is a lack of cohesiveness in the definition and conceptualization of engagement in organizations.

Studies of web analytics and gatekeeping have shown the tools themselves provide little to no information to journalists unless they are socially contextualized (see also Cohen 2019; Nelson and Tandoc 2019). In an ethnographic study of Al Jazeera English online, Usher (2013) found that because, at the time, the Al Jazeera English remained sheltered from the same financial perils the news industry was facing as, it is owned by a rich family, the culture of Al Jazeera English shaped journalistic uses and understanding of metrics. Since Al Jazeera English was not fighting for survival, jour-nalists felt that they were supported by their news organization and were thus capable to ignore analytics and metrics and rather favor their editorial judgement.

Research has also sought to determine the kinds of people and processes that may be "most influential in shaping the social rules and expectations that media workers incorporate in their use and rationalization of audience analytics and metric" (Zamith, Bélair-Gagnon, and Lewis 2019: 1780). In that study of formal and informal socialization mechanisms in US newsrooms (e.g., common training session, shared socialization, comparable on-the-job experiences, and mutual coordination), Zamith, myself, and Lewis also found that while respondents claimed receiving a moderate amount of analytics training and responded mostly to their internal referents (prescriptive learning), particularly superiors, when thinking about metrics, they learned about analytics through observing and communicating with others (non-experiential learning mechanisms) as being particularly influential. At the same time, experience varies across situational contexts and while the organizational context mattered for these journalists, the media workers' position within the institutional hierarchy was also significant (see also Bélair-Gagnon 2018; Petre 2018). This indicates that in the early phase of technological adoption of systems such as analytics, the formation and diffusion of norms are locally situated and less institutionalized (Zamith, Bélair-Gagnon, and Lewis 2019: 1780).

Market orientation forces, and whether news organizations are strongly or more weakly market oriented, has also been shown to have an effect on the uses of web analytics in newsrooms (Ferrucci 2018; Ferrucci 2020; McManus 1994). Such shifts in newsrooms' cultures may transform news organizations that would otherwise have been promoting civic objectives (Tandoc and Thomas 2015; Whipple and Shermak 2018). Indeed, journalists have claimed that audience metrics have been more useful in advancing consumer role orientations than citizen ones (Bélair-Gagnon, Zamith, and Holton 2020: 15). These findings illustrate how organizational context, from ownership to market orientation to organizational culture to technological adoption, impact news metric use in gatekeeping processes.

Social institutions

Fourth, analytics have become part of social institutions influencing journalism, meaning influences that are outside of journalism as an institution, given that they have a mutual dependence. Tandoc (2019) argued from a field theory and gatekeeping perspective that web analytics are meeting points between actors, including technologists, advertisers, journalists, and audiences, each with a set of different interests, motivations and expectations about their function and roles, and each bringing new rules, practices, and interests. Such forms of negotiation are not that straightforward and implicate power relations that involve competition and collaboration. In the context of training, most newsroom training about analytics "comes from the outside, it more often comes from within the immediate field (i.e. a parent organization rather than an outside analytics company)" (Zamith, Bélair-Gagnon, and Lewis 2019: 17). We argued further:

> Thus, while external organizations – and analytics companies in particular – exert ample influence in establishing the technological affordances, their direct influence on how media workers perceive acceptable practices in newsrooms, as measured through training, is perhaps less consequential than previously thought.
>
> *(Zamith et al. 2019: 17)*

Other aspects of analytics remain understudied as they are situated in a "black box" of proprietary software, including social post meta data or algorithms. These are harder to unpack but are nevertheless contributing to the social institutions that are influencing journalism, perhaps in their dark corners (Diakopoulos and Koliska, 2016; Welbers and Opgenhaffen 2018). Furthermore, in the simplest manner, companies producing analytics software significantly affect journalistic practice and, therefore gatekeeping, as choices made about software functionality then impact how journalists do their jobs. In effect, analytics companies, many of which are technology companies in Silicon Valley are most plainly social institutions impacting journalism and gatekeeping (see Russell and Vos chapter in this volume).

Social systems

Finally, the social system refers to macro-level influence of social and cultural structures and societal values (Hallin and Mancini 2017). The different valuations of metrics depend on media environments. Therefore, for example, while software packages may be identical, they vary across national borders. A large amount of English-speaking research emerged from Western examples where professionalism and competition among media organizations can be heightened (Petre 2018; Vu 2014; Anderson 2011). Christin (2018: 156) shows how journalists in two different countries saw the same metrics differently. In the US, editors rely on both metrics (heavily) and the opinion of their peers in decision-making. Conversely, at a French website, editors seemed more conflicted about using metrics while their staff writers were fixated on metrics, seeing these numbers as a reflection of the public sphere within which they were operating.

These differences can be partly explained by the unique journalistic traditions and trajectories of the two countries. In France and the United States, journalists have a different conception of their professional journalistic autonomy, relation with the market, the state, and their public role, with high measures of professionalization in US journalism and a longer history of state support, with latter professionalization, for French journalism. In the Netherlands, the field is professionalized but less market dominated, contributing to a different valuation of analytics (Weblers et al. 2016). Using a survey method of online editors, Tandoc also argued that "journalists' perception of competition in the field and their conceptions of the audience as a particular form of capital lead them to using Web analytics in particular ways" (2015: 782).

Conclusion

This chapter has shown that web analytics have become a cog in the gatekeeping process, across individual, routines, organizational, social institution, and social systems levels. The chapter has also shown their pervasiveness in journalism is complex and yields contradicting results depending on the setting, including within different journalism organizations and cultures, and further has shown their contribution varies according to the case being studied. These systems and tools have become embedded within the tensions that have shaped professional journalism as a field, and further that they are representative of a long-running turn toward the quantification of audiences within journalism.

As Christin (2018: 72) puts it, while editorial journalism values original reporting, background information, and news in dictating the format of the article, click-based journalism driven by metrics values communication with readers, being "webby" or reactive. This latter perspective sees long articles as being boring, with audiences dictating what content is relevant. Signs of editorial success included being followed by competitors' outlets and agencies and compliments by colleagues and competitors, while click-based success was evaluated by the number of page views, likes and tweets, going viral, trending, organic traffic, or "buzzing", suggesting that analytics leave plenty of room for interpretation (see also Bélair-Gagnon 2019).

Before analytics and other measurement tools became commonplace, journalists tended to decide themselves what to report on and publish and in turn imagined that their audience would agree with them and their decision making. Those individual decisions were certainly impacted by a constellation of influences across various levels of analysis, but not by outside institutions such as web analytics impacting all five levels. Now, news organizations track exposure data such as the number of people who visited a site and the amount of time spent on a site, the number of social media mentions, or the number of visits an audience member makes before becoming a subscriber, seeing these metrics as measurements to supplant the journalists' own imagination of the audience. The valuation of these metrics, however, varies from taking these into slower decision-making processes and long-term editorial strategies (i.e., editorial evaluation), to rapid use of real-time analytics (i.e., click-based evaluation). Further, while editorial valuation can be collective (i.e., assessing the metrics at the site or section level), click-based valuation is often individualized (i.e., at the level of the writer or article) (see Petre 2015).

In the end, the way journalists respond to analytics vary across organizations. As Nelson (2021) suggested, the way that journalists make sense of audiences tells us something of the way that audiences have become part of the journalistic institution or not. Analytics are not outside nor are they insiders of journalism, they rather have become a ubiquitous part of the field and the larger process of journalists rationalizing their understandings of the audiences their content reaches. Therefore, it remains vitally important for journalism studies as a field to acknowledge that news metrics are not simply another technological tool, but a disruption affecting practice, and gatekeeping particularly, across all levels of analysis.

References

Anderson, C. W. 2011. "Between Creative and Quantified Audiences: Web Metrics and Changing Patterns of Newswork in Local US Newsrooms." *Journalism* 12 (5): 550–566.

Andersson, Ulrika. 2013. "Contribution or Constrain? Audience Interaction in Swedish Online Newspapers." *Asian Journal of Humanities and Social Studies* 1 (05). https://pdfs.semanticscholar.org/5bcb/35cd2e2c9e1ca9f3257c6d9e04b951387bd8.pdf.

Bélair-Gagnon, Valérie. 2018. "News on the Fly: Journalist-Audience Online Engagement Success as a Cultural Matching Process." *Media Culture & Society* 41 (6): 757–773.

Bélair-Gagnon, Valérie, and Avery E. Holton. 2018. "Boundary Work, Interloper Media, And Analytics in Newsrooms: An Analysis of the Roles of Web Analytics Companies in News Production." *Digital Journalism* 6 (4): 492–508.

Bélair-Gagnon, Valérie, Rodrigo Zamith, and Avery E. Holton. 2020. "Role Orientations and Audience Metrics in Newsrooms: An Examination of Journalistic Perceptions and Their Drivers." *Digital Journalism*, January: 1–20.

Bird, S. Elizabeth. 2011. "Are We All Produsers Now?" *Cultural Studies of Science Education* 25 (4–5):502–516.

Bruns, Axel. 2008. "The Active Audience: Transforming Journalism from Gatekeeping to Gatewatching." http://snurb.info/files/The%20Active%20Audience.pdf.

Bunce, Mel. 2015. "Africa in the Click Stream: Audience Metrics and Foreign Correspondents in Africa." *African Journalism Studies* 36 (4): 12–29.

Carlson, Matt. 2018. "Confronting Measurable Journalism." *Digital Journalism* 6 (4): 406–417.

Cherubini, Federa, and Rasmus Kleis Nielsen. 2015. *Editorial Analytics: How News Media Are Developing and Using Audience Data and Metrics*. Oxford, UK: Reuters Institute for the Study of Journalism.

Christin, Angèle. 2018. "Counting Clicks: Quantification and Variation in Web Journalism in the United States and France." *The American Journal of Sociology* 123 (5): 1382–1415.

Christin, Angèle. 2020. *Metrics at Work: Journalism and the Contested Meaning of Algorithms*. Princeton, NJ: Princeton University Press.

Cohen, Nicole S. 2019. "At Work in the Digital Newsroom." *Digital Journalism* 7 (5): 571–591.

Deuze, Mark. 2008. "Understanding Journalism as Newswork: How It Changes, and How It Remains the Same." *Westminster Papers in Communication & Culture* 5 (2): 4–23.

Diakopoulos, Nicholas, and Michael Koliska. 2016. "Algorithmic Transparency." *Digital Journalism* 5 (7): 809–828.

Ferrer-Conill, Raul, and Edson C. Tandoc. 2018. "The Audience-Oriented Editor: Making Sense of the Audience in the Newsroom." *Digital Journalism* 6 (4): 436–453.

Ferrucci, Patrick. 2018. "Money Matters? Journalists' Perception of the Effects of a Weak Market Orientation." *Convergence: The International Journal of Research into New Media Technologies* 24(4), 424–438.

Ferrucci, Patrick. 2020. "It Is in the Numbers: How Market Orientation Impacts Journalists' Use of News Metrics." *Journalism* 21 (2): 244–261.

Ferrucci, Patrick, Jacob L. Nelson, and Miles P. Davis. 2020. "From 'Public Journalism' to 'Engaged Journalism': Imagined Audiences and Denigrating Discourse." *International Journal of Communication Systems* 14 (2020): 1586–1604.

Gans, Herbert. 1979. *Deciding What's News: A Study of CBS Evening News, NBC Nightly News, Newsweek, and Time*. Chicago, IL: Northwestern University Press.

Hallin, Daniel C., and Paolo Mancini. 2017. "Ten Years After Comparing Media Systems: What Have We Learned?" *Political Communication* 34 (2): 155–171.

Karlsson, Michael, and Christer Clerwall. 2013. "Negotiating Professional News Judgment and 'Clicks.'" *NORDICOM Review* 34 (2): 65–76.

Kim, Jisu, Seth C.Lewis, and Brendan R. Watson. 2018. "The Imagined Audience for and Perceived Quality of News Comments: Exploring the Perceptions of Commenters on News Sites and on Facebook." *Social Media + Society* 4 (1): 1–20.

Lee, Angela M., Seth C. Lewis, and Matthew Powers. 2014. "Audience Clicks and News Placement: A Study of Time-Lagged Influence in Online Journalism." *Communication Research* 41 (4): 505–530.

Lewis, Seth C., and Oscar Westlund. 2015. "Actors, Actants, Audiences, and Activities in Cross-Media News Work: A Matrix and a Research Agenda." *Digital Journalism* 3 (1): 19–37.

Lim, Shawn. 2019. "How the BBC Uses Programmatic Ads to Distribute Branded Content." https://www.thedrum.com/news/2019/05/17/how-the-bbc-uses-programmatic-ads-distribute-branded-content.

MacGregor, Phil. 2007. "Tracking the Online Audience." *Journalism Studies* 8 (2): 280–298.

McManus, John H. 1994. *Market-Driven Journalism: Let the Citizen Beware?* Thousand Oaks, CA: Sage Publications.

Neheli, Nicole Blanchett. 2018. "News by Numbers: The Evolution of Analytics in Journalism." *Digital Journalism* 6 (8): 1041–1051.

Nelson, Jacob L. (2021). *Imagined Audiences*. Oxford: Oxford University Press.

Nelson, Jacob L., and Edson C. Tandoc. 2019. "Doing 'Well' or Doing 'Good': What Audience Analytics Reveal about Journalism's Competing Goals." *Journalism Studies* 20 (13): 1960–1976.

Petre, Caitlin. 2015. "The Traffic Factories: Metrics at Chartbeat, Gawker Media, and *The New York Times*." http://towcenter.org/research/traffic-factories/.

Petre, Caitlin. 2018. "Engineering Consent: How the Design and Marketing of Newsroom Analytics Tools Rationalize Journalists' Labor." *Digital Journalism* 6 (4): 509–527.

Rauch, Jennifer. 2007. "Activists as Interpretive Communities: Rituals of Consumption and Interaction in an Alternative Media Audience." *Media Culture & Society* 29 (6): 994–1013.

Robinson, James G. 2019. "The Audience in the Mind's Eye: How Journalists Imagine Their Readers." https://academiccommons.columbia.edu/doi/10.7916/d8-drvj-wj06.

Ryfe, David. 2019. "The Warp and Woof of the Field of Journalism." *Digital Journalism* 7 (7): 844–859.

Ryfe, David M. 2012. *Can Journalism Survive: An Inside Look at American Newsrooms*. Cambridge, UK: Polity.

Shoemaker, Pamela J., Martin Eichholz, Eunyi Kim, and Brenda Wrigley. 2001. "Individual and Routine Forces in Gatekeeping." *Journalism & Mass Communication Quarterly* 78 (2): 233–246.

Tandoc, Edson C. 2014. "Journalism Is Twerking? How Web Analytics Is Changing the Process of Gatekeeping." *New Media & Society* 16 (14): 559–575.

Tandoc, Edson C. 2015. "Why Web Analytics Click: Factors Affecting the Ways Journalists Use Audience Metrics." *Journalism Studies* 16 (6): 782–799.

Tandoc, Edson C. 2019. *Analyzing Analytics: Disrupting Journalism One Click at a Time*. London: Routledge.

Tandoc, Edson C., and Patrick Ferrucci. 2017. "Giving in or giving up: What makes journalists use audience feedback in their news work?" *Computers in Human Behavior* 68: 149–156.

Tandoc, Edson C., and Ryan J. Thomas. 2015. "The Ethics of Web Analytics." *Digital Journalism* 3 (2): 243–258.

Tuchman, Gaye. 1978. *Making News: A Study in the Construction of Reality*. New York, NY: Free Press.

Tufekci, Zeynep. 2017. *Twitter and Tear Gas: The Power and Fragility of Networked Protest*. New Haven, CT: Yale University Press.

Turow, Joseph, and Nick Couldry. 2018. "Media as Data Extraction: Towards a New Map of a Transformed Communications Field." *The Journal of Communication* 68 (2): 415–423.

Usher, Nikki. 2013. "Al Jazeera English Online: Understanding Web Metrics and News Production When a Quantified Audience Is Not a Commodified Audience." *Digital Journalism* 1 (3): 335–351.

Vos, Tim, and François Heinderyckx. 2015. *Gatekeeping in Transition*. London: Routledge.

Vu, Hong Tien. 2014. "The Online Audience as Gatekeeper: The Influence of Reader Metrics on News Editorial Selection." *Journalism* 15 (8): 1094–1110.

Welbers, Kasper, Wouter van Atteveldt, Jan Kleinnijenhuis, Nel Ruigrok, and Joep Schaper. 2016. "News Selection Criteria in the Digital Age: Professional Norms versus Online Audience Metrics." *Journalism* 17 (8): 1037–1053.

Welbers, Kasper, and Michaël Opgenhaffen. 2018. "Social Media Gatekeeping: An Analysis of the Gatekeeping Influence of Newspapers' Public Facebook Pages." *New Media & Society* 20 (12): 4728–4747.

Whipple, Kelsey N., and Jeremy L. Shermak. 2018. "Quality, Quantity and Policy: How Newspaper Journalists Use Digital Metrics to Evaluate Their Performance and Their Papers' Strategies." *#ISOJ Journal* 8 (1): 67–88.

White, David Manning. 1950. "The 'Gate Keeper': A Case Study in the Selection of News." *The Journalism Quarterly* 27 (4): 383–390.

Zamith, R. 2015. "Editorial Judgment in an Age of Data: How Audience Analytics and Metrics Are Influencing the Placement of News Products." https://conservancy.umn.edu/handle/11299/175385.

Zamith, Rodrigo. 2018. "Quantified Audiences in News Production: A Synthesis and Research Agenda." *Digital Journalism* 6 (4): 418–435.

Zamith, Rodrigo, Valérie Bélair-Gagnon, and Seth C. Lewis. 2019. "Constructing Audience Quantification: Social Influences and the Development of Norms about Audience Analytics and Metrics." *New Media & Society* 22 (10): 1763–1784.

11

JOURNALISM'S INTERACTIONS WITH SILICON VALLEY PLATFORMS

Social institutions, fields, and assemblages

Frank M. Russell and Tim P. Vos

In 2011, National Public Radio journalist Andy Carvin turned to Twitter to make sense of the Arab Spring uprisings (Hermida, Lewis, and Zamith 2014). Carvin used Twitter to identify non-elite, alternative sources – bypassing journalism's usual institutional dependence on elite, official information sources. The platform enabled a place for on-the-scene citizens in the construction of news, challenging traditional gatekeeping habits (Hermida, Lewis, and Zamith 2014). By the end of the decade, particularly after the 2016 US presidential election, this optimism had faded. Social media platforms had become sources of "fake news" (Tandoc, Jenkins, and Craft 2019), or viral misinformation that could dupe citizens as much as empower them. Silicon Valley platforms, especially Facebook, Google, Apple, and Twitter, arguably had eclipsed journalism (Bell et al. 2017). Lasorsa, Lewis, and Holton (2012), Hermida (2013), and others were pioneers in studying journalists' use of platforms. By mid-2020, four leading journalism studies journals had published 182 articles with "Silicon Valley" or the name of one of these platforms in their titles or keywords. These articles paid particular attention to journalistic use of platforms at the individual and organizational levels (e.g., Canter 2015; Engesser and Humprecht 2015). Researchers focused especially on Twitter (e.g., Lewis and Molyneux 2018). More recently, scholars explored journalism's institutional-level relationship with Silicon Valley, noting that actors within each institution develop an approach to the other based on potentially conflicting institutional concerns (Russell 2019a; Vos and Russell 2019).

The purpose of this chapter is to examine more than a decade of research about journalism's relationship with Silicon Valley social media, mobile, and internet search platforms by using three theoretical lenses to highlight a range of concerns across the literature. In doing so, we take a step back and use institutional, field, and assemblage theories as heuristic tools to identify points of agreement and disagreement across this body of literature. Any theory is useful inasmuch as it directs

DOI: 10.4324/9781003140399-15

attention to particular features of a phenomenon, such as the journalism–Silicon Valley relationship, and inasmuch as it suggests an explanation for why things are the way they are. So, drawing from new institutional theory (Hall and Taylor 1996), Russell (2019a) concluded that Silicon Valley platforms interact as a combined institutional-level force that has taken control of exchanges of digital information throughout much of the world. Journalism has relatively weak autonomy as it interacts with Silicon Valley, and both institutions are subject to societal-level influences (Meese 2021; Vos and Russell 2019). Thus, this relationship also might be viewed from perspectives such as field theory (Bourdieu 2005) and assemblage theory (DeLanda 2006), which assume social institutions are less rigid. The next section will briefly review these theoretical perspectives.

Journalism and Silicon Valley as social institutions, fields, and assemblages

A social institution may be defined as "a set of rules that take shape and gain legitimacy over time" (Vos 2013: 39). Journalism in the US has been an institution since at least the 19th century, having met a three-part test: institutional norms governed journalistic practices, these practices endured over time and space, and elites communicated with the public under terms journalists controlled (Cook 2005). Among journalism's enduring norms are objectivity or balance (Schudson 2003). Silicon Valley emerged as a social institution at the turn of the 21st century. Silicon Valley firms also operate based on shared institutional values, among them a technocratic faith in engineers and entrepreneurs to develop solutions for societal problems, a "hacker" ideology blending counterculture idealism with capitalistic wealth creation, and the idea that information wants to be freely accessible (Sadowski and Selinger 2014; Turner and Larson 2015). While Silicon Valley's institutional values have not been in place as long as journalism's, Silicon Valley's control of digital communication has extended over much of the world and has largely superseded journalism as a means by which elites communicate with the public (Russell 2019a; Vos and Russell 2019).

According to new institutionalism, organizations exist mainly to convey institutional or cultural practices, and institutions are relatively fixed structures constrained by history or path dependency (Hall and Taylor 1996). However, institutions can change during critical junctures or transformative moments (Hall and Taylor 1996). Additionally, discourse in the form of "agents' thoughts, words, and actions" is an institutional change mechanism (Schmidt 2008: 314). From this perspective, Vos and Russell (2019) developed a framework to evaluate journalism's relationships with other social institutions. They concluded that: Silicon Valley algorithms apply regulatory pressure on journalistic actors sharing information on platforms; news media respond to a coercive pressure or fear of losing audiences to competitors who post on platforms; Silicon Valley's pressure influences both journalists and news managers; Silicon Valley has a greater effect on journalism as an institution than how individual journalists pursue news stories; and journalism's most likely means of resistance against Silicon Valley is its watchdog role monitoring tech platforms. They argued that societal-level pressure was necessary to change this relationship, but they were pessimistic that regulation protecting journalism could occur in the US political system.

By contrast, Wang (2020: 2) argued that the journalism-Silicon Valley relationship has evolved within a "constantly changing media and tech environment." In this view, interactions between journalism and Silicon Valley developed in a process of differentiation, in which strong demand exists for institutional autonomy, and dedifferentiation, in which institutional boundaries fade (Wang 2020). Silicon Valley's institutional power is indeed contingent, subject to forces such as technological change and government regulation (Meese 2021; Vos and Russell 2019; Wang 2020), suggesting a need for theory allowing more fluidity in institutional relationships. For that reason, we also consider institutional-level interactions from the perspectives of field theory (Bourdieu 2005) and assemblage theory (DeLanda 2006).

As with new institutionalism, field theory recognizes that past struggles have influenced fields such as journalism, but it puts more emphasis on power relations between fields and on their social standing or habitus (Benson and Neveu 2005). Scholars have used field theory to explore how the technological field has pressured journalistic boundaries. For example, Usher (2017) concluded that entrepreneurial news startups adhered to journalistic doxa or assumptions, while also adopting technocratic values of Silicon Valley, which Perrin (2002) described as a "discursive field" with an ideology valuing entrepreneurship and innovation. Similarly, technologists working with journalists learn journalism's rules even as a "Silicon Valley ethos" transforms journalistic practices (Wu, Tandoc, and Salmon, 2019: 1251). Drawing on the idea of institutions as interconnected fields (Bourdieu 2005), Wang (2020) described a push-pull between journalism and Silicon Valley since the 1990s, with dedifferentiation in the form of convergence dissolving boundaries between media and tech, followed by differentiation in which distinct divisions emerged between legacy and digital journalists in newsrooms. A second wave of dedifferentiation blurred boundaries between journalism and platforms in the 2010s, but uncertainty about Silicon Valley gatekeeping control prompted a second wave of differentiation in which journalists became "more strategic" about platforms (Wang 2020: 10).

According to assemblage theory (DeLanda 2016), individuals interact as components of multiple larger assemblages such as organizations, which in turn interact as parts of even larger institutional assemblages. Assemblage theory could help explain shifting dynamics of digital journalism, particularly those taking place within networks transcending levels of influence on news content (Reese 2016). In this view, "an assemblage can be a contingent set of relationships to accomplish shifting social objectives not otherwise defined by formal institutions" (Reese 2016: 821). For example, Anderson (2013) applied assemblage theory to news media in Philadelphia, where a network of blogs both depended on and challenged traditional news organizations. Wang (2020) connected differentiation and dedifferentiation to field theory. However, she also described a "rapidly evolving" news environment with interactions between "'old' and 'new' media actors" (Wang 2020: 509). This echoes the idea that assemblages continually constitute and reconstitute themselves (DeLanda 2016). Furthermore, differentiation and dedifferentiation are similar to assemblage theory's processes of territorialization and deterritorialization, with territorialization referring to interactions which sharpen an assemblage's material or expressive boundaries (DeLanda 2006). Assemblage theory largely rejects "institution" as a noun; instead, institutional organizations have characteristics such as institutional norms or practices (DeLanda 2006). From this perspective, institutional- and societal-level forces influence overlapping journalistic assemblages, some defined by national and other geographic boundaries (Reese 2016). For that reason, an exploration of journalism's relationship with Silicon Valley should take a cross-national approach, considering potential societal-level differences that influence journalists and media.

Taken together, the literature suggests this question: *How could journalism studies research regarding interaction by journalists and news organizations with Silicon Valley platforms be re-evaluated from the perspectives of institutional, field, and assemblage theories?*

The literature analyzed

We explored this question with a textual analysis of four leading academic journals. We examined articles from *Journalism Studies* and *Journalism: Theory, Practice and Criticism* because of their importance in journalism studies as a research field (Carlson et al. 2018), and *Journalism Practice* and *Digital Journalism* based on their affiliation with *Journalism Studies* and the role of *Digital Journalism* in extending journalism studies into the digital realm (Steensen et al. 2019). We selected articles with "Silicon Valley" or Silicon Valley-based platforms "Facebook," "Instagram," "WhatsApp," "Google," "YouTube," "Apple," "Twitter," or "Reddit" occurring in either the title or as a keyword. This resulted in 38 articles from *Journalism Studies,* 28 from *Journalism,* 56 from *Journalism Practice,* and 60 from *Digital Journalism.* For each article, we identified discourse signaling key concepts related to institutional, field, and assemblage theories. We then identified common themes, reported in the next section.

Findings

Scholars in the four journals described journalists' interactions with Silicon Valley platforms largely from three perspectives: (1) normalization of the use of social media, especially Twitter, into journalists' institutional practices and values (e.g., Lasorsa, Lewis, and Holton 2012); (2) as an expansion of journalistic boundaries, with journalists adopting practices more consistent with audience expectations for social media, but not altering the journalistic field substantially by abandoning established routines and principles (e.g., Canter 2015); or (3) as a potential transformation of the way news or other public information is selected, produced, and shared with and by audiences (e.g., Hermida 2013). This section will summarize and critique these findings.

Normalization and the institutional view

Institutional theory suggests journalists will adapt established values and practices to their use of new technologies. Arguably, this is represented in the finding that journalists have normalized Twitter into existing work routines (Lasorsa, Lewis, and Holton 2012). Numerous articles confirmed this assertion for Western journalists. For example, a study comparing Swedish journalists active on Twitter with others who were not found few differences in terms of "professional practices and norms" (Hedman 2015: 287). An examination of Twitter posts by US political journalists during the 2016 election indicated they rarely engaged with members of the public, instead interacting mainly with other journalists or using the reply function to create threads circumventing the character limit of tweets (Molyneux and Mourão 2019). Among journalists for a UK city newspaper, encouraging citizen participation was rare, with journalists "still operating in a traditional gatekeeping manner" (Canter and Brookes 2016: 882). This established gatekeeping approach was evident in studies of organizational-level Twitter practices. For example, two studies concluded that news organizations in countries such as the US, UK, France, Germany, and Italy primarily used Twitter to distribute links to stories (Engesser and Humprecht 2015; Russell 2019b). A large-scale analysis of English-language tweets found news organizations used the platform widely for promotional purposes but have not adopted "the cultural norms of Twitter," particularly "when they conflict with the traditional practice of journalism" (Malik and Pfeffer 2016: 965). Other evidence supporting the concept of normalization was found in countries with differing media systems such as Russia, Lebanon, and Belgium (Bodrunova, Litvinenko, and Blekanov 2018; Kozman and Cozma 2021; Paulussen and Harder 2014). Articles involving journalists' use of WhatsApp noted it as potentially transformative, but also indicated institutional concerns among factors influencing practices on the messaging platform (Boczek and Koppers 2020; Dodds 2019). Similarly, early research about Twitter noted its transformative potential, but additional research tended to confirm the normalization concept.

While journalism studies scholars have examined how institutional values influence news media's interactions with platforms, they could devote more attention to how Silicon Valley's own technocratic institutional values affect this relationship (Russell 2019a; Vos and Russell 2019). In particular, more research could focus on algorithmic gatekeeping, which is central to Silicon Valley's regulative power (Vos and Russell 2019). Such research could follow the example of a study by Machill and Beiler (2009), which concluded that journalists searching for information online were ceding too much power to Google's algorithm, rarely looking past the first few pages of search results. Another study found Facebook's news feed algorithm relies on "personal significance," which differs from traditional news values such as deviance or social significance (DeVito 2017: 767). One article indicated Facebook's algorithm arguably has given too much attention to "fake news" or viral misinformation (Bakir and McStay 2018). A study of the presentation of news images on Instagram concluded that "today's photography is inevitably mediated by computer software – programming codes, data structures and algorithmic auto-mation" (Borges-Rey 2015: 575). Taken together, these articles contribute to a growing body of research demonstrating how platforms have shaped multiple aspects of communication, with consequences at levels from individuals to society (e.g., Gillespie 2010; Karppi and Nieborg 2021; Wajcman 2019). Arguably, platforms' algorithmic gatekeeping role has challenged journalistic boundaries or changed how citizens get news or other civic information, pointing to the need for attention to journalism's interactions with Silicon Valley from field or assemblage theory perspectives, which perhaps have more capacity to explain such transformation than institutionalism.

Expanding the journalistic field

Normalization and institutionalization arguments, above, are consistent with field theory to the extent that normalization of social media platforms is intended to protect journalism's boundaries and habitus. However, journalism studies scholars have also identified cases of individual journalists or news organizations using platforms in ways that expanded or blurred journalistic boundaries. This was evident in studies indicating journalists personalize their use of Twitter or other platforms or have engaged in per-sonal branding that might provide individual standing beyond their identity as news organization employees. For example, Canter intentionally described Twitter use as *personalized* instead of *personal*: Although journalists on Twitter might have crossed boundaries between objectivity and commentary, they did not necessarily reveal details of their private lives (Canter 2015; Canter and Brookes 2016). Other studies indicated that personalized commenting or sharing does not go so far as taking forceful stands on public controversies. A study of retweets by US political journalists, for instance, indi-cated that individuals challenged objectivity somewhat by "dabbling in opinion," but this was not akin to "the strong arguments found on an editorial page" (Molyneux 2015: 927). Twitter personalization by Dutch and Belgian journalists mainly involved "witty" insights and interactions with other journalists (Brems et al. 2017: 452).

Personalization considerations did not necessarily exist for most journalists on legacy platforms. Interviews with health journalists revealed a tension between traditional journalistic practices and personal branding techniques such as using humor in tweets, with journalists seeing "branding as a pathway to a greater level of engagement, one they said their editors and organizations have been pressuring them to explore for years" (Molyneux and Holton 2015: 232). One study indi-cated that Twitter's personalized "social media logic" was partly responsible for branding on the platform by Swedish journalists, who presented "themselves as being more audience oriented, networking, and individualistic, projecting a mixed identity including both professional and personal features" (Hedman 2020: 670). An exploration of branding on Twitter by US political journalists indicated that such features included legitimizing references to employers and journalism schools or other universities where they earned degrees, but also to personal interests and descriptions (Ottovordemgentschenfelde 2017). Journalists expressed mixed feelings about personal branding – e.g., reporters from major US newsrooms viewed personal branding as weakening their organizations in favor of creating "marketable 'stars'" (Chadha and Wells 2016: 1028).

New information assemblages

Given that institutional assemblages constitute themselves from interactions between components (DeLanda 2016), our findings have also been consistent with assemblage theory. Articles from the early 2010s referred to social platforms as potentially transformative for journalism, reinforcing how assemblage theory helps explain changes that occur across social institutions or gatekeeping levels (Reese 2016). For example, Hermida (2013) described Twitter's potential as a networked newsroom of journalists, activists, elites, and non-elite sources who work together to gather and verify information. An early exploration conceptualized Twitter as allowing for "long-term and relatively stable" networks built around connections between followers and "relatively short-term and emergent" networks based on hashtags indicating shared interests (Bruns and Burgess 2012: 803). One study described Twitter as transformative for journalists, who used it to find non-elite voices in coverage of civil unrest in the UK and "as a rich source for story leads and material" (Vis 2013: 43). Later in the decade, another article described a "hybrid normalization" of Twitter in which Italian journalists combined "old practices with new modalities" (Bentivegna and Marchetti 2018: 270). Scholars have found some evidence of transformation within journalism, or at least new hybrid forms of journalism existing alongside legacy media in different societies. One study identified a "hybrid cross-media news environment" in which election stories in Belgium broke on Twitter or newspaper websites, then spread to other platforms, increasing the reach of news (Harder, Paulussen, and Van Aelst 2016: 941). Swedish journalists who were highly active on Twitter described a hybrid environment in which they hold professional values while engaging with audiences and developing a personal brand (Hedman 2015). Indeed, another study described Twitter as a source of audience comment for the BBC in online coverage of terror attacks (Bennett 2016). Arguably, this element would not have existed in the same way without the platform. Other research found Facebook's WhatsApp messaging platform as potentially transformative for reporting and news distribution in Germany, Chile, and Rwanda (Boczek and Koppers 2020; Dodds 2019; McIntyre and Sobel 2019). Ultimately, these studies illustrate the existence of more *potential* for interactions between journalism, citizens, and social platforms rather than what may actually exist in most newsrooms. Instead, as we noted previously, research mostly described journalists integrating Twitter into established gatekeeping practices or personalizing social media by interacting with audiences or other journalists or expressing non-controversial opinions (Canter 2015; Engesser and Humprecht 2015; Lasorsa, Lewis, and Holton 2012; Molyneux 2015).

Nonetheless, scholars recognized that social media platforms have changed how public information is exchanged. However, any transformative news or information assemblages may have adopted media practices or affordances, but not necessarily journalistic values. For example, a study of hyper-partisan news on Facebook indicated audiences share such content more when author bylines are included, but they are even more likely to share stories reflecting frames related to conservative values such as respect for authority (Xu, Sang, and Kim 2020). Other scholars found at least a limited influence on public discourse from sharing of hyper-partisan news and misinformation in the US, Europe, and Africa (Bakir and McStay 2018; Kalsnes and Larsson 2021; Wasserman 2020).

Although articles in the four journals did not present overwhelming evidence that Silicon Valley platforms have transformed journalism, multiple studies indicated that platforms have changed audience interactions with journalism: For example, a powerful news event can disrupt users' visual routines on Instagram from posting original content to sharing images in support of a social cause or in sympathy for a tragedy (Al Nashmi 2018). Furthermore, audiences expect journalists to engage on social media in ways consistent with digital culture and consider journalists who do so as less biased (Diehl, Ardèvol-Abreu, and Gil de Zúñiga 2019). Additionally, news distribution across different types of media including social platforms increases its reach with audiences (Harder, Paulussen, and Van Aelst 2016).

Research also showed social connections beyond journalists' control might be a factor in this expanded reach. A study indicated that if a friend shared a news story on Facebook, a user could perceive it as more relevant than they would have otherwise (Kümpel 2019). Another study found citizens could use hashtags to take a secondary gatekeeping role in sharing news on Twitter (Masip, Ruiz, and Suau 2021). An exploration of Black Twitter in the aftermath of the 2014 police shooting of a Black man in Ferguson, Missouri, concluded it gave marginalized communities a virtual public sphere not provided by traditional media (Richardson 2017). Focusing on Reddit, Straub-Cook (2018: 1319–1320) described the r/Seattle subreddit forum as "an important social news site" in a city with "unique sources of localized, online information," suggesting the presence of a news assemblage similar to what Anderson (2013) described in Philadelphia. Audiences and journalists are not the only participants in these information assemblages; algorithms are also factors influencing what news stories users can find or share. For example, different factors influence Google search results for news events, including IP address, language settings, and country search domain – e.g., Google search sites for Denmark, Germany, and Austria (Ørmen 2016).

TABLE 11.1 Institutional, field, and assemblage theory perspectives

	Institutional-level relationships	Journalism-Silicon Valley relationship
Institutional theories	1. Social institutions are relatively fixed structures.	1. Journalists normalized social media use based on existing values and practices.
	2. Interactions between institutions are based on established institutional values and practices.	2. Silicon Valley claimed an algorithmic gatekeeping role based on technocratic values.
	3. Discourse and critical junctures are change mechanisms.	

	Institutional-level relationships	Journalism-Silicon Valley relationship
Field theory	1. Social institutions are shaped by habitus, doxa. 2. Social institutions have varying levels of autonomy or dependence on other social forces. 3. Internal and external forces protect, expand, or blur a social field's boundaries.	1. News media adopted Silicon Valley's market/innovation logic when it did not conflict with journalism's established values and practices. 2. Journalists personalized posts or branded themselves on platforms, accepting elements of social media logic.
Assemblage theory	1. Institutions do not exist, but institutional organizations or assemblages do. 2. Interactions occur across gatekeeping levels and decentralized networks. 3. Assemblages continually constitute and reconstitute themselves.	1. Some cases exist of journalists using platforms to embrace citizen participation, relinquishing gatekeeping control over news. 2. Audiences, sources, and misinformation promoters have bypassed journalism, but platforms control information distribution as algorithmic gatekeepers.

Discussion

This systematic review examined research about journalism's interactions with Silicon Valley platforms from three perspectives: new institutionalism (Hall and Taylor 1996; Vos and Russell 2019), field theory (Benson and Neveu 2005; Bourdieu 2005), and assemblage theory (DeLanda 2006; Reese 2016). These theories proved to be useful in understanding a range of findings across the body of literature we analyzed.

From a new institutionalism perspective, we can see that research indicates news media and journalists have normalized their use of Silicon Valley platforms by adopting existing institutional practices. This is especially the case for Twitter, which was by far the most studied platform (e.g., Hedman 2015; Lasorsa, Lewis, and Holton 2012; Molyneux and Mourão 2019). Additionally, research pointed to the role of algorithms shaped by Silicon Valley's own institutional values in controlling journalism's interactions with audiences. Taken together, these findings are consistent with the argument that journalism's relationship with Silicon Valley might be relatively fixed, but societal-level pressure could change the power dynamic between them (Vos and Russell 2019).

However, much of the research indicated that this relationship is influenced by varying approaches of individual journalists or news organizations within countries with different media systems. While the articles did not necessarily point to paths between differentiation and dedifferentiation as described by Wang (2020), they revealed that individual journalists and news organizations have experimented within a changing media and tech environment, in some cases discursively constructing expanded journalistic boundaries without fundamentally altering journalistic values (e.g., Canter 2015; Hedman 2020; Molyneux 2015). Tension was apparent between innovations of individual journalists such as Andy Carvin (Hermida, Lewis, and Zamith 2014), and the normalization of social media that dominated the journalistic field. This underscores field theory as a useful lens for studying journalism's interactions with Silicon Valley. In particular, as Wang (2020) argued, differentiation and dedifferentiation are concepts that could be incorporated into research concerning journalism and other institutions, complementing and extending the Vos and Russell (2019) framework.

As for assemblage theory, it provides a means to assess further contingencies or influences in the relationship between journalism and Silicon Valley platforms. This too was evident in our analysis. As Reese (2016) suggested, assemblage theory might be particularly helpful when journalism and other social institutions interact together with gatekeeping forces beyond the institutional level or with deinstitutionalized networks. For example, even as many articles concluded that journalists adapted existing practices to their social media use, others showed that Silicon Valley platforms have clearly transformed audience interactions with news and other civic information (e.g., Diehl, Ardèvol-Abreu, and Gil de Zúñiga 2019; Richardson 2017; Straub-Cook 2018).

Ultimately, scholars studying journalism's relationships with other social institutions might benefit from incorporating institutional, field, and assemblage theories into their research. This chapter's analysis considers how societal-level differences and similarities existed in interactions between journalists and platforms in countries with varying media and political systems, advancing our understanding of how these are theorized. However, even greater emphasis on cross-national research is possible, given that most articles focused on the US (e.g., Chadha and Wells 2016; Molyneux and Mourão 2019), UK (e.g., Canter and Brookes 2016; Vis 2013), or Northern Europe (e.g., Boczek and Koppers 2020; Kalsnes and Larsson 2021). Scholars could pay more attention to interaction with Silicon Valley platforms by journalists in Latin America, Africa, Asia, and elsewhere. This observation points to a limitation of the present study, suggesting that further analysis of journalism studies research should consider articles published in English and other languages in journals focusing on these parts of the world.

We summarize the contributions evident in our application of institutional, field, and assemblage theories to institutional-level relationships, and to the journalism-Silicon Valley relationship, in Table 11.1. We note, however, that on a basic level, the three theoretical lenses shared a common outlook: While some of the literature we analyzed seemed to construe the platforms as simply technologies, all three theories see journalism's relationship with Silicon Valley platforms as a social relationship among agentic actors. A selection of different theoretical lenses might draw our attention to different understandings of the journalism-Silicon Valley relationship.

Our journalism studies focus also may have put too much attention on how journalism actors interact with Silicon Valley platforms and not enough on the role of Silicon Valley actors or those outside either social institution. Journalism studies scholars could look closer at research in journals such as *New Media & Society* (e.g., Gillespie 2010), which has put more emphasis on institutional concerns of Silicon Valley platforms and actors. For example, Karppi and Nieborg (2021) analyzed discourse of prominent Silicon Valley actors who expressed regret over platforms' complicity in the spread of misinformation during the 2016 US presidential election, but the *mea culpa* writers did not go so far as to abandon their positions and accompanying values within the technology industries. On a more functional level, Wajcman (2019) explored how digital calendar developers reflect Silicon Valley's work-centric culture. Ultimately, research focusing on Silicon Valley and its values can help explain its influence on journalism and other institutions in a way that studies focusing solely on those influenced cannot. Additionally, media economics scholars (e.g., Napoli and Caplan 2017) have drawn attention to potential regulation of platform firms to change the power dynamic between Silicon Valley and journalism. Although we have argued that Silicon Valley has emerged as a powerful social institution and expressed pessimism about the prospect of societal-level intervention in the US media system (Russell 2019a; Vos and Russell 2019), greater regulation of platform firms now seems possible – signaling a possible critical juncture putting Silicon Valley and other social institutions on a new path. Federal and state regulators in the US have filed antitrust claims against Facebook and Google (Ryan 2020), and conservative politicians, long resistant to regulation, now claim they have been "silenced" by Twitter and Facebook and are more willing to impose government control (McKinnon and Ryan 2020). Regardless of the outcome of these regulatory attempts, this potential for change reinforces the need to incorporate institutional, field, and assemblage theories into research about journalism's institutional-level interactions with Silicon Valley platforms.

Conclusion

This chapter explored how Silicon Valley platforms have influenced journalistic practice. It underscores our previous conclusion that journalism and Silicon Valley interact with each other based on potentially conflicting institutional-level concerns (Russell 2019a; Vos and Russell 2019). In particular, journalists resisted expanded gatekeeping participation made possible by platforms and instead normalized their use of Twitter, protecting their traditional gatekeeping authority (Lasorsa, Lewis and Holton 2012). However, our findings also support the view that the journalism-Silicon Valley relationship is more fluid (Wang 2020). Multiple articles showed journalists adopted social media values when they did not conflict with traditional journalistic values such as objectivity. This hybrid model arguably blurred or expanded journalism's boundaries (see Hepp and Loosen, this volume). We did not find much evidence beyond some notable exceptions that journalists welcomed transformations enabled by digital media assemblages. However, audiences embraced Silicon Valley platforms to engage with news and other information, requiring news media to interact with platforms, regardless of whether journalists are willing participants.

References

Al Nashmi, Eisa. 2018. "From Selfies to Media Events: How Instagram Users Interrupted Their Routines After the Charlie Hebdo Shootings." *Digital Journalism* 6 (1): 98–117.

Anderson, Christopher William. 2013. *Rebuilding the News: Metropolitan Journalism in the Digital Age*. Philadelphia: Temple University.

Bakir, Vian, and Andrew McStay. 2018. "Fake News and the Economy of Emotions: Problems, Causes, Solutions." *Digital Journalism* 6 (2): 154–175.

Bell, Emily J., Taylor Owen, Peter D. Brown, Codi Hauka, and Nushin Rashidian. 2017. *The Platform Press: How Silicon Valley Reengineered Journalism*. New York: Tow Center for Digital Journalism.

Bennett, Daniel. 2016. "Sourcing the BBC's Live Online Coverage of Terror Attacks." *Digital Journalism* 4 (7): 861–874.

Benson, Rodney, and Erik Neveu. 2005. "Introduction: Field Theory as a Work in Progress." In *Bourdieu and the Journalistic Field*, edited by Rodney Benson and Erik Neveu, pp. 1–28. Malden, MA: Polity Press.

Bentivegna, Sara, and Rita Marchetti. 2018. "Journalists at a Crossroads: Are Traditional Norms and Practices Challenged by Twitter?" *Journalism* 19 (2): 270–290.

Boczek, Karin, and Lars Koppers. 2020. "What's New about WhatsApp for News? A Mixed-Method Study on News Outlets' Strategies for Using WhatsApp." *Digital Journalism* 8 (1): 126–144.

Bodrunova, Svetlana S., Anna A. Litvinenko, and Ivan S. Blekanov. 2018. "Please Follow Us: Media Roles in Twitter Discussions in the United States, Germany, France, and Russia." *Journalism Practice* 12 (2): 177–203.

Borges-Rey, Eddy. 2015. "News Images on Instagram: The Paradox of Authenticity in Hyperreal Photo Reportage." *Digital Journalism* 3 (4): 571–593.

Bourdieu, Pierre. 2005. "The Political Field, the Social Science Field, and the Journalistic Field." In *Bourdieu and the Journalistic Field*, edited by Rodney Benson and Erik Neveu, pp. 29–47. Malden, MA: Polity Press.

Brems, Cara, Martina Temmerman, Todd Graham, and Marcel Broersma. 2017. "Personal Branding on Twitter: How Employed and Freelance Journalists Stage Themselves on Social Media." *Digital Journalism* 5 (4): 443–459.

Bruns, Axel, and Jean Burgess. 2012. "Researching News Discussion on Twitter: New Methodologies." *Journalism Studies* 13 (5–6): 801–814.

Canter, Lily. 2015. "Personalised Tweeting: The Emerging Practices of Journalists on Twitter." *Digital Journalism* 3 (6): 888–907.

Canter, Lily, and Daniel Brookes. 2016. "Twitter as a Flexible Tool: How the Job Role of the Journalist Influences Tweeting Habits." *Digital Journalism* 4 (7): 875–885.

Carlson, Matt, Sue Robinson, Seth C. Lewis, and Daniel A. Berkowitz. 2018. "Journalism Studies and its Core Commitments: The Making of a Communication Field." *Journal of Communication* 68 (1): 6–25.

Chadha, Kalyani, and Rob Wells. 2016. "Journalistic Responses to Technological Innovation in Newsrooms: An Exploratory Study of Twitter Use." *Digital Journalism* 4 (8): 1020–1035.

Cook, Timothy E. 2005. *Governing with the News: The News Media as a Political Institution*. 2nd ed. Chicago: University of Chicago Press.

DeLanda, Manuel. 2006. *A New Philosophy of Society: Assemblage Theory and Social Complexity*. London: Continuum.

DeLanda, Manuel. 2016. *Assemblage Theory (Speculative Realism)*. Edinburgh: Edinburgh University Press.

DeVito, Michael A. 2017. "From Editors to Algorithms: A Values-based Approach to Understanding Story Selection in the Facebook News Feed." *Digital Journalism* 5 (6): 753–773.

Diehl, Trevor, Alberto Ardèvol-Abreu, and Homero Gil de Zúñiga. 2019. "How Engagement with Journalists on Twitter Reduces Public Perceptions of Media Bias." *Journalism Practice* 13 (8): 971–975.

Dodds, Tomás. 2019. "Reporting with WhatsApp: Mobile Chat Applications' Impact on Journalistic Practices." *Digital Journalism* 7 (6): 725–745.

Engesser, Sven, and Edda Humprecht. 2015. "Frequency or Skillfulness: How Professional News Media Use Twitter in Five Western Countries." *Journalism Studies* 16 (4): 513–529.

Gillespie, Tarleton. 2010. "The Politics of 'Platforms'." *New Media & Society* 12 (3): 347–364.

Hall, Peter A., and Rosemary C. R. Taylor. 1996. "Political Science and the Three New Institutionalisms." *Political Studies* 44 (5): 936–957.

Harder, Raymond A., Steve Paulussen, and Peter Van Aelst. 2016. "Making Sense of Twitter Buzz: The Cross-media Construction of News Stories in Election Time." *Digital Journalism* 4 (7): 933–943.

Hedman, Ulrika. 2015. "J-Tweeters: Pointing Towards a New Set of Professional Practices and Norms in Journalism." *Digital Journalism* 3 (2): 279–297.

Hedman, Ulrika. 2020. "Making the Most of Twitter: How Technological Affordances Influence Swedish Journalists' Self-branding." *Journalism* 21 (5): 670–687.

Hermida, Alfred. 2013. "#Journalism: Reconfiguring Journalism Research about Twitter, One Tweet at a Time." *Digital Journalism* 1 (3): 295–313.

Hermida, Alfred, Seth C. Lewis, and Rodrigo Zamith. 2014. "Sourcing the Arab Spring: A Case Study of Andy Carvin's Sources on Twitter during the Tunisian and Egyptian Revolutions." *Journal of Computer-Mediated Communication* 19 (3): 479–499.

Kalsnes, Bente, and Anders Olof Larsson. 2021. "Facebook News Use During the 2017 Norwegian Elections – Assessing the Influence of Hyperpartisan News." *Journalism Practice*, 1–17.

Karppi, Tero, and David B. Nieborg. 2021. "Facebook Confessions: Corporate Abdication and Silicon Valley Dystopianism." *New Media & Society*. 23 (9): 2634–2649.

Kozman, Claudia, and Raluca Cozma. 2021. "Lebanese Television on Twitter: A Study of Uses and (Dis) Engagement." *Journalism Practice* 15 (4): 508–525.

Kümpel, Anna Sophie. 2019. "The Issue Takes It All? Incidental News Exposure and News Engagement on Facebook." *Digital Journalism* 7 (2): 165–186.

Lasorsa, Dominic L., Seth C. Lewis, and Avery E. Holton. 2012. "Normalizing Twitter: Journalism Practice in an Emerging Communication Space." *Journalism Studies* 13 (1): 19–36.

Lewis, Seth C., and Logan Molyneux. 2018. "A Decade of Research on Social Media and Journalism: Assumptions, Blind Spots, and a Way Forward." *Media and Communication* 6 (4): 11–23.

Machill, Marcel, and Markus Beiler. 2009. "The Importance of the Internet for Journalistic Research: A Multi-method Study of the Research Performed by Journalists Working for Daily Newspapers, Radio, Television and Online." *Journalism Studies* 10 (2): 178–203.

Malik, Momin M, and Jürgen Pfeffer. 2016. "A Macroscopic Analysis of News Content in Twitter." *Digital Journalism* 4 (8): 955–979.

Masip, Pere, Carles Ruiz, and Jaume Suau. 2019. "Contesting Professional Procedures of Journalists: Public Conversation on Twitter after Germanwings Accident." *Digital Journalism* 7 (6): 762–782.

McIntyre, Karen, and Meghan Sobel. 2019. "How Rwandan Journalists Use WhatsApp to Advance Their Profession and Collaborate for the Good of Their Country." *Digital Journalism* 7 (6): 705–724.

McKinnon, John D., and Tracy Ryan. 2020. "Zuckerberg, Dorsey Tout Progress in Combating Political Misinformation: Senators Warn Facebook, Twitter CEOs about Tougher Regulation of Social Media." *Wall Street Journal*, November 17. https://www.wsj.com/articles/facebook-twitter-ceos-brace-for-another-grilling-before-senate-committee-11605620848.

Meese, James. 2021. "Journalism Policy Across the Commonwealth: Partial Answers to Public Problems." *Digital Journalism* 9 (3): 255–275.

Molyneux, Logan. 2015. "What Journalists Retweet: Opinion, Humor, and Brand Development on Twitter." *Journalism* 16 (7): 920–935.

Molyneux, Logan, and Avery Holton. 2015. "Branding (Health) Journalism: Perceptions, Practices, and Emerging Norms." *Digital Journalism* 3 (2): 225–242.

Molyneux, Logan, and Rachel R. Mourão. 2019. "Political Journalists' Normalization of Twitter: Interaction and New Affordances." *Journalism Studies* 20 (2): 248–266.

Napoli, Philip, and Robyn Caplan. 2017. "Why Media Companies Insist They're Not Media Companies, Why They're Wrong, and Why It Matters." *First Monday* 22 (5). doi:10.5210/fm.v22i5.7051.

Ørmen, Jacob. 2016. "Googling the News: Opportunities and Challenges in Studying News Events through Google Search." *Digital Journalism* 4 (1): 107–124.

Ottovordemgentschenfelde, Svenja. 2017. "'Organizational, Professional, Personal': An Exploratory Study of Political Journalists and their Hybrid Brand on Twitter." *Journalism* 18 (1): 64–80.

Paulussen, Steve, and Raymond A. Harder. 2014. "Social Media References in Newspapers: Facebook, Twitter and YouTube as Sources in Newspaper Journalism." *Journalism Practice* 8 (5): 542–551.

Perrin, Andrew J. 2002. "Making Silicon Valley: Culture, Representation, and Technology at the Tech Museum." *The Communication Review* 5 (2): 91–108.

Reese, Stephen D. 2016. "The New Geography of Journalism Research: Levels and Spaces." *Digital Journalism* 4 (7): 816–826.

Richardson, Allissa V. 2017. "Bearing Witness While Black: Theorizing African American Mobile Journalism after Ferguson." *Digital Journalism* 5 (6): 673–698.

Russell, Frank Michael. 2019a. "The New Gatekeepers: An Institutional-level View of Silicon Valley and the Disruption of Journalism." *Journalism Studies* 20 (5): 631–648.

Russell, Frank Michael. 2019b. "Twitter and News Gatekeeping: Interactivity, Reciprocity, and Promotion in News Organizations' Tweets." *Digital Journalism* 7 (1): 80–99.

Ryan, Tracy. 2020. "More States Hit Google over Alleged Monopoly Conduct: Case Follows Probe into Search Business by Colorado and Other States." *Wall Street Journal*, December 17. https://www.wsj.com/articles/states-file-antitrust-lawsuit-against-google-11608228334.

Sadowski, Jathan, and Evan Selinger. 2014. "Creating a Taxonomic Tool for Technocracy and Applying it to Silicon Valley." *Technology in Society* 38 (1): 161–168.

Schmidt, Vivien A. 2008. "Discursive Institutionalism: The Explanatory Power of Ideas and Discourse." *Annual Review of Political Science* 11: 303–326.

Schudson, Michael. 2003. *The Sociology of News*. New York: W.W. Norton.

Steensen, Steen, Anna M. Grøndahl Larsen, Yngve Benestad Hågvar, and Birgitte Kjos Fonn. 2019. "What Does Digital Journalism Studies Look Like?" *Digital Journalism* 7 (3): 320–342.

Straub-Cook, Polly. 2018. "Source, Please? A Content Analysis of Links Posted in Discussions of Public Affairs on Reddit." *Digital Journalism* 6 (10): 1314–1332.

Tandoc, Edson C., Joy Jenkins, and Stephanie Craft. 2019. "Fake News as a Critical Incident in Journalism." *Journalism Practice* 13 (6): 673–689.

Turner, Fred, and Christine Larson. 2015. "Network Celebrity: Entrepreneurship and the New Public Intellectuals." *Public Culture* 27 (1): 53–84.

Usher, Nikki. 2017. "Venture-backed News Startups and the Field of Journalism: Challenges, Changes, and Consistencies." *Digital Journalism* 5 (9): 1116–1133.

Vis, Farida. 2013. "Twitter as a Reporting Tool for Breaking News: Journalists Tweeting the 2011 UK Riots." *Digital Journalism* 1 (1): 27–47.

Vos, Tim P. 2013. "Historical Mechanisms and Journalistic Change." *American Journalism* 30 (1): 36–43.

Vos, Tim P., and Frank Michael Russell. 2019. "Theorizing Journalism's Institutional Relationships: An Elaboration of Gatekeeping Theory." *Journalism Studies* 20 (16): 2331–2348.

Wang, Qun. 2020. "Differentiation and De-differentiation: The Evolving Power Dynamics between News Industry and Tech Industry." *Journalism & Mass Communication Quarterly.* 97 (2): 509–527.

Wajcman, Judy. 2019. "How Silicon Valley Sets Time." *New Media & Society* 21 (6): 1272–1289.

Wasserman, Herman. 2020. "Fake News from Africa: Panics, Politics and Paradigms." *Journalism* 21 (1): 3–16.

Wu, Shangyuan, Edson C. Tandoc, and Charles T. Salmon. 2019. "When Journalism and Automation Intersect: Assessing the Influence of the Technological Field on Contemporary Newsrooms." *Journalism Practice* 13 (10): 1238–1254.

Xu, Weiai Wayne, Yoonmo Sang, and Christopher Kim. 2020. "What Drives Hyper-Partisan News Sharing: Exploring the Role of Source, Style, and Content." *Digital Journalism* 8 (4): 486–505.

CONCLUSION

Understanding the institutions influencing journalism: Ideas for future work

Patrick Ferrucci

In 2007, filmmaker Michael Moore was enjoying, inarguably, the most cultural capital of his career to date.

The documentarian, in 2002, released his critically acclaimed examination of gun violence in the United States, *Bowling for Columbine*, a work that won an Academy Award and took in more than $58 million at the box office in the United States, while also becoming the highest-grossing documentary in the history of the United Kingdom, Austria, and Australia. Moore followed this up with 2004's *Fahrenheit 9/11*, another feature-length documentary that this time critically examined the George W. Bush presidency, while also spending time critiquing media coverage of the then-ongoing war in Iraq. *Fahrenheit 9/11* only increased Moore's cultural capital and public profile as the film won the coveted Palme d'Or from the Cannes Film Festival, and went on to become, by far, the highest-grossing documentary of all time, earning more than $222 million in worldwide box-office receipts.

Therefore, when it became public knowledge that Moore's 2007 documentary *Sicko* would critically scrutinize the United States' healthcare industry, many in that industry became nervous. The industry's lobbying/political action arm, America's Health Insurance Plans (AHIP), began fermenting "a multipronged strategy to discredit both Moore and his movie" (Potter 2010: 32). This plan involved bringing together dozens of well-regarded public relations executives to brainstorm a multifaceted campaign. One of the main components of the enacted plan included the incorporation of Health Care America, a completely fake 'astroturf' organization created by public relations executives "for the sole purpose of attacking Moore" and talking about "the shortcomings of government-run (healthcare) systems" to the press (Potter 2010: 37).

The strategy worked. Numerous elite press organizations, including *The New York Times*, quoted Health Care America as if it was a real grassroots organization. "Astroturfing the press" is, of course, nothing new. The Nixon administration did it almost for sport (Feldstein 2010). But what Health Care America shows, and

DOI: 10.4324/9781003140399-16

even more so what the public relations industry's decision to use this campaign reflects, is just one example of an institution on the periphery of journalism nefariously and intentionally influencing journalistic practice. For decades, journalism research, particularly work around ethics, focused extensively on strategic communication institutions such as public relations and advertising and how those influenced journalism practice (Baker 1994). This book illustrates how a whole host of other institutions, in addition to strategic communication, are now lurking on the edges – or within – the journalism ecosystem. These institutions do not simply wish to assist the journalism industry in ways amendable to practitioners. Saliently, then, each of this work's chapters elucidates how various institutions on the periphery of the industry have some agency to impact journalism, sometimes for the good and sometimes for the bad.

In the introduction to this book, Eldridge states that in this tome "we posit that these interlopers are now firmly within the field" (Eldridge, this volume: 1). In effect, using public relations as an exemplar institution, historically journalism studies conceptualizes the institution as something interacting and potentially influencing journalism practice, but always with journalists making decisions. *The New York Times* could have done some research and discovered the true origin story of Health Care America, but instead AHIP nefariously leveraged its knowledge of journalism's historic norm of objectivity to manipulate press coverage of *Sicko*. Public relations, as an institution, also traditionally influences the press in numerous positive ways. Gandy (1982) illustrated how public relations often acts as information subsidies for the press, effectively providing the press with needed story ideas and access to official sources (Vos 2011). In summation, in the case of *Sicko*, while public relations clearly affected practice, *journalism* made a choice and failed. When I was a music journalist, I also relied on information subsidies from public relations employed by the music industry, through which they provided both story ideas and access to artists, very much embodying the journalism Gandy (1982) describes. But, again, ultimately I wielded decision-making power, or autonomy, over what received coverage and the frames utilized … even if those decisions were primarily governed by social system controls (Shoemaker and Reese 2014). In their seminal *Mediating the Message*, Pamela J. Shoemaker and Stephen D. Reese provide a model depicting how influence manifests itself on journalism practice. In their original hierarchal model, they put what they call the influence from "outside journalism" on a level below only ideology; more recently, they call this level of influence the social institutional level. That chapter, really, provides the blueprint for this book: We wanted to provide expanded scholarly work focusing on individual social institutions clearly influencing practice. One main point of this book, then, is to identify these interlopers, and then illustrate how journalism's historic autonomy over how these interlopers impact practice is now long gone, a relic from a past continuously romanticized.

Studying the groups formerly known as the outsiders

If, as stated previously, many actors we formerly considered outsiders to the field of journalism are now firmly within the field, and, if we as journalism researchers typically focus on journalism, then future research needs to account for this. This translates into a research agenda under which we can no longer just study the perceptions of journalists concerning various formerly outside institutions, but need to now study those institutions as well.

For example, in a study of discourse I co-authored relatively recently, we looked at how industry trade magazine defined both the public journalism movement of the 1990s and the engaged journalism movement of recent times (Ferrucci, Nelson, and Davis 2020). Public journalism, though, primarily came from insiders, practitioners such as Buzz Merritt or academics like Jay Rosen (Merritt 1998, Rosen 1996). Researchers understood the motivations of public journalism evangelists (Corrigan 1999); this was possible because it was clear the original purveyors, at least, had little to none financial motivation. But while public journalism and engaged journalism, according to our study, is seemingly two sides of the same proverbial coin according to journalists, the motivations are very different. As Nelson and Wenzel (this volume) point out in their chapter, organizations profiting off selling engagement resources or software to newsrooms have an economic incentive.

And this is the key. While much prior work acknowledges the existence of peripheral or interloping actors within the field of journalism (Bélair-Gagnon and Holton 2018; Eldridge 2018), the vast majority of the rich body of literature applying these concepts takes a decidedly journalistic perspective. What this means, then, is that, for the most part, research embodies the perceptions of journalists. In the case of advertising, that means most research approaches influence in the negative. With engagement organizations such as Hearken or Agora, they are treated as potentially positive, helping in the pursuit of a more democratically inclined institution of journalism. But should this be the default?

In the case of advertising, as the chapter by Li (2022) illustrates, advances such as native advertising certainly embolden and strengthen heteronomous forces impacting journalism practice. But Li also shows that, occasionally, competing goals can align and result in a positive outcome for all. However, with engagement companies, because many founders and team members come from a journalistic background, most journalists, and especially journalism studies researchers, not only perceive these companies as a no-doubt positive partner, but do not even entertain the possibility for competing goals. But as Nelson and Wenzel (this volume) show, while engagement companies absolutely have the potential to catalyze processes that change the trajectory of a news organization for the better by providing systems and frameworks to create more positive and lasting relationships with the public, ones that will definitively improve journalism, they can also entirely alter normative notions of the field. As they argue, engagement companies typically are not in the business of assisting with journalism, but rather transforming journalism in a way that fits *their* notions of what journalism should be, not necessarily what professional journalists themselves think. As their chapter notes,

> the future of journalism is not solely a matter of ideas people have about how best to fix the profession, but also a matter of how effectively they are able to

persuade both journalistic stakeholders and community members to embrace and subsequently implement those ideas

(Nelson and Wenzel 2022: 149)

What this means for journalism studies research can be articulated in multiple ways. First, if outside organizations always desire to "fix" journalism, then that fixing is simply an alternate way of saying that these outside institutions want journalism to reflect their values, not competing ones, including competing ones that might be at the heart of historical normative notions of journalism. Second, these organizations engage in rhetorical and discursive processes aimed at defining journalism in a manner that embodies their ideas of journalism. For example, in this book, Peters elucidates how, in the United States and over the last several years, a legal system emboldened by a conservative and populist administration enacted a series of laws and decisions aimed at forcing the press to align with very specific ideals. These laws and decisions seem practical and necessary to a large segment of Americans, due primarily to a decades-long discursive strategy from conservative politicians and organizations aimed at weakening the press. This plays out not only in traditional courtrooms, but also in the court of public opinion. Therefore, when, for example, conservatives want to weaken journalistic authority, they do not first take issues to traditional courtrooms, but rather debate these issues in the press as to avoid any public outcry over these inarguably negative challenges to journalistic authority when they do make it to traditional courtrooms.

With all this in mind, it seems not only correct but obvious that the terms "peripheral actors" or "interlopers" or the like do not begin to fully describe the roles of these outside institutions.

Earlier in this book, Baack, Cheruiyot and Ferrer-Conill made a powerful argument for not just focusing on how outside institutions impact journalism, but also on how journalism impacts outside institutions. They wrote that "journalism is not a one-way street, and those at the periphery, while exerting their influence, are often heavily influenced by journalism as well. Sometimes, even at a foundational level" (2022: 113). This is absolutely correct and an important contribution of this book. The belief here, though, is this call does not go far enough, as evidenced by so many chapters here. This call, like so much research in our field, sees the institution of journalism through a perspective that prioritizes and privileges its centrality. To truly understand the influence of both outside institutions on journalism and journalism on outside institutions, we must do away, occasionally, with research that puts journalism in the center of all webs of influence. As noted by Blumler and Cushion, due its explosion as a field of inquiry, journalism studies research seems to "focus more and more on the complex inner workings of journalism at the expense of attention to its external ties, impacts and significance. In other words, journalism studies could become too inward-looking" (2014: 260).

Future research in journalism studies must independently study these outside institutions. That means not only studying outside institutions when they come into contact with journalists, in the newsrooms where they are enacting their processes, but also when they are fully independent of newsrooms. We need to study these organizations that make up outside institutions sometimes on their own as that is often the only way to truly understand their culture. This responds to a frequent call from organizational theorists who argue the optimal manner to investigate an organization's mission and goals requires studying that organization on multiple levels of analysis and utilizing numerous methodological tools (i.e., Argyris 2004, Weick 2012), something impossible when prioritizing journalism. As noted in Banjac's (this volume) chapter, the field of journalism often, and correctly, considers its audience an outside institution that influences journalism in a variety of ways. Due to this, we often study the audience independently from journalism. But we don't do that when considering other outside institutions both discussed in this book and elsewhere. As this book's chapters demonstrate, this path-dependent approach to research needs to end if we are to stretch our scholarly reach from focusing solely on institutions *through* the view of journalism, to understand how institutions see themselves *and* journalism.

In summation, if this book can catalyze only one positive outcome, we hope that it is a new focus from journalism studies researchers on studying these inter-loping institutions not from a journalism perspective, but from their own.

Revisiting normative ideas

As previously argued, the outside institutions identified in this book and within journalism studies as a whole often enter the field of journalism with a goal of reimagining journalism practices or normative processes in some manner. What separates the journalism industry from so many other fields is, of course, the nor-mative philosophies that undergird its practice. Ryfe (2009) encapsulated how, historically, if either an outside institution or even actors from within journalism attempt to alter or remove normative ideas at the center of the industry, the results tend to be disastrous. As Ryfe argued, most journalists believe that "the purpose and practice of journalism are and ought to remain constant" and, therefore, "it should not be surprising that reporters react with moral indignation when they perceive restrictions on their freedom to produce such journalism" (2009: 212–213).

Despite technological and economic disruptions facing the field in recent dec-ades, the normative ideas that theoretically guide journalism practice do not seem to change (Christians et al. 2009). Journalism studies as a field is an "inescapably normative domain. That is, it is inescapably involved in the realization of, or failure to realize, collectively self-determining processes of citizenship and democracy" (Blumler and Cushion 2014: 261–262). Yet, while the central normative idea that completely braces the foundation of journalism studies is that journalism is a public good, one that indisputably strengthens citizenship and democracy, the many nor-mative processes making this undergirding possible consistently shift or remain fluid (Ferrucci and Taylor 2019; Bertrand 2018).

Therefore, research into outside institutions' influence on journalistic practice should engage with normative ideas of journalism in multiple ways. First, our work should not simply reify historical ideas without first interrogating whether those ideas make sense. For example, much prior work in the area of web analytics' influence on journalism practice tends to highlight two main viewpoints: that web analytics either are entirely a market-driven entrant into the field or that they can potentially assist in various democratically focused goals such as understanding citizen needs (Ferrucci 2020, Tandoc 2019). But, as the chapter by Bélair-Gagnon in this book displays, web analytics companies affect journalism practice in myriad ways that go beyond simply how journalists utilize information gleamed from them. Yet while normative ideas of journalism "might vary by differences of media system and journalistic culture," it remains true that "certain challenges might be more common across the journalism board" (Blumler and Cushion 2014: 267). So, then, if web analytics as an institution, similar to many more highlighted in this book and beyond, violate normative ideas of journalism, researchers should not immediately assume those ideas sacrosanct. As Usher's (2021) recent book implicitly documents, many of the normative ideas at the center of the field led us to an institution that inarguably never served all constituents in an equitable manner. It is the explicit contention of this book that journalism studies researchers must begin grappling with the normative ideas at the center of the field openly. When an outside institution catalyzes change, change that will no doubt be fought by insiders as Ryfe (2009) illustrates, our research must begin with a question: Is this change altering a normative notion that actually and empirically strengthens democracy or have we just historically assumed it as such?

Second, and more obviously, for scholars to truly and fully understand influence from outside institutions, we must clearly identify the normative ideas at the center of journalism. Blumler and Cushion (2014) highlight some of these ideas, but argue that one way to better identify these notions is to ascertain what journalists perceive as challenges and then grapple with what those challenges are impeding. In this book, Konieczna demonstrates this by examining how foundations have increasingly become a larger part of the journalism funding ecosystem and how with that influence comes expectations. She highlights how research has pointed to aligning logics of journalism and journalism-focused foundations as a benefit that might impact journalism practice on a micro level, but not at the macro level where the normative goals of these institutions align. But do they? If, historically, autonomy has been needed for journalism to truly accomplish its mission (McDevitt 2003), then how can foundations not be a negative addition to journalism? However, what if control over a story should not be a normative ideal, what if ceding some control to like-minded foundations or citizens themselves would improve journalism? I do not pretend to know this answer, and I believe that is a significant admission.

In short, with more outside institutions influencing journalism, many of the normative ideas of the field are, understandably, under attack. The question journalism scholars must continue asking is whether these normative ideas should be protected or not. The only way to do this is to both identify the idea and study its impact on practice.

Who gets to set boundaries?

One of the many ways that we can identify and study normative practices is through the examination of journalism's boundaries. Carlson and Lewis (2015), in *Boundaries of Journalism,* a book that directly influenced the thinking going into this one, present a work that identifies numerous boundaries of journalism. But what that tome does not do, primarily because it was not part of its scholarly purview, is explore who sets those boundaries.

In their edited collection, Carlson and Lewis (2015) join colleagues in identifying various boundaries of the field, places where primarily insiders wage battles for the power of definitional control, and authority over practice. Inarguably these battles continue. For example, despite widespread digital change, insiders remain steadfast in discursively articulating the boundary between who is and who is not a journalist, oftentimes utilizing entirely antithetical and fluid definitions to mark the boundary (Ferrucci, Taylor, and Alaimo 2020; Ferrucci and Vos 2017). However, most of this work incorrectly gives insiders, primarily "professional" journalists, greater agency in terms of marking these distinctions. In contrast, the chapters in this book provide a more macro-level investigation not into what these boundaries are, but which institutions really have the power to determine whether these even exist and where they are located.

In that sense, Konieczna's (this volume) chapter tells a familiar story: An economically precarious industry very willingly accepting funds that come with enormous strings attached. Do some newsrooms try to implement practices meant to maintain independence of news? Some salient prior work that I've done illustrates how some news organizations try to insulate themselves from unwanted influence from foundations (Ferrucci 2015; Ferrucci and Nelson 2019). But it cannot be overstated: Newsrooms are, more and more, taking money from foundations and actively changing how they practice journalism based around the wants and needs of said foundations. This precarity allows the "pioneer journalism" conceptualized in the chapter by Hepp and Loosen (this volume) the ability to shape what journalism looks like both now and into the future.

In their contribution, Hepp and Loosen describe how numerous outsiders, such as pioneer journalists, often enter the field implicitly as an interloper and are originally treated as such, as actors with a discreet amount of agency when attempting to reconfigure normative aspects of the field. Thinking institutionally, though, better identifies the foundation of power in these relationships. In other words, while the institution of journalism, through its many normative ideas, may seem like the institution wielding the power to set its boundaries, in the case of pioneer journalism and numerous other outside institutions, that is not the circumstance. As described in the chapter, in many instances these pioneer journalists enter an organization with a mind toward the institution of journalism as a whole, and then attempt to discursively contest boundary markers. Hepp and Loosen write that pioneer journalism "is fundamental for these transformations" (2022: 131), transformations in practice that no doubt also redraw boundaries.

One can see this also clearly in the chapter from Li (2020) on native advertising. Not long ago, Coddington (2015) wrote about the "boundary" between advertising and journalistic practice, a boundary that historically was represented by a literal wall between the two departments. Coddington (2015) theorized that maybe the wall, or boundary, had become a curtain. But Li's chapter illustrates that any pretense of a boundary between the institutions of advertising and journalism is not there due to a determined show of authority on the part of journalism, but rather a lack of insight on the part of advertising. In other words, whatever boundary remains between the two institutions exists solely because advertising has yet to determine a financially lucrative means of destroying it.

Succinctly, then, if in the case of advertising or the technological change that comes with pioneer journalism, these outside institutions have the agency over journalism to determine where boundaries sit, to determine boundary markers, then we must not only study those outside institutions and how their work impacts normative ideas of journalism, but also what they see as the boundaries of journalism.

Innovation as panacea

The manner in which so many outside institutions seek to attain influence over journalism practice comes through what many inside and outside the field of journalism consider innovation. There's a certain segment of both journalism practitioners and, more saliently, journalism studies researchers who view innovation as an unqualified good, as something journalism must incorporate or it will meet its deserved death (i.e., Picard 2013). Carey (2008: 198) described this phenomenon as a "nostalgia for the future," a viewpoint common within journalism that envisions technological innovation as a positive given that it will help the industry meet its normative goals. In a sense, this view of innovation sees it as a panacea, as a solution to each and every problem facing the industry. The underlying notion is that all of journalism's failures lie with the field's unwillingness to fully embrace and harness the power of technological innovation (Siegelbaum and Thomas 2016). We can see this in numerous areas of research, in work that paints journalists unwilling to innovate as stereotypically crotchety old fogies hindering the field's progress (Usher 2014).

While admittedly this type of mindset seems to have lessened in recent years, much of it as the faith in the Silicon Valley ethos described in this book's chapter from Russell and Vos has also eroded, it still exists. We've recently seen an uptick in research on "product," a body of work that often "requires that academia and media professions make accommodations to adapt and adjust" (Royal et al. 2020: 597). However, to view journalism or specific journalism stories as product requires a market-driven mindset, one that so clearly invites undue economic influence on news. Innovation does not arise from within journalism; it comes from the outside, from outside institutions that, as previously noted, wish to transform journalism into something that enriches them. The chapter from Russell and Vos (this volume) describes how more than a decade ago, many within journalism saw Silicon Valley firms such as Facebook or Google as a potential solution to the journalism industry's increasing economic precarity. Of course, what these innovation evangelists got wrong was that Facebook or Google never really cared about strengthening democracy or journalism as a public good. In fact, as Figenschou and Ihlebæk (this volume) illustrate in their chapter, these Silicon Valley firms actually have played a large role not only in undermining the authority of journalism, but also in weakening democracy worldwide. Why? Because doing the nefarious latter things became more profitable.

Separating innovation from economics is simply impossible. That, of course, does not mean innovation should be conceived as universally negative. Many outside institutions identified in this book have done much good bringing innovation to the field of journalism. As described by Konieczna (this volume), foundations such as the Knight Foundation in the United States truly desire a more robust and omnipresent version of journalism that continuously fortifies democracy. To accomplish that goal, which clearly aligns with the journalism industry's, Knight and others of its ilk have helped fund both small- and large-scale innovations within newsrooms. But when those innovations fail to, or even do not try to, accomplish the foundation's desired goals, it often leaves a reimagined newsroom in the lurch, a newsroom that might have reorganized around a failed product which now lacks the funding to re-establish prior practices. We can see similar examples of both the good and bad of innovation throughout this book. For example, if journalism is truly going to serve its community, as normative notions of the field demand, then understanding those communities is imperative. Earlier in this book, Banjac (this volume) described how recent technological innovation forever changed the audience-journalism relationship in ways both productive and not. Bélair-Gagnon (this vollume) illustrated how analytics help journalism understand audiences in a way completely inconceivable to the reader surveys described decades ago by researchers illustrating how journalism aims to understand audiences (McManus 1994).

As the journalism industry across the world continues to shrink due to more pronounced economic precarity, though, it is important to note the increased role universities play in innovations. Hermida, Varano, and Young (this volume), in their chapter, recounted how *The Conversation Canada* emboldens academics to take on the role of journalist. This innovation provided Canadian citizens, and those around world, a nonprofit news organization specializing in much-needed explanatory reporting around a global pandemic. With, in most cases, far more resources and less of a downside to failure, universities are becoming more and more of a site for experimenting with various innovations in journalism.

The key here is understanding how all of these various factors come together when studying innovation in journalism. First, we must not uncritically assume innovation or product in journalism is inherently good, as a rich body of literature illustrates how much of that scholarship presumed positive turned out to be the opposite. Second, if, as noted, the majority if not all innovation comes from institutions outside of journalism, we as scholars must attempt to identify and understand the motivations of those outside institutions, detecting both where mutual goals arise and where divergent ones occur also. Third, we as scholars must seek to study these innovations in practice, making sure to train a keen focus toward how the innovation impact normative notions providing the framework for journalism. Finally, we as scholars must determine how this innovation ultimately shapes boundaries, allowing outsiders agency in the boundary demarcation process.

Conclusion: Is journalism an institution?

After considering the increasingly many ways outside institutions enact influence over the journalism field, it feels important to end this book speculating on where the institution of journalism stands, as presently constituted.

It is within this context, then, that Eldridge's introduction to this book presents the thought experiment of the "Ship of Theseus" as a metaphor for the journalism industry, a field that remains in such a slow but constant state of flux, it is important to ask whether it is even the same thing scholars studied decades ago (Scaltsas 1980). If we assume it is not, then, we are left with what Baudrillard (1994) would label a simulacrum, a journalism industry that is not simply only, to many, an unrecognizable copy of what it was, but actually an industry where this copy is now considered the real thing. This would be a scenario where, according to the sociologist George Ritzer, "the true and real have disappeared in an avalanche of simulation" (1999: 114).

This leaves glaring blind spots in journalism studies research. In professional journalism, groups such as the Society of Professional Journalists often warn of the unintended consequences that come from conflicts of interest, stating you should not report on something you are personally connected to since it might shape how you interpret the world around you. Journalism studies research is no different. Blind spot No. 1 can be seen in the "Ship of Theseus" metaphor: We are studying a simulacrum of the journalism industry, but treating it like it's the same industry as the one, for example, that flourished in decades prior. This means we as researchers continue bestowing on it the power of an institution, even as it lacks many of the traits we'd need to operationalize it as such.

Second, the majority of us in this field, the editors of this book included, came to academia after some career in professional journalism. Many of us still consider the profession part of our professional identity. It is within this centrality of journalism studies researchers to the field at large that problems present themselves. First, a deep allegiance to many of the normative beliefs of journalism, many reflected in practice, leave us unwilling to explore possible improvements to the field. In her recent work, Usher (2021) articulates how some deep-seated beliefs about what journalism is, many originally grounded not in journalistic but rather economic decisions, result in the privileging of certain types of people and news important to them and only them. In prior study I conducted with my colleague Mike McDevitt, we analyzed professional journalists' evaluations of media coverage surrounding the 2016 US presidential election. In our conclusion, we highlighted an almost third-person effect that happens when journalists talk about their field: They simply believe in established practices and routines, so much so that they refuse to place any blame for journalistic shortcomings on journalism itself (McDevitt and Ferrucci 2018). Speaking of true reflexivity, Ahva (2013: 791) contends "journalists' capacity for self-awareness; their ability to recognize influences and changes in their environment, alter the course of their actions, and renegotiate their professional self-images as a result" simply does not happen often enough. Schultz (2007) even contends that reflexivity in journalism is essentially impossible due to the strength of the doxa, or rules, within the field. This seems to also be the case in journalism studies research. So much work takes the perceptions of journalism as an institution as sacrosanct. Most criticism of journalism practice tends to take a more macro view or reifies normative practices. More importantly, and saliently for this book, most work scrutinizing the intersection of journalism and outside institutions examines, for good reason, the journalistic point of view, how journalists see these institutions or how they impact journalism. What we don't research is how journalism impacts outside institutions, save for the audience. That viewpoint could give us more insight into why these institutions enter the journalistic field. In essence, study the outsider and its relation to the insider, rather than the insider and its relation to the outsider. With all this in mind, it's imperative that we use this book's chapters as a jumping off point for future research in the field.

Therefore, if we entertain the notion that the institution of journalism is currently a version of the "Ship of Theseus" (Scaltsas 1980), or merely a simulacrum of what it once was (Baudrillard 1994), then it becomes increasingly important to revisit ideas of journalism as an institution altogether. March and Olsen (1989) defined an institution as an enduring set of rules and practices that exist across a field; these rules and practices are so embedded within the field that they remain amazingly resilient to individuals within or outside the field who aim to make changes. It is within these rules and practices where directions for how practitioners can act appropriately are seated (March and Olsen 2011). And, of course, research on journalism from across sub-disciplines, but especially media sociology, revolve around the notion of journalism as an institution, as a field with a set of doxa or fixed routines (e.g., Shoemaker and Reese 2014; Benson 1999; Bourdieu 1999). But with various outside institutions unequally altering and influencing journalism practice in disparate manners across the large field of journalism globally, arguably some of the truisms that sit at the center of the idea of journalism as institution no longer hold up.

This is not a definitive argument for journalism de-institutionalizing or the like. But, rather, a call for more research into the idea that, perhaps, the field of journalism is now more of a constellation of a normative ideals dispersed based on how much outside institutions have affected it. If we agree that both the main doxa of journalism comes in the form of autonomy over news (Kovach and Rosenstiel 2007), and that outside institutions are absolutely eroding that autonomy, for both good and bad, maybe conceptualizing journalism as an institution needs to be revisited, revisited in a way that makes salient how these institutions outside of journalism – these barbarians – are now completely inside of journalism's gates.

References

Ahva, Laura. 2013. "Public journalism and professional reflexivity." *Journalism* 14 (6): 790–806.

Argyris, Chris. 2004. *Reasons and Rationalizations: The Limits to Organizational Knowledge.* Oxford, UK: Oxford University Press.

Baker, C. Edwin. 1994. *Advertising and a Democratic Press.* Princeton, N.J.: Princeton University Press.

Baudrillard, Jean. 1994. *Simulacra and Simulation.* Ann Arbor, MI: University of Michigan Press.

Bélair-Gagnon, Valérie, and Avery E. Holton. 2018. "Strangers to the game? Interlopers, intralopers, and shifting news production." *Media and Communication* 6 (4): 70–78.

Benson, Rodney. 1999. "Field theory in comparative context: A new paradigm for media studies." *Theory and Society* 28 (3): 463–498.

Bertrand, Claude-Jean. 2018. *Media Ethics and Accountability Systems.* New York: Routledge.

Blumler, Jay G, and Stephen Cushion. 2014. "Normative perspectives on journalism studies: Stock-taking and future directions." *Journalism* 15 (3): 259–272.

Bourdieu, Pierre. 1999. *On Television.* New York: New Press.

Carey, James W. 2008. *Communication as Culture: Essays on Media and Society.* New York: Routledge.

Carlson, Matt, and Seth C. Lewis. 2015. *Boundaries of Journalism: Professionalism, Practices, and Participation.* New York: Routledge.

Christians, Clifford G., Theodore Lewis Glasser, Denis McQuail, Kaarle Nordenstreng, and Robert A. White. 2009. *Normative Theories of the Media: Journalism in Democratic Societies, The History of Communication.* Urbana, IL: University of Illinois Press.

Coddington, Mark. 2015. "The wall becomes a curtain: Revisiting journalism's news–business boundary." In *Boundaries of Journalism: Professionalism, Practices, and Participation*, edited by Matt Carlson and Seth C. Lewis, pp. 67–82. New York, NY: Routledge.

Corrigan, Don H. 1999. *The Public Journalism Movement in America: Evangelists in the Newsroom.* Westport, Conn.: Praeger.

Eldridge, Scott A. 2018. *Online journalism From The Periphery: Interloper Media and the Journalistic Field.* New York: Routledge.

Feldstein, Mark. 2010. *Poisoning the Press: Richard Nixon, Jack Anderson, and the Rise of Washington's Scandal Culture.* New York: Farrar, Straus and Giroux.

Ferrucci, Patrick. 2015. "Follow the leader: how leadership can affect the future of community journalism." *Community Journalism* 4 (2): 19–35.

Ferrucci, Patrick. 2020. "It is in the numbers: How market orientation impacts journalists' use of news metrics." *Journalism* 21 (2): 244–261.

Ferrucci, Patrick, and Jacob L Nelson. 2019. "The new advertisers: How foundation funding impacts journalism." *Media and Communication* 7 (4): 45–55.

Ferrucci, Patrick, Jacob L. Nelson, and Miles P. Davis. 2020. "From" Public Journalism" to" Engaged Journalism": Imagined Audiences and Denigrating Discourse." *InternationalJournal of Communication* 14.

Ferrucci, Patrick, and Ross Taylor. 2019. "Blurred boundaries: Toning ethics in news routines." *Journalism Studies* 20 (15): 2167–2181.

Ferrucci, Patrick, Ross Taylor, and Kathleen I. Alaimo. 2020. "On the boundaries: Professional photojournalists navigating identity in an age of technological democratization." *Digital Journalism* 8 (3): 367–385.

Ferrucci, Patrick, and Tim Vos. 2017. "Who's in, who's out? Constructing the identity of digital journalists." *Digital Journalism* 5 (7): 868–883.

Gandy, Oscar. 1982. *Beyond Agenda-Setting: Information Subsidies and Public Policy.* Norwood, NJ: Ablex.

Kovach, Bill, and Tom Rosenstiel. 2007. *The Elements of Journalism: What Newspeople Should Know and the Public Should Expect*. 1st rev. ed. New York: Three Rivers Press.

March, James G, and Johan P. Olsen. 1989. *Rediscovering Institutions: The Organizational Basis of Politics*. New York: Free Press.

March, James G, and Johan P Olsen. 2011. "Elaborating the "new institutionalism"." In *The Oxford Handbook of Political Science*, edited by Robert E Goodin, pp. 3–20. Oxford, UK: Oxford University Press.

McDevitt, Michael. 2003. "In defense of autonomy: A critique of the public journalism critique." *Journal of Communication* 53 (1): 155–164.

McDevitt, Michael, and Patrick Ferrucci. 2018. "Populism, journalism, and the limits of reflexivity: The case of Donald J. Trump." *Journalism Studies* 19 (4): 512–526.

McManus, John H. 1994. *Market-Driven Journalism: Let the Citizen Beware?*Thousand Oaks, Calif.: Sage Publications.

Merritt, Davis. 1998. *Public Journalism and Public Life: Why Telling the News is Not Enough*. 2nd ed, LEA's communication series. Mahwah, NJ: Erlbaum.

Picard, Robert G. 2013. "Killing journalism?" In *Journalism and Media Convergence*, edited by Heinz-Werner Nienstedt, Stephan Russ-Mohl and Bartosz Wilczek, pp. 19–28. Boston, MA: de Gruyter.

Potter, Wendell. 2010. *Deadly Spin: An Insurance Company Insider Speaks Out on How Corporate PR is Killing Health Care and Deceiving Americans*. New York: Bloomsbury Publishing USA.

Ritzer, George. 1999. *Enchanting a Disenchanted World: Revolutionizing the Means of Consumption*. Thousand Oaks, CA: Pine Forge Press.

Rosen, Jay. 1996. *Getting the Connections Right: Public Journalism and the Troubles in the Press, Perspectives on the News*. New York: Twentieth Century Fund.

Royal, Cindy, Amanda Bright, Kirstin Pellizzaro, Valérie Bélair-Gagnon, Avery E. Holton, Subramaniam Vincent, Don Heider, Anita Zielina, and Damon Kiesow. 2020. "Product management in journalism and academia." *Journalism & Mass Communication Quarterly* 97 (3): 597–616.

Ryfe, David M. 2009. "Broader and deeper: A study of newsroom culture in a time of change." *Journalism* 10 (2): 197–216.

Scaltsas, Theodore. 1980. "The ship of Theseus." *Analysis* 40 (3): 152–157.

Schultz, Ida. 2007. "The journalistic gut feeling: Journalistic doxa, news habitus and orthodox news values." *Journalism Practice* 1 (2): 190–207.

Shoemaker, Pamela J., and Stephen D. Reese. 2014. *Mediating the Message in the 21st Century: A Media Sociology Perspective*. 3rd ed. New York, NY: Routledge.

Siegelbaum, Sasu, and Ryan JThomas. 2016. "Putting the work (back) into newswork: Searching for the sources of normative failure." *Journalism Practice* 10 (3): 387–404.

Tandoc, Edson C. 2019. *Analyzing Analytics: Disrupting Journalism One Click at a Time*. New York: Routledge.

Usher, Nikki. 2014. *Making News at The New York Times*. Ann Arbor, MI: University of Michigan Press.

Usher, Nikki. 2021. *News for the Rich, White, and Blue: How Place and Power Distort American Journalism*. New York: Columbia University Press.

Vos, Tim P. 2011. "Explaining the origins of public relations: Logics of historical explanation." *Journal of Public Relations Research* 23 (2): 119–140.

Weick, Karl E. 2012. *Making Sense of the Organization, Volume 2: The Impermanent Organization*. Vol. 2. New York: John Wiley & Sons.

INDEX

Page numbers in italics refer to figures. Page numbers in bold refer to tables. Page numbers followed by 'n' refer to notes.

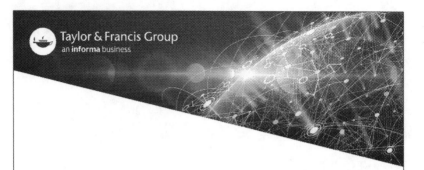

Printed in the United States
by Baker & Taylor Publisher Services